HELLO BABY!

Hello BABY!

Parenting with Confidence

A Tresillian Guide

Cathrine Fowler

Published by Tresillian Family Care Centres
www.tresillian.net

First published 2014

A Cataloguing-in-Publication record is available from the
National Library of Australia.

ISBN: 978 0 992 52770 9 (pbk)
       978 0 992 52771 6 (ebk–epub)
       978 0 992 52772 3 (ebk–mobi)

Designed, typeset and printed by Palmer Higgs
palmerhiggs.com.au

Cover image by bigstock.com

Illustrations by Ariana Urs

WELCOME NOTE

It gives me great pleasure to introduce Tresillian's new parenting guide, *Hello Baby! – Parenting with Confidence*. We wish it the same success as our two previous publications, *The Parents' Book* and *How to Stay Sane in Your Baby's First Year* which both went on to become bestsellers.

This book is simply an amazing and comprehensive resource for those with a new baby. It offers practical, hands-on advice on issues such as getting baby to sleep through the night, breastfeeding, weaning, travelling with baby and much more. Presented in everyday language, *Hello Baby!* essentially provides guidance and advice for new mums and dads, along with reassurance and solutions to many common parenting problems. What's more, because it's been written by Tresillian's very own Professor Cathrine Fowler, all information is based on the very latest research.

Since 1918 Tresillian Family Care Centres has been supporting families through the early years of their baby's life, so we understand the challenges parents face. We hope this book will help new parents enjoy the very first year of their baby's life by allaying fears and building confidence.

We're sure you'll find *Hello Baby! – Parenting with Confidence* a rich and invaluable resource.

Robert Mills
Chief Executive Officer
Tresillian Family Care Centres

CONTENTS

Foreword by Annabel Crabb   ix

Introduction   xi

PART ONE   1
GETTING STARTED AS A PARENT

Chapter 1   Getting Ready for Parenthood   3
Chapter 2   Caring for Yourself as a Parent   19
Chapter 3   Baby Needs   33
Chapter 4   Appearance and Basic Physical Care   55

PART TWO   75
INFANT DEVELOPMENT AND GROWTH

Chapter 5   Sleep and Early Brain Development   77
Chapter 6   Building Your Relationship With Your Baby   103
Chapter 7   Your Baby's Development   121
Chapter 8   Supporting Your Baby's Development   145

PART THREE   159
INFANT FEEDING AND NUTRITION

Chapter 9   Food for You and Your Baby   161
Chapter 10   Breastfeeding   171
Chapter 11   Breastfeeding Problems   195
Chapter 12   Bottle Feeding   213
Chapter 13   Weaning   231
Chapter 14   Time for Solid Foods   241

PART FOUR   261
BABY'S HEALTH AND SAFETY

Chapter 15   Child Health   263
Chapter 16   When Baby is Unwell   289
Chapter 17   Leaving Your Baby   313
Chapter 18   Travel and Outings with Your Baby   329
Chapter 19   Frequently Asked Questions   339
Chapter 20   Your Baby's First Foods – Recipe Ideas   353

Websites   367
References   377
Acknowledgements   381

FOREWORD BY ANNABEL CRABB

TRESILLIAN FAMILY CARE CENTRES are a precious public asset and a treasure-trove of expertise; the very whisper of the Tresillian name inspires confidence in the chronically sleep-deprived.

I myself have never experienced first-hand the HUSHED efficiency of its residential service, fabled for hard-to-crack infants and their parents, who spread the word to their friends: "I can't believe it. They got the baby to sleep! Plus there was cake!"

Human beings are rational creatures. Except when they have just reproduced, in which case we can become needy, confused and unable to distinguish wise counsel from utter guff. Sometimes, this is because we are paralysed with terror at the vast new responsibility of looking after a baby, and cannot reconcile it with our equally vast feeling of inadequacy. Or perhaps because we haven't slept more than a 40-minute block in several weeks. Often, it's the bombardment of information and opinion from everywhere that proves so disorienting.

The internet now enables a fretful parent to check (typing one-handedly) his or her child's symptoms at any hour of the day or night, rendering spot diagnoses of typhoid, lupus or irritable bowel syndrome at 3am a very real and exciting possibility.

Fad parenting books offer a debilitating array of warnings, carrying with them the glutinous baggage of parental guilt: Carry your baby at all times, or risk damaging him for life. Don't spoil him by carrying him everywhere, for God's sake. Construct a sleep schedule and observe it to the minute. Don't terrorise your baby with sleep schedules; just put her to bed when she pulls her ears, or grimaces. (I always found this one a bit difficult. Babies look to me as if they are grimacing a lot of the time. Or maybe it's just my kids. They got put to bed a lot.)

And of course, the confusing and ancient tradition of baby advice from family and friends continues to thrive. "I can't believe you're feeding her like that. She's obviously got colic. You need to burp her more." "Mine slept through the night from six weeks!" "Just give him some formula. I don't know why you're so obsessed with this breastfeeding."

In these circumstances, the value of consistent and sensible advice – free of any commercial or personal agenda – is far above rubies.

I have on a number of occasions called the Parents' Help Line, and have invariably found it to be staffed by pleasant and sensible experts who will say reassuring things while they wait for you to stop sobbing.

They assist with myriad practical and health issues, but they also offer the best thing any stressed parent can encounter: Perspective. A cool-headed answer on what to worry about and what not to; a reminder that this too shall pass, and some bankable tips on what to do in the meantime.

Twenty-two years ago, my wonderful colleague Geraldine Doogue wrote the Foreword to the first edition of the second Tresillian book, in which she welcomed its advice, among other things, on how to make the practical lifestyle changes and compromises that come with new babies.

"The earlier the changes, the earlier you'll become expert at flexibility, the more you'll realise that anything is possible with a baby – it just takes a little longer and you may not be able to achieve it all in one day," she wrote.

"But after one year, you'll be astonished at how efficient you become. This book offers optimism because it gives practical advice, and that's what new parents need most."

I second that sentiment. Having a baby is like taking delivery of an intricate and temperamental high-performance vehicle. It induces wonder, admiration, pride, feelings of inadequacy, and rank existential terror that one might inadvertently crash it. After a few years, all the tricks and techniques will be second nature, much of your terror will be forgotten, and you will be fanging about the place with ease.

But in the meantime, there's nothing quite like a good, honest instruction manual.

Annabel Crabb

INTRODUCTION

IT IS AMAZING HOW A BABY can change so many lives in so many ways. Having a baby means your life will probably never be the same again. At times during the early months it may feel as if the constant demands will never stop.

Many first-time parents are surprised by the intensity of parenting. They frequently ask others: why didn't anyone tell me it would be like this? Reassuringly, the initial rollercoaster ride of emotions from overwhelming joy to sheer panic is soon over. The time will fly and very quickly an inquisitive toddler will replace the early months of nights broken by a baby who needs regular feeding, nappy changing and reassurance that you are there to calm and keep them safe. The good news is that parents survive and thrive as they settle into their parenting role, developing confidence and competence in caring for their baby; or in some families, two or more babies.

Babies need parents to keep them safe and provide all the necessities of life. This is not always easy, as babies don't come with a manual to guide parents. Though if parents take the time to watch their babies they will find out lots of interesting information as babies are very skilled communicators, providing signals to guide you in providing the care that is needed. An important strategy is to ask: what might my baby be experiencing; and how are they feeling?

Tresillian has supported the writing of this book to provide parents with information that whenever possible is underpinned by research evidence. The book has four sections:

- Section 1 will assist you to prepare for the early months of parenthood, covering important topics that include: managing fatigue, perinatal mental health, parenting alone, having more than one baby, and introducing your baby to their siblings and pets.

- Section 2 provides information about babies to help you prepare for their arrival, how to assist your baby in learning to regulate their behaviour and feelings, learning to read baby cues or signals, sleep and settling especially what is normal for a baby, and building and enhancing the relationship with your baby. This section also explores the amazing skills babies are born with and develop during their first year of life, and how you can support your baby's development.
- Section 3 aims to guide parents through the essentials of infant and family nutrition. A constant theme through this section is that feeding your baby is an excellent opportunity to enhance the relationship between your baby and you. During the first year of life, feeding is one of the most frequent and important periods of interaction you will have with your baby. Practical information on breastfeeding, infant formula feeding, weaning and the introduction to solid foods are provided.
- Section 4 focuses on your baby's health and safety. Crucial information about protecting your baby's health is provided including regular developmental checks, immunisation, dental care and common health concerns. Common childhood illnesses and prevention measures are described. To assist you in returning to paid work or having short periods of time away from your baby, strategies are provided to ease the stress of separation. Travelling with a baby and frequently asked parenting questions complete this section.

We would like to wish you well on your new adventure as a parent. Maintain your sense of humour and have lots of fun as you wonder in awe at your amazing baby.

THE TRESILLIAN STORY

Funded by the NSW Ministry of Health, Tresillian's history dates back to 1918 when the Royal Society for the Welfare of Mothers and Babies (the Society), now known as Tresillian Family Care Centres, was originally formed to coordinate early childhood and maternal services in New South Wales. Our organisation was then incorporated by an Act of Parliament in 1919. The Society's primary aim back then was to make a real difference to the high mortality rate of children under the age of five who were losing their lives through poverty, disease and lack of hygiene. As well as saving lives, the Society's other aims as outlined in the 1920–21 annual report, were:

- To coordinate all agencies dealing with mothers and babies;
- To ensure proper nursing conditions for every mother prior and subsequent to childbirth;
- To establish welfare centres and committees in the metropolis and country;
- To establish rest homes for mothers;
- To establish a Corps of Mothers' Aids;
- To care for and bring under supervision all children up to school age; and
- To provide certified and humanised milk and ice.

In 1921, Dr Margaret Harper, the first medical director, established an 'Infant Welfare Training' school at Shaw Street, Petersham, to educate baby health centre nurses, so they could be more effective in helping parents address basic problems such as a lack of hygiene and institute immunisation programs.

The building at Petersham had been named 'Tresillian' by the previous owners who originated from the village of the same name in Cornwall, England. From that moment on, the Royal Society for the Welfare of Mothers and Babies was referred to as 'Tresillian'.

These days Tresillian has four Family Care Centres across Sydney at Willoughby, Wollstonecraft, Penrith and Belmore with a mix of services designed to provide professional support and practical advice to families with a baby or toddler.

Tresillian's tradition of education has also continued over the years. Courses for both nurses and parents are still offered but the emphasis has changed from infant survival to health promotion and meeting the changing needs of parents.

We are proud of Tresillian's fascinating history and honoured to have Her Majesty Queen Elizabeth II as our patron.

HELLO BABY! Parenting with Confidence

Part One

GETTING STARTED AS A PARENT

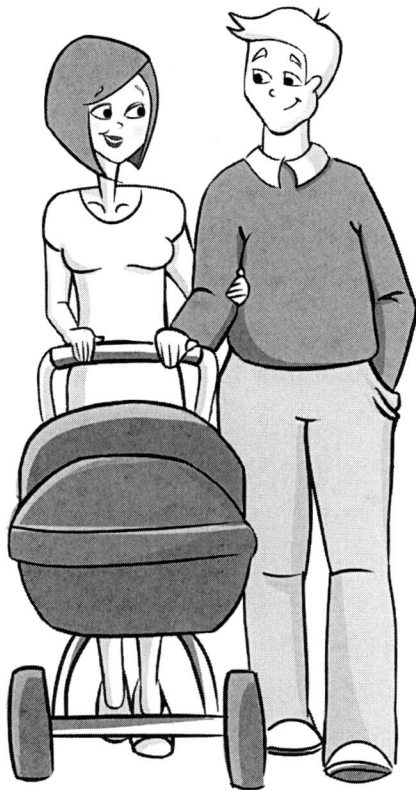

Chapter One
GETTING READY FOR PARENTHOOD

THE BIRTH OF YOUR CHILD is one of life's most amazing life-changing events. You may have planned and eagerly anticipated your baby's birth or your pregnancy may have been a big unplanned surprise. Excitement, joy, amazement and wonder are often mixed with feelings of exhaustion, anger, fear and sadness. The important thing to know is that these fluctuations of feelings are normal for most new parents. Becoming a parent takes time, support, and a sense of humour and fun as you head off on your big adventure.

Parents need to know they don't have to be the perfect parent. It is all right to get things wrong or misread what your baby is trying to tell you (as long as they are safe). Remember, you are both on a huge learning curve, especially in the first few months of your baby's life.

YOU WERE BORN TO BE A MOTHER OR FATHER!

You were born to be a mother! How often have you heard that women are "born with a maternal instinct"? Interestingly, there is minimal research that supports the idea of maternal instinct. Maternal instinct is a frequently used throwaway term; "she is very maternal", or conversely, "she has no maternal instinct" when describing a woman who is not interested in having a baby or when things start to go wrong with parenting. Rarely are negative comments about fathers linked to their lack of paternal instinct. So rather than talking about maternal instinct as being something you are born with, it is much more productive to think about the ability to parent as a learnt skill.

Yes, there are some things nature provides that help women to become mothers and men to become fathers. The wonder of being a parent, for example, helps you to focus on your pregnancy and your unborn child. A baby's appearance and behaviour also have a positive impact on parents. A baby's big eyes (just like any baby mammal), an extended gaze when they stare into your eyes, the ability to grasp your finger or turn to your nipple when you stroke their cheek, their smell after a bath, and the beauty and vulnerability of a sleeping baby all help to make parents feel a sense of love, care and protection.

Nature also contributes to enhancing your connection with your baby. During pregnancy there are changes in hormones to support pregnancy, childbirth and breastfeeding. Oxytocin is one of these hormones and it is known to play a crucial role during childbirth and lactation. Oxytocin, sometimes referred to as the 'love hormone', has now been demonstrated through research to have a key role in the development of relationships. It is thought to assist in breaking down normal social barriers and thus enhances the development of the parent–infant relationship.

We learn to parent in many different ways. The main way, of course, is from our own childhood and our experience of being parented, as you will learn in the section on early brain development in Chapter 5. Our very earliest experiences of being nurtured, loved and cared for by our parents have set up the templates for our own parenting abilities and style. We all wish for our children to receive these positive parenting experiences.

The key focus of your child and family health nurse is to support the development of your relationship and interactions with your baby; assist you in monitoring your baby's development and general health; and if appropriate, help you manage the situation.

BEFORE THE BABY IS BORN

Pregnancy is the ideal time to start to do some forward planning when it comes to parenting. But it is never too late to start. There are obvious tasks to do and decisions you will need to make. There are also several less obvious but equally important decisions that are needed as a parent, such as:

1. What type of parent will I be?
2. What type of parent will my partner be?
3. What are our preferred parenting styles? If we have different styles, how will we provide consistent care to our child?
4. What are the parenting behaviours and other things you want to keep or discard from your own childhood?
5. How will my relationship with my partner, family and friends change?
6. How will my lifestyle change?
7. What are the activities I need to do, to keep myself physically and emotionally well?
8. Who can I call for support and help in times of distress, or when I am experiencing overwhelming fatigue?
9. Will I be returning to the paid workforce?
10. If so, who will care for my baby while I am at work?
11. How am I going to feed my baby?

WHAT KIND OF PARENT DO YOU WANT TO BE?

Parents come in all shapes and forms. No two parents will be the same. As we have already discussed, the way you parent is a reflection of your own experiences during childhood. There are also many other things that impact on your ability to parent, such as your temperament, personality, cultural background, childhood experiences, physical and emotional health, education level and financial capacity. The list of parenting influences is endless.

There are lots of ways to parent that are safe for your baby and are workable. Parenting books usually favour one style over another. Some of the parenting choices include using a *behavioural* approach or an *attachment* parenting style.

A behavioural approach is usually parent or adult focused, requiring the child to comply with the needs of the parents. This type of parenting approach often neglects to understand the developmental stage or needs of the baby.

An attachment approach is focused on the baby. Parents using this style require a great deal of commitment to enable them to always be available for their children. Having a well functioning support network for the parent is absolutely necessary for those considering using the attachment parenting approach.

A parenting style that is a blend of both the attachment and behavioural styles of parenting is probably the most realistic. Importantly, as adults and parents, our responsibility is to "keep the baby in mind". That means asking ourselves questions such as, "How would this feel if I were a baby?"

In this book, the parenting style being promoted is one that is caring, kind and safe for both baby and parents. It requires understanding and sensitivity to the needs of baby. It also encourages parents to maintain their emotional and physical health, so they can be actively engaged with their baby. Importantly, it is accepted that parents do not always get their responses right when trying to work out their baby's needs. This book also acknowledges that parents will often shift their style of parenting, depending on the circumstances.

PARENTING ALONE

Single parenthood is more common today than in previous decades. Some parents have chosen this situation, while others have been forced into single parenthood. In some situations, parenting alone is a temporary situation because of their partner's work situation.

It's a good idea to check with the appropriate government agencies to see if you are entitled to some financial assistance. These entitlements may include childcare payments. Maternity or paternity leave will provide you with paid leave for a short period of time. Checking with your employer during pregnancy will ensure you receive all your benefits.

Parenting can take a major toll on your health. Keeping physically and mentally healthy must be a key priority, rather than treating it as a luxury. Eating nutritious meals, keeping up regular exercise and staying in touch with friends and family are a must. Equally important is creating a workable and sustained support network of family, friends and community services. Your local child and family health nurse will be able to put you in touch with other mums in a similar situation in your local area and keep in mind that many organisations like Tresillian hold group programs for single parents.

MORE THAN ONE BABY

Finding out you are having more than one baby can pose a real challenge for most parents. If you have first-hand knowledge of other family members with twins or triplets, you will understand some of the experience of having more than one baby.

Twins or more babies will attract a great deal of attention from family, friends and strangers. People are often intrigued by the prospect of twins or more babies, but many have little knowledge about multiple births.

FACTS ON MULTIPLE BIRTHS:

- Fraternal or dizygotic (two zygotes) twins pregnancy occurs when there are two separate eggs fertilised. The similarities between the babies are like those you would expect from siblings born at different times. They maybe alike and the same sex (boy/boy or girl/girl) or a boy and girl. Having fraternal twins is like having two separate pregnancies.
- Identical or monozygotic (one zygote) twins have a shared egg that splits into two separate but identical fetuses. These fetuses share the same genetic material and have many similar characteristics.
- If you are having triplets or more than three, they can be a mix of identical and fraternal multiples. Triplets can be a combination of two identical babies and a fraternal baby.

Start to build a relationship with your babies during pregnancy. Imagine each of the babies as an individual. Talking to each of your babies is important as they can hear your voice. Getting to know their movements and imagining what they might look like or what their personalities will be, is always an enjoyable activity for expectant parents. Asking for a copy of your ultrasound pictures will make the idea of more than one baby real and help you to connect with them.

It's important to be organised by arranging lots of support before you leave hospital. Asking for and accepting help will be an important skill to cultivate. If family and friends offer to help, get one of them to organise a timetable and a list of tasks they can do in order to allow you to focus on your babies. Contacting the Australian Multiple Birth Association will get you in touch with other parents with experience of having a multiple pregnancy and babies. They will provide you with access to information and, if you want to participate, suggest social activities and a support group. Information is easily obtained from the Australian Multiple Birth Association website or through your child and family health nurse.

PARENTING PRACTICES

Being a parent requires you to adopt sensitive practices to care for your baby. These four basic practices will get you off to a good start:

1. Be sensitive to your baby's cues. (Rubbing eyes and grizzling means they need to sleep.)
2. Respond to your baby's distress. (Crying can mean a number of things, from hunger, needing a nappy changed or 'I'm lonely'.)
3. Support their social-emotional growth. (Label your baby's emotions – 'you look happy today' or 'you're crying, do you feel sad?')
4. Support their cognitive growth. (Sing, talk and read to your baby.)

For every good relationship to work, it requires an interaction from at least two people. Your baby will provide you with some feedback, such as give you clues about their needs and be responsive to you when you try to reduce their distress or meet one of their needs. Sometimes this is not always possible. Both babies and parents can experience a glitch in this arrangement due to sleep deprivation, illness, prematurity and lack of support.

A great starting point for gaining confidence as a parent is the ability to talk about your needs, concerns and desires. You will find that there are lots of parenting experts. Do not be discouraged by this, as much of the advice you will receive is often very similar, it just sounds different. An easy way to handle it is to listen, thank the person, and either accept or discard the advice.

If you were born in the 1980s or after, you are a digital native. The world you grew up in has always contained some form of digital technology. There are lots of very positive things about digital technology, starting with the amazing amount of information you can access about parenting and child health. But there are also lots of dilemmas that can occur with the use of digital technology.

Ask yourself, is the website you're visiting Australian based? Is the advice best practice in Australia? Try and stick to credible websites such as Tresillian (www.tresillian.net). If you have any concerns about your baby, it's always better to discuss it with your child and family health nurse or family doctor.

GRANDPARENTS

Grandparents are a great source of information and play an important role in the family. At Tresillian we advocate the role of the extended family in raising a child, but to be successful, all family members need to be open and honest with each other from the start.

Developing a relationship between your child and their grandparents can enrich both their lives. Grandparents often have a little more time to just be with their grandchildren. They have very different responsibilities than parents and can occasionally bend family rules. Generally, grandparents really enjoy being involved in the lives of their grandchildren.

Here are some ways grandparents can be involved:
- Asking them to read books to your child and tell them stories, especially ones about their parents!
- Ask grandparents to babysit occasionally.
- They may also want to join you on a pick up from child care or preschool.

- Have some special toys at 'Grandma's' place.
- Let grandparents know when special events are on in your child's life so they can attend (e.g. Grandparents' Day at preschool, dancing concerts, etc.). This goes a long way towards building the relationship between grandparent and child.

If you're planning on going back to work when your baby is only a few months old you may want to ask grandparents to help with childcare. This can be a wonderful way for grandparents to connect and get to know your child. Once again though, it's a time to be honest and open with each other and talk through issues such as:

- The hours you intend working (will you be working long days, full time, part-time?)
- Will you bring baby to their place or do you want them to look after baby in your home?
- How do you want your baby cared for? (i.e. if you wrap your baby before bedtime, this needs to be communicated to grandparents so they can replicate this when baby is in their care)
- What happens if they get sick or baby is sick?
- What happens if they find it too much?
- Are you comfortable with grandparents driving your child places?

The good news is that most parent/grandparent arrangements work out extremely well, particularly when grandparents are looking after a grandchild a few days a week rather than full time. It's important to be aware of the grandparents' health and age when considering their suitability as regular babysitters. Despite good intentions, some grandparents simply are unable to give their grandchildren the best of care due to their health, their age and living situations that are not ideal for babies. These issues need to be discussed openly and honestly for the benefit of baby's health and wellbeing.

Other ways to involve grandparents on a less hands-on basis may be:

- Asking for advice – you don't need to take the advice, but being listened to makes grandparents feel wanted and respected.
- Involving grandparents in family activities like birthdays and other celebrations.

- Involving them in decisions about the way you want to parent your children.
- Use of digital technologies like Skype to keep in touch and assist your baby to become familiar with their grandparents. This will make it so much easier if they need to come and babysit occasionally.
- Send regular pictures and movies of your baby.

KEEPING YOUR BABY SAFE

Safety extends to your home and a good time to check if you have a childproof and friendly home is during pregnancy, well before your baby is mobile. Learning to anticipate your baby's development will make it much easier to care for your baby.

An effective method of identifying the danger spots is to get down on the floor with your baby. From this vantage point, you will be able to see potential dangers such as heavy objects, power cords, splinters in your timber floor or nails and other baby hazards. It's good practice to put away clutter, locking away chemicals, poisons and medications, and assessing potential water risks that can cause drowning.

Removing dangers well in advance of your baby gaining the skill to explore their world will allow you to relax and enjoy being with your baby. There are many simple pieces of safety equipment you can buy for your home to improve safety – locks for kitchen cupboards, curly cords for jugs and other electrical equipment, plugs for power points, and safety gates for stairs and areas you don't want your baby to enter.

Involving other people, including grandparents, with child safety activities is essential, especially if your baby is going to be visiting or left in other people's homes.

Throughout this book safety precautions will be highlighted. Nevertheless, it is impossible to identify every child safety risk in every home or setting. Be vigilant at all times. You will need to be one step ahead of your baby's developmental skills. This will make a huge difference in keeping your baby safe from accidental injury.

NO LONGER THE BABY IN THE FAMILY

When a toddler becomes a big brother or sister, it can be very upsetting for them. All of a sudden, they are no longer the baby in the family. The age of your toddler or preschooler will usually determine how they react to the news or of the arrival of a new brother or sister. Some toddlers and preschoolers revert back to baby-like behaviours:

- If toilet trained they might start wetting their pants or demanding they are put into a nappy – this is usually short-lived as it's not very comfortable wearing a nappy.
- They may want to try to breastfeed or demand a bottle – usually if you allow them to try, they will then stop asking.
- They may want to sleep with you or wake in the middle of the night to check you are still at home.
- They might have a few more tantrums to get your attention to help manage their feelings.

These problems are usually short-lived if you don't make too much of a fuss. Praising positive behaviour and trying to ignore unwanted behaviour usually works well with most toddlers.

Helping your toddler or preschooler prepare for the arrival of a new baby can make the first weeks or months a lot easier to manage for everyone. Here are some methods that might help:

- Not telling your child about the new baby too far in advance – you may get very tired of telling them that it is still many months before the baby arrives.
- Getting them to help with the preparations of the baby's room.
- Read books about the arrival of a new baby in the house – you may find some appropriate books on new babies in your local library.
- Visit friends who have new babies.
- Practise staying with the person who will be caring for them while you are in hospital – an overnight stay is always a good idea.
- When you're in labour and leaving for the hospital make sure you say goodbye – never sneak out of the house.
- Leave something you always have with you and ask your child to bring it to the hospital when they come to visit.

- Have your arms free when they come to visit and give them your full attention.
- Have a present for them such as a small edible treat or book.
- Allow them to touch their baby sister or brother. If you think they are old enough and interested, allow them to hold the new baby (strictly supervised, of course!)
- When you are ready to go home let someone else carry the baby so you are free to be with your elder child.
- Ask visitors to remember you have another child, and not just a baby.
- Try and organise some special one-on-one time with your toddler or preschooler.

PETS

Dogs and cats are important members of many families. However, bringing a new baby into the house when there is a dog or a cat will require vigilance and preparation. Dogs and cats are curious animals and their investigations of the new and interesting smells in your home could cause your baby harm.

Before your baby is born make sure your pet has the appropriate immunisations, and is treated for worms, fleas and ticks. The health of your pet is important, as babies do tend to get up close and friendly with pets.

To make sure your baby is safe around your pets:
- Make changes to your dog's routine before your baby is born.
- Maintain established routines like a daily walk with your dog or normal greeting when arriving home.
- Wash your hands well after touching your pet.
- Never leave your baby alone with a dog or cat. Cats, in particular, like to sleep in warm cozy areas, and a bassinet is a perfect area for sleeping. There is a potential suffocation risk for your baby.
- Introduce your baby to your dog when you arrive home.
- Feed your dog or cat in an area away from your baby, especially when your baby becomes mobile.

- Do not allow your baby to play near your pet's food or bedding.
- Even if you know the cat or dog and believe they are harmless, keep a close eye on your baby. Babies can unknowingly harm animals by pulling fur, ears or tails.

WHEN THINGS DON'T TURN OUT AS EXPECTED

Having a baby comes with some risks. Sometimes babies are born too soon or they are born with physical problems and challenges. Some problems are minor, while others can be life threatening. Regardless, a normal response is to be upset when finding out there may be a problem with your baby. You might feel very distressed, confused, frustrated and angry.

Some parents want time alone and withdraw from family and friends until they have time to control their emotions. Other parents have lots of questions that need to be answered. Unfortunately, answers are not always available. Being provided with accurate information is essential. Make sure you write down your questions for when you consult your doctor or nursing staff.

Your baby may be separated from you at birth or shortly after birth. Every time you go to the neonatal intensive care unit (NICU), you might feel overwhelmed or that you are in the way but don't let that stop you visiting your baby. The nursing and medical staff in the NICU expect you to be with your baby. They also understand how upset you may be feeling. Don't be afraid to ask to touch or hold your baby. If at all possible they will allow you to hold your baby.

Even though you may feel you are not contributing to your baby's care while they are in the NICU, just being there with your baby will provide them with comfort. You will be encouraged to express breast-milk or breastfeed your baby (if baby is well enough). Breastfeeding will be allowed as soon as your baby is strong enough to suck. As your baby's condition improves, you will be encouraged to increase the amount of time spent touching and holding your baby.

Talking about how you are feeling often helps manage your emotions. All hospitals have social workers who will be available to assist you to work through your emotions. Fathers greatly benefit from talking to someone about how they are feeling. Often they feel they must remain strong, but most times they are just as confused and upset as mothers. Social workers can also provide very practical assistance, ensuring you are receiving all the appropriate benefits and assistance that are available.

Being a parent is not always easy and experiences vary greatly from one person to another. Don't be too hard on yourself and expect to have good days and not so good days.

As well as guiding you through some of those inevitable parenting dilemmas, this Tresillian book will also give you lots of tips on how to build a meaningful relationship with your baby. However, in order to achieve that relationship, you need to look after yourself as a parent. If you think that sounds impossible, read our next chapter on 'Caring for Yourself as a Parent'.

INTRODUCTION SUMMARY

- Learning to parent takes time, support and a sense of humour and fun.
- You don't have to be a perfect parent but you need to be willing to learn.
- Being organised and prepared makes a real difference, especially if you are a single parent or having more than one baby.
- Asking for help and learning to accept help is really important during your baby's first year.
- Grandparents can be a great source of support and parenting information.
- Learning to anticipate your baby's next development stage will make it much easier to parent your baby and keep them safe.
- When a new baby comes into the home, toddlers and preschoolers can become upset. The good news is that this is usually short-lived.
- If you have pets you need to remain vigilant to keep your baby safe.
- Being a parent is not always easy and experiences vary from one person to another. Don't be too hard on yourself.
- As a parent there will be lots of good days and some difficult days.

Chapter Two

CARING FOR YOURSELF AS A PARENT

A HAPPY AND HEALTHY PARENT is necessary for your baby's health and wellbeing and one of the most precious gifts you can give your baby. There are lots of things you can do to make sure you maintain and improve your mental and physical health as a parent.

Like all new jobs, it requires time to adjust to the demands of parenthood. It means being prepared for the unexpected, keeping your sense of humour and fun, and having realistic expectations of what you will achieve each day.

DEVELOPING A STRONG SUPPORT NETWORK

Having a strong, supportive and readily available network of family and friends can really make a difference. However, for many parents this is not a reality. Being a new mother or father can be a very isolating experience. Feeling exhausted, not wanting friends to know you are struggling with parenthood, or that you are feeling sad or distressed, can mean you avoid contact with the people who love and care about you. Many mothers and fathers use parenting forums, blogs and social media to share their experiences, gain reassurance and to answer parenting questions. Before posting experiences or questions on parenting forums or blogs read some of the posts to ensure that you are comfortable with the responses received by others. We do not recommend posting information or photos that will identify you or your family.

The reality is that it's never too late to develop a support network and there's no better time to start than right now.

Regardless of the level of support you have, the challenge is to make sure it is the right kind of support. A great starting place is with your child and family health nurse who will be able to provide you with services and support groups within your local community. New parents' groups are a great way to meet other mums (and dads) in your local area with a child the same age as yours. Many strong and life-long friendships start as a result of a new parents' group.

LEARNING TO ASK FOR HELP

A regular comment made to parents by friends and family is to ask for help if you need anything. The difficulty for many new parents is that they don't like to ask for help as it can seem like they are imposing on an already busy friend or family member. One way to get around feeling awkward when asking for help is to make a list.

When people ask you what they can do to help, suggest they choose something from the list as it also provides them with some choice as to what they do. Partners also find this useful. Instead of having to ask you or just guess what needs to be done, you have given your partner some ideas on how they can best assist you.

HELLO BABY! Parenting with Confidence

HEALTHY EATING AND EXERCISE

Many new mums put on weight during pregnancy, and some dads-to-be think they're eating for two as well, so it's not uncommon for both parents to be overweight after the birth of their baby. Pregnant women are strongly advised not to drink alcohol due to the potential risks to the developing fetus. If you are breastfeeding you are also advised to avoid alcohol (see Chapter 9).

By role modelling good eating and exercising habits from the very start, you are giving your child invaluable life skills. In Australia, as in many parts of the developed world, there is an obesity epidemic, so making healthy diet choices and exercising is of even more importance.

Fad diets are rarely the answer for losing or sustaining a healthy weight and they are not recommended for breastfeeding mothers. The answer lies in having a balanced diet with foods from each food group (see Chapter 9).

If you are overweight or obese, see your local doctor for advice and support. Your doctor will either work out a diet and exercise program for you or refer you to a dietician or nutritionist.

If you simply want to drop back to your pre-baby weight, give it time and remember sensible eating goes hand in hand with regular exercise, so take every opportunity to be active. Put your baby in the pram and walk when you can. The minimum recommendation of moderately-intensive exercise is 30 to 60 minutes every day. This doesn't have to be done all at once but can be broken up during the day. Of course, before starting any new exercise program it's best to have a talk to your doctor.

To maintain motivation, there's nothing like exercising with others. A morning or evening walk with your partner (and your baby) can be an enjoyable daily activity. Some communities have pram-walking clubs. These clubs are also a great way to meet other parents. Walking groups often advertise for members through local libraries or local councils. Joining a gym with a crèche, doing yoga or pilates can also be a good way to exercise with other mums and have timeout from your baby. If lack of childcare is stopping your involvement in an exercise class, some communities have exercise programs that include your baby.

SMOKE-FREE ENVIRONMENTS

Living in a smoke-free environment benefits everyone. There is no longer a debate about the negative effects of smoking. The damage done by smoking and the inhalation of second-hand smoke is well documented. If you are thinking of having a baby and you are a smoker, if at all possible, now is the time to stop. Smoke does cross the placental barrier and impacts on the future health of your baby.

If you have family members or friends who are smokers, encourage them to smoke outside the house. Always keep smokers away from your baby. There are now lots of options and supports for people wanting to stop smoking. Many of these are free or subsidised by the government. Your local doctor or child and family health nurse will be able to provide you with information and support.

PHYSICAL RECOVERY AFTER PREGNANCY AND CHILDBIRTH

Some women recover very quickly, but for most women it takes several weeks, even months, to recover from the impact of pregnancy and childbirth. By your six-week check-up with your obstetrician or at the postnatal hospital clinic, your body should be returning to normal. If you have urinary incontinence (e.g. leaking urine when you laugh, cough or sneeze), or back pain, it's a good idea to discuss these symptoms with your doctor or midwife. A referral to a physiotherapist may be necessary to assist you to improve the situation. Incontinence can be and should be treated as it is debilitating and can be very embarrassing.

Before your six-week check-up you need to see your doctor if you are feeling unwell or experiencing:

- A vaginal discharge that is increasing, not decreasing; is smelly and/or contains blood (it is normal to have a bloody discharge in the first week)
- Pain or burning when passing urine
- Fever
- Joint pain.

Ensuring you are physically well is essential. Babies need healthy parents.

TIME FOR SEX

Having sex in the days or even weeks after the birth of your baby may be the very last thing you are thinking about or looking forward to. There are no strict rules about when to resume sexual relations with your partner. You can start when you are feeling ready. Some women who have had an episiotomy or tear or a traumatic birth experience, may require more time to feel able to be intimate with their partner.

Using a lubricant can make it easier to commence intercourse. Take it slowly, if it is too painful stop and try again in the next week or so, or when you have healed. Commencing pelvic floor exercises will assist in returning the muscle tone of your pelvic floor.

Oxytocin is involved in sexual arousal, so don't be surprised if breastmilk starts to leak or spurt from your breasts.

It is normal not to be interested in sex for several weeks or months. Many parents are just too tired. Some partners are concerned about causing their partner pain or harm. Talking through any fears or concerns with your partner is important.

Equally, many couples are very interested in resuming intercourse or at least an intimate relationship. There are lots of other ways to show your love for each other other than sex.

If you are starting to have intercourse, it is essential you consider the need for contraception. If you are fully breastfeeding, have not started to menstruate or your baby is younger than six months of age it will provide some protection against conception, but there is not a 100% guarantee you will not get pregnant. It is always wise to talk to your doctor about this at the six-week check up. If you are not fully breastfeeding or are offering your baby an infant formula, it is important to discuss your contraception needs before leaving hospital or in the early weeks after the birth of your baby.

LACK OF SLEEP

Lack of sleep can be a problem for many new parents, as caring for a baby requires an incredible physical effort. Dealing with fatigue while you're caring for a baby, going to work or needing to drive a car, can be extremely difficult and dangerous. Severe lack of sleep can feel like you are drunk. It can have an impact on your coordination and unwanted mood swings can develop.

Avoid working right up to your due date if you possibly can. Having a few weeks off before the birth of your baby will help you recover more fully after the birth. Many women tend to start their motherhood journey feeling tired.

Communication between parents is essential at all times, however, when one or both parents are fatigued this becomes critically important. Figuring out ways to enable extra sleep and time out needs to become a key priority. During pregnancy, it is helpful to talk about strategies you can put in place once your baby arrives. Questions to explore include:

- If you are the parent working in the paid workforce, how much time will you be able to spend sharing the care of your baby?
- Are there family members or friends who can come and stay for at least a week to assist in caring for the other children, help with cooking and housework and allow you to rest?
- What are the house maintenance or cleaning activities that need to be completed on a regular basis? Who will take responsibility for ensuring they are completed?
- Are there activities or tasks that you can do before your baby arrives that will make your home easier to manage?

Many parents change their attitude about using extra time catching up on housework or shopping, and use it to catch up on sleep or rest and do something pleasurable and relaxing. For other parents this is not an option as they are unable to rest if the house is a mess. If you find it too difficult to ignore the housework, work out ways to reduce your workload. Reducing clutter (if possible during pregnancy) can make housework easier to complete, for example.

Other ways you can catch up on sleep or relax include:

- Organise Occasional Care for your baby and other young children, and use the time to go home and have a sleep. Most councils operate Occasional Care Centres.
- When the baby is asleep, use the time to put your feet up and have a nap.
- If family or friends offer to look after your baby, ask them to take the baby out for a couple of hours. This will allow you to switch off and sleep.

If you are finding it difficult to sleep, even just lying down for half an hour and closing your eyes can help you regain some energy. Cutting down or eliminating caffeine (coffee, cola) from your diet can also help you sleep.

FEELING ANGRY

Anger is a normal human emotion. Being tired, and having a baby who seems to be crying for long periods of time can be extremely upsetting and scary. Feelings of anger usually occur for a good reason. These feelings are a warning sign to stop and think about what might be happening to you, even though it is not always possible to isolate the cause. Anger can be a serious outcome of feeling exhausted. Feelings of anxiety, fear, exhaustion, frustration and not feeling valued, can all combine until you are at breaking point.

Get to know your body signals that you are getting angry. Ask yourself:

- What am I experiencing at the moment?
- What am I feeling?
- What do I need to do to feel calmer and less angry?

Acting early to relieve these feelings, rather than waiting until you are out of control and ready to explode, is a good way to short circuit tension build-up.

The real concern with feeling anger is that it is easy to temporarily lose control of your behaviour. Sometimes you strike out at the people you love the most, including your baby.

What to do if you feel that you're just not coping:

- Phone a friend or support person. They might be able to come and provide you with some reassurance.
- Call a parents help-line such as Tresillian's.
- Visit your child and family health nurse who can assist you develop a plan to help manage the situation.
- Go outside for a walk or run. If there is no one to look after your baby take them with you in the pram.
- Talk to your partner, a family member or friend to see if they can give you some free time, where you can sleep or just relax.

If you become angry or lose control frequently, talking to a professional counsellor will usually make a huge difference to the way you may be feeling and provide ways to manage your feelings.

PARENTAL HEALTH

It is well documented that a parent's mental health has a significant impact on a baby's brain development. The first three months after the birth of your baby is a time when you need to emotionally and physically care for yourself to ensure you recover from the enormous emotional and physical changes that come with having a baby. A baby needs to have a parent who is able to be responsive to their needs. This is difficult to do if you are distressed, anxious or depressed.

In Australia, there is an increased recognition of the importance of early identification of risk factors that may trigger the onset of emotional distress, postnatal depression and anxiety. The aim is to enable health professionals to support women during pregnancy and into the first year after giving birth. Partners also need to be mentally healthy to effectively parent and provide the necessary support to their partner and children.

During pregnancy your midwife will ask you a series of questions related to your social and emotional wellbeing. They will also ask you to complete an Edinburgh Depression Scale questionnaire. Your responses to the questions will assist the midwife and you to discuss and explore your feelings. These questions will also enable you to discuss concerns or anxieties you may have about becoming a mother. It's well documented that women with a pre-existing mental illness prior to pregnancy are more likely to experience some form of mental illness after the birth of their baby. We also know that many women (and men) can develop anxiety and depression during pregnancy. These assessments will be repeated several times during your baby's first year.

Early supportive interventions such as counselling and, in some instances, medication are recommended in such cases. Talk to your doctor before becoming pregnant or during pregnancy if you have a pre-existing mental illness or have had a previous episode of mental illness. This will allow time to review your current health status and put in place lots of support to ensure you stay healthy.

BABY BLUES

The baby blues occur on or around the third day after giving birth. Up to 80% of women experience the baby blues, and it can be confusing and distressing for the mother. You may be:

- Teary
- Irritable
- Oversensitive when interacting with other people
- Having mood swings, from feeling happy to bursting into tears, for no known reason.

Fortunately, most mothers begin to feel better after a couple of days, especially as the tasks involved in being a new parent start to feel less daunting and, of course, if they are able to get some all important regular sleep. A new father's emotions can also feel a little out of control as the responsibility of being a parent can be overwhelming. You might be feeling very confused about how your partner is acting, and that you can't seem to do anything right or helpful.

As a couple, you need to talk about your feelings and work out ways in which you can be provided with adequate support. Being kind to each other and being forgiving of each other's mistakes is a great place to begin gaining control of the situation.

If your feelings of distress and rapid mood changes do not start to diminish within a week, it is time to seek professional support. Your child and family health nurse is a great starting point. The nurse will know what is available in your community and how to access these services. The nurse may also advise you to seek medical attention.

POSTNATAL DEPRESSION AND ANXIETY

Postnatal depression and anxiety are the most commonly occurring mental illnesses after the birth of a baby. A definition for postnatal depression is that it develops from one month to one year after the birth of a baby.

In Australia, it has been identified that 10% of women develop antenatal depression during pregnancy and up to 16% of women develop postnatal depression during the first year after the birth of their baby. It is very common to feel symptoms of anxiety along with depression.

If you are experiencing some of the following symptoms for two weeks or more, it is time to ask for help.

1. Feeling inadequate. This can include feeling like a failure, guilty, ashamed, worthless, hopeless, helpless, empty or sad.
2. Having a low mood, feeling numb.
3. Frequently feeling close to tears.
4. Feeling angry, irritable or resentful (this can include feeling easily irritated by your partner or other children, and friends and other family members).
5. Having trouble sleeping (being unable to fall asleep or get back to sleep after night feeds) or sleeping for excessive amounts of time, or having nightmares.
6. Having decreased energy and feeling exhausted most of the time (this symptom on its own may be due to a lack of sleep and not depression).
7. Feeling fearful for your baby; fear of being alone with the baby or baby being unsettled.
8. Losing interest in things that you usually enjoy.
9. Appetite changes – either not eating or over-eating.
10. Lacking motivation and being unable to cope with the daily routine.

11. Fear of being alone or going out of the house.
12. Withdrawing from social contact; not looking after yourself properly.
13. Having trouble thinking clearly or making decisions, lack of concentration and poor memory (these symptoms are not uncommon for new mothers due to fatigue and other stressors).
14. Having thoughts about harming yourself or the baby, ending your life (you must seek help immediately), or wanting to escape or get away from everything.

It is quite common to experience symptoms of anxiety, as well as depression. Several of the above symptoms on their own may be a normal response to being a new parent and the resultant lack of sleep and increased physical demands.

Talking to your child and family health nurse or doctor can assist you to work out what are normal feelings associated with being a new parent and the increased workload, and what is possibly depression or anxiety.

Regardless of the diagnosis these are some basic guidelines:
1. Arrange for some assistance with your baby and household chores, so you can get some extra daytime and night-time sleep.
2. Be realistic in what you can achieve in a day.
3. Take a daily walk. This is an activity you can do as a family each day.
4. Ask and accept help from health professionals, family and friends.

Your baby will also need some special time and additional input during each day. It is important throughout each day that you:
1. Respond when your baby makes a sound, cries or smiles at you.
2. Look at and smile at your baby.
3. Talk and sing to your baby.
4. Touch and hold your baby.
5. Take the time to get to know each other.

These seem simple things to do, but it is surprising how easy it is to go all day without paying very much attention to, let alone enjoying, being with your baby when you are feeling distressed, anxious and depressed.

All parents want to be the best parents they can be and sometimes that means acknowledging there might be some difficulties and getting advice and treatment sooner rather than later. This helps parents get back into their role of being effective parents as soon as possible. A common statement by many mothers is, "Why did I wait so long before getting help?"

If you have thoughts that the baby or your family would be better off without you, you have thoughts of suicide, or you think you might harm yourself or your baby, seek help immediately.

If your partner is having any of the above thoughts or is acting out of character, it is vital you seek medical help for them. You will need to play a key role in initiating assistance and ongoing care for your partner. You will also need to act to ensure the safety of your baby and other children.

CHAPTER SUMMARY

- A happy and healthy parent is essential for a baby's health and wellbeing.
- Give yourself time to adjust to the demands of parenthood; you are on a huge learning curve with your baby.
- If you do not have a strong and supportive network, remember it is never too late to start to develop this type of network. Your child and family health nurse is a great starting point.
- Eat a healthy diet, have regular exercise and time to relax each day to keep you healthy and physically and emotionally well.
- Anger is a normal human emotion. Try and act early to deal with feelings and concerns that are making you feel angry.
- Up to 80% of new mothers experience the baby blues around day three. Most mothers feel better after a couple of days.
- Postnatal depression occurs in up to 16% of women after the birth of the baby. It can also occur during pregnancy. Seeking family and professional help and support will assist you to become healthy again.
- If you are having thoughts about harming yourself or the baby, or ending your life, you must seek help immediately.

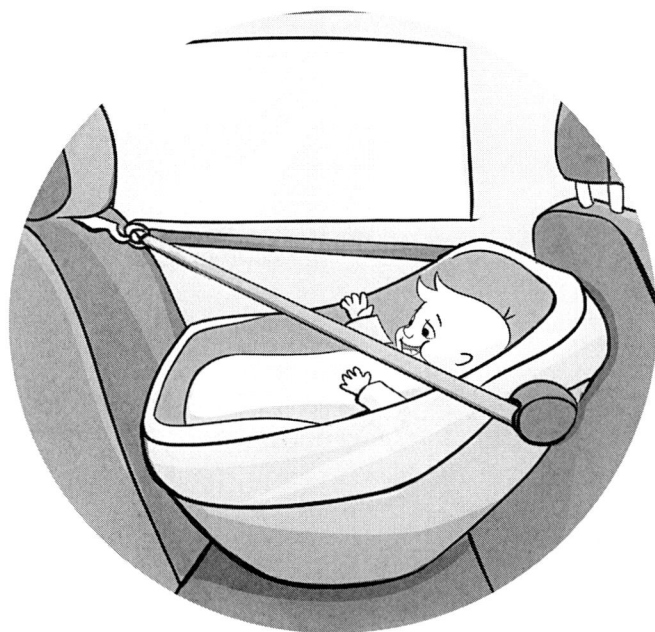

Chapter Three
BABY NEEDS

PREPARING FOR THE ARRIVAL of your baby is lots of fun, but it can be an expensive exercise and it's easy to get carried away with the latest trend in baby equipment and baby clothing.

Before committing yourself to lots of equipment, remember that babies grow rapidly, and equipment and clothing become obsolete very quickly. Babies also don't know that they are wearing hand-me-downs or sitting in a second-hand high chair. If you are buying or being given second-hand equipment, as a safety measure, it is worthwhile checking the Australian government website that provides information about equipment that has been recalled due to safety problems (www.recalls. gov.au) or check with the *Product Safety Australia* website for safety information (www.productsafety.gov.au).

Having a safe place for your newborn baby to sleep is essential. Baby furniture stores and buy, swap and sell websites all provide a great range when it comes to baby bassinets, cots and bedding. Regardless of your choice, safety has to be a major consideration.

BASSINETS

In the first six to eight weeks after birth many parents choose to sleep their baby in a bassinet. After that time, most babies have outgrown the bassinet and are ready to move into a cot. Whether you're buying a brand new bassinet or borrowing one, there are safety features you need to be aware of:

- Is it the right size and style to suit your baby's age, length and weight?
- Does it have a wide and stable leg base (as this will assist in reducing the risk of it tipping over)?
- Is the bottom of the basket sturdy enough to support baby's weight and movement?
- Is the mattress firm and snug fitting – it should be no thicker than 75 mm as this reduces the risk of suffocation.
- The sides of the basket should be at least 300 mm higher than the mattress to stop your baby falling out.
- Remove any loose ribbons, pillows and protective coverings from the sides of the cot to reduce the risk of choking and sudden infant death.
- If you're purchasing a bassinet second-hand, make sure it is painted with lead-free paint.

The main risks to your baby from a bassinet are *suffocation* and *falls* so make sure the bassinet is stable. Move your baby to a cot as soon as they show any signs of being able to roll over or if they show any signs of outgrowing the bassinet.

BABY HAMMOCKS

At Tresillian we do not advise parents to sleep their babies in a hammock as there are no standards for the production of hammocks and babies can easily fall. Tresillian recommends cots or bassinets that meet the latest guidelines to prevent Sudden Infant Death Syndrome (SIDS).

COTS

Many parents save money by buying a cot and using this for their baby from birth.

When purchasing a cot make sure it has a label confirming that it meets current Australian Standards. Check that it's stable, does not wobble and that all the safety catches are in working order and not likely to trap tiny fingers. Slats (or bars) should be at least 50 mm apart.

Your baby's cot should be a clutter-free environment to reduce the risk of suffocation and choking. This is easily achieved by avoiding the placement of bumpers, pillows and stuffed toys inside the cot. In fact, toys of any kind are best saved for times when baby is awake and you can supervise their use.

Where should I position the cot? It's not about décor when it comes to baby and safety. Where the cot is placed in your baby's room needs to be carefully considered. Babies quickly learn how to climb and pull and love putting things in their mouth.

Tresillian recommends you place your cot in the middle of the room (not near a window where your baby can potentially pull on blinds, curtains and cords, including electrical cords) as these can result in strangulation. All other furniture should be placed well away from the cot – you don't want to help your baby or toddler to climb out!

PORTABLE COTS

Portable cots, like regular cots, have potential safety hazards. While there is an Australian Standard that covers the construction of portable cots, there are also things as a parent you can do to keep your baby safe.

- If your baby can undo the latches stop using the cot.
- If your baby weighs more than 15 kg stop using the cot.
- Regularly check the cot is in good repair, e.g. tears in cot fabric or vinyl, loose or broken locks or tears that could result in the cot collapsing.
- Place the cot away from potential hazards like cords, windows, curtains and so on.
- Never use a portable cot for long-term sleeping arrangements.
- Never use a mattress that is not intended for the cot.
- Never use an extra mattress, pillows, or toys in a portable cot as they are a potential safety risk for you baby that could result in suffocation, or provide a foothold that may result in a fall.

TWINS AND COTS

If you are a parent of twins, in the early days you can place each baby in the same cot with their feet facing towards the centre. Sleep your twins in nightwear that has a sleeping bag bottom. This avoids the use of bedclothes and makes the environment much safer. The added advantage is that they are less likely to wake up because they have uncovered and become cold. As they grow, you will have to move your babies into separate cots.

If you have two or more babies or toddlers in cots in the same room, make sure there is a good distance between them to reduce the risk of climbing.

NOTE: Antique cots are not safe for baby. They **do not** meet the current Australian Safety Standards.

MATTRESSES AND BEDDING

A mattress can be a potential safety risk. A mattress needs to:
- Fit the bassinet or cot snugly, leaving no gaps between the mattress and the bassinet or cot.
- Be firm; a serious risk is present if a mattress is soft and your baby happens to roll over and their face becomes trapped or covered.
- Be clean; special attention to checking the mattress is necessary if the mattress has been used by other children.
- Be used flat, not tilted or elevated.
- Have no covering such as plastic.

> **NOTE:** Babies should never be placed on a soft mattress, waterbed, beanbag or pillows to sleep with or without a parent sleeping with them. These are extremely dangerous for babies.

BED COVERINGS

Some bed coverings have the potential to cover your baby's face or restrict airflow in the bassinet or cot. When your baby is put into bed to sleep, a very minimalist approach is the safest and best.
- Sheets, blankets, wraps and baby sleeping bags are best if made of natural fibres, e.g. cotton, bamboo and wool.
- The bottom sheet should be fitted so that it doesn't come loose and cause a suffocation risk.
- Choose subtle colours, such as white or pastels; these are calming and less stimulating for your baby.

Bedding or other items that can result in harm include:
- Bassinet or cot liners or padding
- Quilts or doonas
- Sheepskins
- Items that are meant to stop baby rolling over in their sleep, e.g. rolled up towels, nappies or commercial devices

- Mattress covers that are made of plastic or rubber that can be a suffocation risk
- Pillows (babies don't need a pillow and they cause a substantial risk) and pillow cases
- Toys
- Hot water bottles, electric blankets or wheat bags in your baby's bed.

See Chapter 5 for further information on safe sleep and sleep environments.

LIFTING AND CARRYING YOUR BABY AND EQUIPMENT

Having a baby involves regular and prolonged lifting and carrying. Parents who have already experienced back injuries need to take greater care and avoid aggravating or compounding their back, shoulder or knee problems or injuries.

When lifting a baby or baby equipment, the same principles as for lifting any object should be applied. It's a good idea to remember your BACK:

Back straight – keep the natural curve in your back

Avoid twisting – never twist and lift

Close to body – keep your baby or other load close to your body

Keep smooth – lift in a smooth movement – never jerk

Avoid carrying your baby on your hip as this can result in long-term musculoskeletal injuries. Use chairs or furniture with upper back support when holding or rocking your baby.

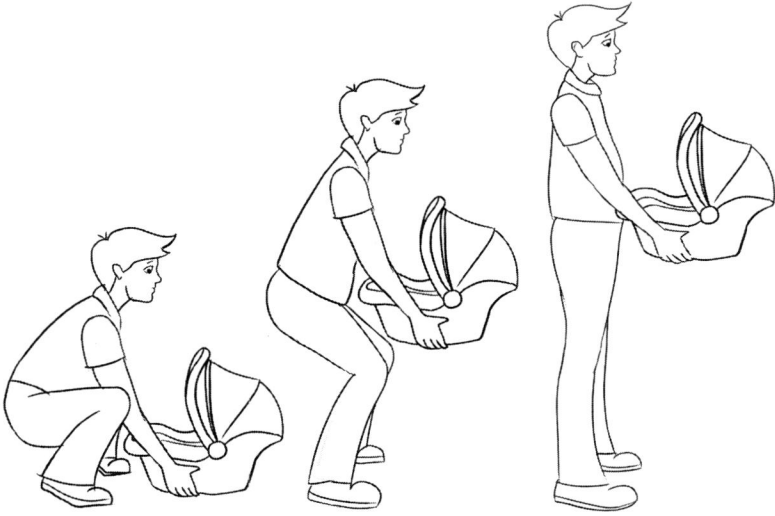

EQUIPMENT AND BABY CLOTHING BASIC RULES

In this chapter, some of the issues you need to consider when selecting equipment and clothes for your baby will be highlighted. Only the everyday necessary equipment will be discussed. However, we would strongly advise that equipment such as baby exercise jumpers and baby walkers are not used due to the high risk of injury.

There are potential problems that may occur with a baby's physical development and ability to walk. For example, babies do not learn to balance while they are in a walker or jumping; they can also bypass the all important skills of crawling, and pulling up on furniture that build the muscles needed for walking. They often have a tendency to walk on their toes as their leg muscles may have become tight from jumping or propelling themselves by their toes.

Importantly, all the information in this chapter has been checked against the Australian Standards when available. These standards do change over time, so if you are in doubt about any product you are buying or have been given for your baby, please check the most recent update on the Product Safety Australia website.

There are a few basic rules when selecting equipment and baby clothing. These are:

- ✓ Is it safe?
- ✓ Does it meet Australian Standards?
- ✓ Is it a low fire risk? Natural fibres are the best
- ✓ Are there cords or strings that can harm? For example, strangulation or constriction of blood flow to baby's fingers or toes can occur.
- ✓ Will you be safe using this equipment? Is it too heavy or bulky to lift?
- ✓ Are there small parts that are a potential choke risk?
- ✓ Are there gaps between mattress and cot railings that will pose a risk?
- ✓ Is the paint used non-toxic, e.g. lead-free?
- ✓ How often will you use this piece of equipment? Do you have another piece of equipment that does a similar job? Or can you borrow this piece of equipment from a friend?
- ✓ Is it developmentally appropriate and safe for your baby?

BABY CLOTHING

Most babies end up with more clothing than they can wear. Gifts of lovely new and pre-loved clothes will arrive, so you might want to wait before you rush out and fill your baby's wardrobe. It is fine to buy more than just a few items of clothing without going overboard, especially since it often helps make your pregnancy feel real. Most parents, as well as having the basics, also buy a couple of cute pieces of clothing for their baby when they go on a special outing.

Whenever possible buy or ask for clothing made from natural fibres – cotton, wool, silk and bamboo. The simpler the clothes you dress your baby in, the easier it is to manage changing and the more comfortable the clothing will usually be for your baby. Your baby will need some basic clothing. A good starting point is to have:

- • Five to six singlets.
- • Six pairs of socks or bootees.

- Two bonnets or beanies.
- Six to eight jumpsuits – these are the most practical articles of clothing. In winter or cooler nights choose long leg and sleeve jumpsuits. In summer you can use a short-sleeve suit that does not have legs. They are easy to get your baby dressed or undressed and can be washed frequently without losing their shape (see below for safety features).
- Two baby sleeping bags for sleeping (see below for safety features). Baby sleeping bags are very useful in winter, and especially as your baby becomes more active. They also work well if taking your baby out on a cold winter's day to keep socks on and their legs and feet cosy.
- Three to four jackets or cardigans.
- Three to four gauze wraps (in summer), or flannelette/brushed cotton in winter.
- Leggings will help keep your baby warm in winter .
- Four to six bibs of a reasonable size to protect clothing.

Babies grow very quickly, so unless you have a very small baby, size 00 or 0 will allow for your baby's growth.

BABY'S DAY AND SLEEPWEAR SAFETY

Your baby's sleepwear needs to be comfortable, safe and easy to use. There is an Australian and New Zealand Standard for baby sleepwear and some daywear, but essentially, when choosing baby day or sleepwear, look for clothing that:
- Is close-fitting with a low fire danger rating
- Makes it easy to dress and undress your baby
- Is easy to wash and no ironing needed
- Has no fiddly fastenings – zippers, Velcro or studs are the best
- Has no ribbons or material ties
- Is front fastening so it is comfortable for your baby to lie on their back
- If fitted around the neck, wrists or ankles with elastic or elasticised bands, is not too tight.

After washing, always check for loose threads that may cause a danger to tiny fingers or toes by restricting circulation. If there are buttons, check they are securely sewn on – they can become a major choking risk.

CHANGE TABLES

A change table provides a solid base at the right height to change your baby's nappies and protect your back.

The main hazard with a change table is baby falling. To minimise the risk of this happening, make sure that it is a safe change table that has these features:
- Ends and sides raised at least 100 mm to help prevent your baby from falling.
- Is stable and correctly assembled.
- Is easy to clean.
- Is at the right height to avoid back problems or injuries .
- No gaps in the change table or close to the table that will trap or injure your baby's fingers, arms, head, legs or toes.
- Secure locking devices if it is a folding table.

Safety habits that will help to keep your baby safe:
- Never leave your baby unattended on the change table even for a 'couple of seconds'.
- Always keep one hand on the baby when they are on the change table.
- If you need to get something you have forgotten take your baby with you.
- Ignore any interruptions like phone calls.
- Have everything ready before you place your baby on the table.
- Make sure harmful items like tubes of cream are out of your baby's reach. Don't use these items to distract your baby.
- Use a safety harness if available on the table (but never leave your baby alone on the table).
- Remember to wash your hands after you have disposed of the nappy.

NAPPIES

There is a debate about what is the best type of nappy to use – cloth or disposable nappies. Really the choice is yours. It may help you to make the decision by considering:
- Cost
- Convenience
- Environmental concerns
- Work involved in buying or laundering them
- And finally the look and feel of the nappy.

Your baby will use approximately 60 nappies a week in the first few months of their life. The number of nappies needed then decreases after four to six months of age. Most babies spend some time of the day or night in nappies until they are two years old and some, a little longer.

Some parents use a combination of disposable and cloth nappies. This is especially helpful if you are returning to the paid workforce or have other demanding obligations you need to manage.

CLOTH NAPPIES

Cloth nappies require an initial outlay of money but work out being cheaper in the long term as they can be reused for your next baby. Of course if you choose to dry them using a clothes dryer or you use a nappy service, this can significantly increase the cost. Drying nappies in the sunlight is the most cost effective method.

If you decide to use cloth nappies you will find a large range available. These include nappies made from terry towelling, flannel and bamboo. Some nappies are flat requiring you to fold each time they are used – just like grandma did. Or they are already pre-formed so no folding is needed. Some have a plastic covering to assist in reducing the risk of leakage.

As a minimum you will need two dozen nappies but three dozen allows you to manage on rainy days or when you are very busy.

Some parents like to use a nappy liner and this makes cleaning the nappy slightly easier. Make sure you do not flush these liners into your toilet. Some liners can be washed with the nappies and reused especially if only wet from urine. If the cloth nappy you choose doesn't have an attached fastener, it is probably safer to use a plastic fastener in preference to a metal nappy pin.

WASHING CLOTH NAPPIES

- Disposing of your baby's poo prior to washing is essential (this has to be done with disposable nappies as well).
- Some parents have a hose attached to their toilet to help rinse the poo and urine off the nappy.
- Place the nappy in a bucket with a tightly fitting lid (make sure the lid cannot be removed by a young child). You can either dry store (no water in the bucket) the nappies or have water in the bucket (because you have rinsed the nappies, further soaking is not necessary).
- Once the bucket is full of nappies you can empty the nappies into your washing machine. If you soaked the nappies, remember not to empty the water used into the washing machine.
- Dry nappies in the sun.
- Remember to wash your hands after touching dirty nappies and before doing any other tasks.

DISPOSABLE NAPPIES

If you choose disposable nappies, the brand you use will be determined by some of the things previously mentioned such as cost, appearance, ease of access and environmental claims the companies make about their nappies.

To use a disposable nappy:
- Follow the instructions on the package.
- Make sure you wash off any poo before disposing of the nappy.
- Don't flush nappies down the toilet.
- Place in a plastic bag that you can seal before disposing of the nappy.
- Remember to wash your hands after touching dirty nappies and before doing any other tasks.

PRAMS AND STROLLERS

Prams and strollers can have a considerable price tag and you can pay anywhere from hundreds to thousands of dollars. At the end of the day, you want a pram to suit your needs, for example, if you're a regular jogger, a three-wheel pram may be your preference. If possible, buy a pram or stroller that allows your baby to face towards you. Whatever pram you decide on be sure it meets the Australian Standards and that it's light. Remember, you'll be lifting it in and out of cars and public transport for at least the next few years. Prams and strollers are a wonderful invention for parents but, as with all baby equipment, read the instructions or manual before use.

SAFETY ISSUES

- Stay with your baby while they are in their pram or stroller.
- Do not cover the front of the pram with blankets as this can reduce the airflow to your baby.
- Do not allow your baby to stand up or lean out of the pram or stroller.
- Always apply the safety brakes when the pram is stationary.
- Always position the pram or stroller parallel to hazards such as road crossings, water or railway tracks.
- Use the tether strap and harness to keep your baby safe.
- Regularly check frame latches and fabric fasteners are in good condition and locked before use.
- Regularly check the brakes to make sure they are in good condition and function well.
- Only use the pram or stroller for the intended number of babies.
- Don't allow other children to stand, climb on or lean over the pram or stroller.
- Always remove your baby from the pram or stroller before adjusting its position or any moving parts.
- Make sure other children outside the pram or stroller keep fingers away from the folding and unfolding parts of the pram or stroller.

There are several precautions that need special mention:

- A pram or stroller is never to be used as a substitute for a cot – there is a potential for the baby to become trapped and seriously injured or even die due to strangulation and suffocation.
- Always put your baby down on their back in a pram – this is the safest position for them if they fall asleep.
- Pillows, cushions or bumpers should never be used.
- Do not allow other young children to push the pram or stroller without your assistance.
- Do not hang shopping on the handles – the pram or stroller can easily tip over.
- Always use the brakes and wrist tether straps when you stop the pram or stroller – there have been some terrible accidents when brakes and tether straps have not been used at appropriate times, for example, when waiting to cross the road or on train platforms.

BABY SLINGS

Baby slings have regained popularity in recent years. These are usually made of a material sash and come in several different designs. It is now being advised that slings should not be used for babies under four months of age. Babies need a straight back to safely breathe and very young babies under four months do not have the head control to allow them to easily move their head if they get into breathing difficulties.

BABY POUCHES AND BACKPACKS

Baby pouches and backpacks come in many styles and can be designed to carry your baby on your front or back. A pouch or backpack can be a very useful piece of baby equipment as:

- They allow you to carry your baby and leave your hands free.
- Babies often calm more quickly in a carrier due to the physical contact with their parent. Babies respond to the parent's smell, the movement and the ability to snuggle into the parent.
- They allow greater mobility in crowded situations or when there is uneven ground.

As with all equipment consider whether or not it is safe for your baby:

- Make sure it is designed for your baby's developmental age and there is adequate head support (this is especially important when your baby has limited head and neck control).
- It is appropriate for your baby's size and weight (there should be a tag attached with this information).
- All body and limb straps, ties or buckles are in good condition and you use them every time baby is placed into the pouch or backpack.
- Test the pouch or backpack by trying on before buying, make sure it is comfortable and practical for your needs.
- Ensure the padding on any metal frame is adequate and will not cause any injury or discomfort to your baby or you.
- When putting your baby in or taking them out of the pouch or backpack carrier take care baby does not get injured.

BABY DUMMIES

Using a dummy provides a baby with non-nutritive sucking which is a natural thing for babies to do and it often helps calm and soothe them. Dummies are also called pacifiers or soothers in some countries. Professional and community opinion is divided about the use of dummies. In particular it is not recommended a dummy be used when breastfeeding is still being established.

If used correctly most dummies are safe, but as with all baby equipment there are safety risks of choking, strangulation and infection. The main safety concerns are:

- Strangulation due to the dummy being attached to a cord or chain.
- Choking, if parts are smaller than recommended size or the dummy is damaged or poorly constructed (does not meet the Australian Standards).

- Cuts and abrasions if your baby falls over while walking with a dummy in their mouth.

It is important the dummy you are purchasing meets Australian Standards. They must:
- Have a shield with ventilation holes to prevent suffocation if the entire dummy enters your baby's mouth.
- Be strong enough not to break into small pieces that can cause a choking hazard.
- Not have strings or ties that could become wrapped around your baby's neck. This has the potential to cause your baby to be strangled.

If your baby uses a dummy ensure you:
- Check the dummy prior to giving it to your baby. It is advised you pull firmly on the teat while tugging on the dummy handle to ensure that under pressure it does not come apart.
- Buy a new dummy at regular intervals as they weaken with use and cleaning.
- Clean the dummy regularly by sterilising the dummy or washing in hot soapy water, rinsing and then air drying.
- If you are concerned about the condition of the dummy throw it away and use a new dummy.
- If your baby can remove the dummy watch them to make sure they don't put the whole dummy in their mouths.
- If your baby is teething or chewing, avoid using the dummy, as chewing might cause damage to the dummy and cause it to be a choke hazard.

CAR SAFETY RESTRAINTS

Safely restraining your baby is a legal requirement. Restraints that are correctly fitted and meet the Australian Standards are more likely to reduce the impact of an accident on your infant. This means that restraints bought from overseas may not meet Australian Standards. The Australian Standards are one of the most stringent in the world as they require all restraints to be tested in side and rear impact tests and some with inverted test for roll-over protection.

Car safety restraints are required by law to be used to transport infants and young children in a vehicle. The current rules require:

- Children under the age of six months must use an approved, properly fastened and adjusted rearward facing restraint (also known as a baby capsule).
- Children aged between six months and under four years must use an approved, properly fastened and adjusted rearward facing child restraint or a forward facing restraint.
- Children aged between four years and under seven years must use an approved, properly fastened and adjusted forward facing restraint or an approved booster seat which is properly positioned and fastened.

If your baby is very small it is advised to keep them in their current restraint until they reach the required height and weight for the next size restraint. It's best to follow the manufacturer's instructions.

Additional rules about transporting children in vehicles:

- If a car has two or more rows of seats, then children under four years must not travel in the front seat.
- If all seats other than the front seats are being used by children under seven years, children aged between the age of four and six years (inclusive) may travel in the front seat provided they use an approved restraint or booster seat that is properly fitted.

The driver is responsible for making sure all passengers are correctly restrained. Penalties are issued if they are not. For more information check with your local road and traffic authority.

BUYING A CAR RESTRAINT

The mandatory standard applies to all car restraints. Ensure the Australian Standards label is on the restraint.

When buying a child car restraint, make sure they have the following mandatory warnings:

- Use the restraint exactly as shown in the instructions.
- Always supervise children because they can undo buckles.
- Don't alter or modify the restraint.
- Have repairs made only by the manufacturer or agent.
- Don't allow the restraint to come into contact with polishes, oil, bleach and other chemicals.
- Destroy the restraint if it has been in a severe crash, even if no damage is visible.

The restraint you choose may also have additional manufacturer warnings and it is important these are followed.

IMPORTANT: DON'T LEAVE CHILDREN UNATTENDED IN THE CAR.

SECOND-HAND RESTRAINTS

If you are given or buying a second-hand restraint it is essential you check the following to ensure it will provide the necessary protection for your baby if an accident occurs. The restraint must:

- Have the Australian Standards label attached.
- Never have been in a crash.
- Be in good condition with no frayed or broken straps or buckles.
- Come with the original instruction booklet.

FITTING AND USING THE CAR RESTRAINT

It is highly recommended that you have your child's car restraint fitted at an approved fitting station. To find out the location of the nearest fitting station, contact your local road and traffic authority.

When placing your baby in the restraint make sure it fits snugly with no twisted or slack straps.

HIGH CHAIRS

A high chair is designed for your baby to be safely contained when eating. Being at table height allows your baby to be part of family meals. Using a high chair gives them more independence as they start to explore their food and learn to feed themselves.

When buying a high chair make sure:

- It has a strong and sturdy framework.
- The base is wide and stable.
- It has a five-point harness that goes over the baby's shoulders, around their waist and between their legs.
- The backrest is fixed – it needs to remain stable and not move.
- All the locks work and are locked in place when putting your baby in each time you use the high chair.
- There are no moving parts to trap and crush fingers, or sharp edges that could cut your baby.
- If there are wheels or castors on the chair, at least two of the wheels have well functioning brakes.

The height of a high chair makes it a potential fall hazard, so developing safety habits is essential.

- Always make sure your baby is strapped in.
- Always supervise your baby.
- Make sure you move your baby's hands, arms and legs out of the way when fitting the tray.
- Do not allow your baby to stand or climb into or out of the high chair.
- Regularly check for broken or loose parts, exposed padding or torn material these can be a choking hazard for your baby.
- Make sure your baby can't touch or pull on electrical cords, tablecloths, curtains, blinds or cords from the high chair.
- Never allow other children to climb on or play near the high chair.

SAFETY GATES

Safety gates can provide an effective barrier to prevent your exploring baby from coming to harm. Babies love trying to go up and down stairs so having a safety gate at the bottom and top of the stairs gives you a level of security. In high-risk areas such as the kitchen, the use of a wall-mounted gate is the safest option.

PLAYPENS

Playpens help keep your baby safe as they become mobile and you are busy doing housework (such as ironing) or if you have other young children or pets. When buying a playpen make sure:

- It is stable, sturdy and remains rigid when your baby leans over the side so it won't tip.
- Spaces between the bars are no larger than 95 mm, as larger gaps may trap your baby's head.
- Sides are at least 500 mm high.
- Latches and locks can be locked securely and cannot be undone by your baby.
- It is easy to clean.
- It has a non-toxic finish.

Remember to:

- Always supervise your baby while they are in the playpen.
- Never use a portable cot as a playpen.
- Make sure the playpen is assembled correctly using the manufacturer's instructions and all latches or locks are secure.
- Place the playpen away from curtains, blinds and stairs.
- Stop using the playpen once your baby can undo the latches or starts to climb.

TOY BOXES

Toy boxes are a great way to store your baby's toys. When you buy a toy box, choose one without a lid, or if there is a lid, choose one that has stoppers on the lid that leave a gap of 12 mm or more when the lid is closed. This will keep your baby's fingers and hands safe. As with all baby equipment, toy boxes should be placed away from hazardous areas such as windows, stairs and balconies.

TOYS FOR BABIES

You will be amazed at the number of toys your baby will accumulate. There are many claims made about the educational value of some toys and fortunately there are lots of alternatives that provide equal or more value educationally to your baby. Your baby's most important toy is you, their parent – you have the highest educational value of all baby toys. A baby will quickly throw aside a toy if a parent is willing to involve them in a game or conversation.

Are you aware that all toys should meet a mandatory Australian and New Zealand Standard? This standard aims to make toys safe for children aged from 0–36 months.

For specific toys:
- Stuffed toys need to be carefully checked to ensure that all seams are intact and there are no small parts such as eyes or buttons. The toy should also be easily washed.
- If a push or pull toy has a rigid handle, make sure it is well fixed to the toy. Toys with strings or ropes to pull them along can be a risk for strangulation. If it does have a string attached it should be no longer than 220 mm.
- Balloons (including burst balloons) should be kept away from babies. If you want your baby to play with a balloon always closely supervise and never leave unattended. Always tie a knot in the end instead of using a plastic balloon tie.
- Floating devices for use in a pool need to be sturdy. Remember these are not safety devices – babies need to have an adult with them, and be supervised at all time when near or in water.

- Toys that are strung across playpens, prams or strollers with cords, elastic, straps or string should be assembled using the manufacturer's instructions. Do not string toys across the cot or bassinet.

If you find a toy has become unsafe, throw it out so it no longer poses a risk to your baby. Make sure you destroy the toy to stop it becoming a risk to another young child.

In Chapter 6 you will find information about developmental stages and the type of toy that is suitable.

KEEPING YOUR BABY SAFE – A SUMMARY

- Ensure your baby is positioned on their back to sleep. This is known to reduce the risk of Sudden Infant Death Syndrome (SIDS).
- Check that their sleep environment is safe by keeping their bassinet or cot clear of bumpers and toys that could be a potential suffocation hazard.
- Dress your baby in nightwear with a sleeping bag bottom – avoid bed clothing that baby can wriggle underneath or that can cover their head.
- If your baby is on an elevated surface (change table, bed), keep one hand on their body at all times. This will stop them wriggling or falling off the edge.
- Make sure the car capsule or seat are safely attached and always strap your baby in to the capsule or seat.
- Never leave your baby with a feeding bottle propped up.
- Check all toys and baby equipment for potential choking or strangulation hazards.

Chapter Four

APPEARANCE AND BASIC PHYSICAL CARE

SOME NEWBORN BABIES can look beautiful and perfect at birth, while others look a little battered and a bit scrunched up. Remember, they have been in a watery environment and a very compact position for much of the nine months of your pregnancy. Labour for your baby requires many hours of being squeezed as they progress down the birth canal. Don't worry, squashed heads, ears and noses regain their normal shape within hours or days of birth. Bruises also fade and disappear fairly quickly. It is normal to worry about your baby's imperfections but if you are concerned speak to your doctor or midwife.

Learning to provide the basic care for your baby can be daunting in the first few weeks as a parent. It seems impossible to do it all, but juggling the feeds, bathing, nappy changes and all the other care your baby needs fall into place with time and support. It can be particularly difficult to master it all if you have had minimal previous contact with babies. The good news is that it's great fun caring for a baby and watching them grow and develop.

YOUR NEWBORN BABY

Newborn full-term babies are very resilient and robust. The fetus develops with a body structure that is flexible, to enable a safe arrival through the birth canal.

Your baby can be very alert shortly after birth. If you watch carefully you will see their eyes focusing and following the action in the room. The other action that is common and exciting for new parents is the intense gaze of your baby as they look at your face. If you have had painkillers or anaesthetic during labour, this can affect your baby's alertness and it may take a couple of hours or days for them to reach an alert state (see Chapter 5).

This period of alertness can sometimes only last for a short period and they are then likely to become very sleepy for the next 24 hours. You may have to wake them every three to four hours to feed.

HEAD
Your baby's head might be misshapen or have an oblong shape at birth due to the sutures in their skull over-riding (molding) to allow passage through the birth canal (see Chapter 15 on Child Health for further information). Their head may also be sporting some bruises with a large area that may have become swollen. This swelling on their head is usually due to the collection of fluid and blood in and around the scalp (*caput succedaneum*). It is usually the point of contact for prolonged impact during the labour. The good news is most babies look very normal within days, while others can take a few weeks.

If you have a planned caesarean section, your baby's head is likely to look round and otherwise well shaped.

EYES

Your baby's eyelids can look puffy for a few days after birth. This is a result of the pressure as they come through the birth canal. You may also notice that your baby may have a red area on the white part of their eye due to a minor bleed during birth. This should clear within a couple of days. Most babies are not born with their permanent eye colour. By six months, your baby's eye colour will usually be established.

NOSE

Newborn babies can look as if they have been in a boxing ring. Your baby's nose may be flattened at first, but this should correct itself within days of birth.

EARS

Ears, like noses, can get very squashed during birth. At birth, the cartilage in the ears is very soft and pliable. It can take up to a month for the cartilage to harden and your baby's ears will take on a more normal shape.

LANUGO (HAIRY BODY)

Lanugo is downy, very fine and soft hair that starts to cover the body of a fetus from about five months. It is normally shed prior to birth, but can still be present at birth. A newborn baby will usually shed the remaining lanugo within a few days or weeks of birth. Pre-term infants will usually have lanugo on their bodies at birth.

HEAD HAIR

Some babies are born with a very thick and shiny head of hair. This will usually fall out over the first weeks or months and be replaced with permanent hair. Some babies have minimal head hair at birth, and it can take many months before they have a reasonable head of hair. Don't be disappointed if your baby starts to develop a bald patch at the back of their head. This hair will grow back once your baby is able to change position and sit up.

FINGER AND TOENAILS

Fingernails and toenails are very soft and often appear paper thin and quite long. Baby's toenails can look like they are ingrown, but as long as they are not red or inflamed, they need no treatment except regular cutting.

SKIN

Your baby's skin appearance will usually depend on their gestation (time in the womb). Babies can be born with a white creamy (*vernix caseosa*) covering. This can be seen mainly in the creases of their arms and hips. This protects babies while they are in the amniotic fluid of the womb. Some babies can look very wrinkly, others will look very dry with flaking skin, especially if they were overdue (if your pregnancy has been longer than 42 weeks).

Within days, your baby may have lots of red splotches and blotches, or a fine rash. These will usually vanish as quickly as they appeared. No treatment is usually needed.

MILIA

If you notice what looks like tiny pimples on your baby's nose and cheeks, it's most likely to be *milia*. Milia are caused by blockages in the skin's sebaceous glands. They usually appear on a baby's nose and cheeks, but they may occur anywhere on the face. Milia do not cause your baby any discomfort. There is no treatment and they will disappear without leaving any marks. Milia are hard to prevent, though it can be helped by not allowing your baby to overheat.

UMBILICAL CORD

The umbilical cord plays an essential role during pregnancy. It enables oxygen and food to go from mother to baby and it assists with the removal of waste products. At birth, it is a creamy colour and is soft and thick. Within days it becomes shrivelled and gets darker. During this period, it might ooze a little and can have a slight smell. It falls off within about 10 days to two weeks, leaving the umbilicus or belly button. If the area around the belly button becomes red, hot or swollen and your baby develops a fever, take your baby to the doctor as sometimes this area can become infected.

SNEEZING AND NOISY OR SNUFFLY BREATHING

Babies often have noisy breathing and will sneeze. A sneeze helps your baby clear their noses of mucous and this will reduce the noise or snuffling they make in their nose when they breathe.

KEEPING BABY CLEAN

Bathing provides a wonderful opportunity to connect with your baby, however, some babies take a little time before they start to enjoy having a bath.

Importantly, babies rarely need to be bathed every day as long as you regularly clean their skin in the nappy area, and their neck folds if they are dribbling, spitting up (posseting) or vomiting. These areas can become very inflamed and sore.

You can bathe your baby at anytime of the day. Some parents like to bathe their baby in the morning, while others bathe just before bedtime as it relaxes their baby and becomes part of the night-time ritual.

You do not need to use lotions, powders, shampoos or oils on your baby's skin. Plain water is fine and a washer to help gently remove any lint or other grime works well too. A non-perfumed soap is fine if baby is really dirty from a messy bowel motion.

If your baby's skin is very dry, a small amount of non-perfumed baby lotion or cream on these dry areas is usually enough to reduce the dryness. Reducing the frequency of bathing can also assist. If the dryness continues, ask your child and family health nurse, doctor or pharmacist for their advice.

Some babies don't enjoy being bathed, especially when they are newborns. It may be due to your baby not liking being uncovered, or that they are feeling unsafe without the reassuring security of their arms and legs being contained by a wrap. You may also be feeling insecure and concerned you will not be able to hold a slippery wet baby. If you are lacking in confidence, use only a small amount of water in the bath until your confidence increases.

If bath time is turning into an unpleasant experience, you can top and tail your baby for a few days or weeks. Once you have gained confidence in handling your baby you can then start to try giving your baby a bath again. There are lots of novel bathing equipment on the market, but these are really an unnecessary expense and there are significant safety issues related to their use.

Tresillian does not advise the use of any bathing equipment that is used to support your baby in the water, e.g. a bathing chair. The only time you may need to use a bathing aid for your baby is if you have a physical disability – in this situation your occupational therapist will provide you with guidance. Never leave your baby unattended in a bath even just for a moment. Babies can die very quickly in minute amounts of water.

By three months of age most babies love having a bath. It may even become one of the highlights of your day. As with most things when caring for your baby, this is a great learning opportunity for your baby and can be lots of fun. Dads or partners often enjoy bathing their babies too and it's a wonderful way for them to give some practical help while spending time with baby.

As your baby grows, you can use the family bath. If you live where there is no bath the laundry sink will also work well. Some parents like to shower with their baby and this is fine, but have your partner help by handing you the baby once you are in the shower and to take your baby once you have finished. This will help keep you both safe from slips and falls.

SAFETY AT BATH TIME

Water and babies and young children are a dangerous combination. Even very small amounts of water pose a danger.

- Never leave your baby alone in or near water. If you need to answer the phone or you have forgotten something, take your baby with you.
- Never leave your baby with another child to watch over them during bath time. This is dangerous and too much responsibility for the other child.

- Do not be distracted by talking or texting on your mobile phone if your baby is in the bath, even if they can sit unsupported and are playing happily.
- Always check the water temperature. Use the inside of your lower arm before putting your baby into the water.

Parents also need to be careful when bathing their baby. It's so easy to injure yourself, especially your back:

- Make sure water spills are wiped up to avoid slipping.
- If using a baby bath away from a tap and sink, use containers to fill and empty the bath, rather than trying to carry a heavy bath full of water.
- If possible, when using a baby bath, position it on a bench or table so you do not have to bend.

PREPARING FOR THE BATH

Being well prepared is the key to a relaxing bathing experience for both you and your baby. Before you start, place your baby somewhere safe, such as in their bassinet or cot.

- Collect all the things you will need for bath time and put them in an easy to reach place. Some of the equipment will need to be in arms reach of the bath, e.g. washer, cotton wool (if used), bath toy (not necessary for a newborn), towel and soap or lotions you are using (if any).
- Other equipment, nappy and clothing will need to be ready next to the area you will dry and dress your baby.
- Remove your watch and any jewellery that might get in the way or scratch your baby.
- The bath can be made less slippery by placing a hand towel, nappy or small rubber bathmat in the bottom of the bath.
- If the baby bath is a distance from the tap, use a jug to fill and empty the bath. Always start with cold water first, then top up with hotter water. If using a bathtub, make sure you finish by running the cold tap for a moment or two. This will ensure the water outlet is not going to burn your baby if they touch it.

- The amount of water used will depend on how confident you are. Start with a small amount if you are lacking in confidence. Over the next couple of weeks gradually increase the amount of water you use.
- Test the water temperature using your wrist or the inside of your lower arm. As most adults' elbows have a thicker layer of skin, they are usually less sensitive to heat.
- Once your baby is in the bath don't add extra water.
- If you are using a non-perfumed bathing lotion add this to the water before putting your baby in the bath.

DRESSING AND UNDRESSING YOUR BABY

- Babies can become upset when being dressed and undressed. Use a change table, a change pad or folded towel on a bed or table as the place to dress or undress your baby.
- Make sure you have all the items of clothing you will use before putting your baby on the change table or area.
- Do not leave your baby unattended on the change table, bed or table.
- Talk to your baby as you undress or dress them, using a gentle tone in telling them what is happening. This helps to regulate their emotions.
- If undressing baby to put them in the bath, leave the nappy on until last. When dressing, put the nappy on first.
- Rolling up the body of a top will help you to put on and remove the top without dragging it across your baby's face. Check sleeves are rolled down and comfortable, especially if layering your baby's clothes.

If your baby becomes distressed at bath time:
- Gently talk or sing to your baby.
- Position yourself so your baby can see your face. Use facial expressions to reassure your baby.
- Make eye contact.
- Slow down your movements and avoid sudden or jerky movements
- When dressing or undressing your baby, place them on their side to dress and undress or keep a hand on their chest to give the baby a sense of containment. Newborn babies generally feel uncomfortable being on their back and exposed.

BATHING YOUR BABY

Things to do if your baby is very young or you are not feeling confident:
- Avoid using soap on your baby's face – warm water is fine.
- You can use either a clean soft washer (a thin washer is easier to manage) or cotton balls moistened with clean warm water.
- Start with your baby's eyes, wiping from the inside corner to the outside of the eye. The tear duct is on the inside corner near their nose. Wiping from their nose outwards stops debris being wiped into the tear duct.
- Use a different part of the damp washer or a new damp cotton ball for each eye.
- Wipe gently around each nostril. Do not poke anything into their nose (including cotton buds), as you are likely to cause damage to the nasal mucosa, resulting in bleeding.
- Wipe gently around your baby's ears, paying special attention to behind the ears as this area can become crusty and red. Do not poke anything into your baby's ear as it is very easy to damage the internal structure of the ear.
- Wipe your baby's chin and neck creases. It is amazing how easily milk and other debris can collect in the neck creases.

IN THE BATH

Once you are confident handling your baby, you can include the cleaning of baby's head and face whilst they are in the bath.

Washing tips:

- Make sure you have a firm grip on your baby; place your arm around their back and hold them under the arm; with your other hand under their buttock, gently grasp the top of their leg; lift and gently lower into the bath.
- Gently support your baby at all times while they are in the bath.

- Supporting baby's head, lay your baby down in the bath so the back of the head is submerged. Gently splash some water onto baby's head – using the washer can help.
- If washing your baby's face and head in the bath, do as described in the previous section.

- Wash your baby's hair once or twice a week. Shampoo is not needed for newborn hair.
- Gently wash your baby's genitals and bottom last, using water only. Also clean out any bits of poo or vomit from body creases.
- Place your arm around their back and hold them under their arm; with your other hand under their buttock, gently grasp the top of their leg; lift your baby out of the bath then place on their back on a clean, dry, soft towel.
- Wrap your baby in the towel and pat dry. Pay attention to drying skin creases, around the neck, under the chin, behind the ears, armpits, and groin.
- If your baby's skin is dry a non-perfumed moisturising cream or lotion, or if your baby has a red bottom you can apply a mild barrier lotion such as zinc and castor oil (if your baby has a nappy rash see Chapter 15).
- Dress your baby, putting their nappy on first.
- Place your baby in a safe place, such as in their bassinet or cot.
- Empty the bath water.

CLEANING YOUR BABY'S GENITAL AREA

Your baby's genital area will require regular cleaning at each nappy change if soiled or if they have developed a nappy rash. There are lots of commercial products on the market that are useful if you are away from home. Avoid any product that is perfumed – in most instances, a warm wet washer is just as effective as commercial products.

Even though your baby does not need to be bathed each day, as a precaution at least once a day wash their bottom using a washer and warm water. This will help remove old creams and ointments that build up in the groin creases.

CLEANING YOUR SON'S UNCIRCUMCISED PENIS

Your baby's penis and foreskin do not need any special care other than bathing with water as part of his regular bath. The foreskin is connected by tissue to the penis head or glans. You should *not* try to retract the foreskin, as this will cause your son pain and may damage the penis head. You should occasionally watch your baby wee to see that the hole is adequate to allow a normal stream. If you are concerned, your doctor or child and family health nurse needs to check your son's penis. It will be several years before it is safe for the foreskin to be retracted and allow cleaning of the penis head. As your son gets older, you will need to teach him how to retract the foreskin to clean his penis and then pull the foreskin back over the penis head.

CLEANING YOUR SON'S CIRCUMCISED PENIS

If you have chosen to have your son circumcised, your doctor will instruct you in how to manage care of the wound. The important thing is to keep the area as clean as possible. The penis head will look quite red for the first few days, and there may be a yellowish secretion. The redness and secretion should disappear within a week. If there is bleeding, swelling, persistent redness or secretion, especially if the area becomes smelly, there may be an infection; your baby will need to see your doctor.

Once the circumcision has healed, regular bathing is all that is necessary. No special care is needed.

CLEANING YOUR DAUGHTER'S LABIA

At bath time (and during nappy changing if necessary):

- Use a washer or cotton ball moistened with warm water to clean your daughter's labia area
- Gently part your daughter's legs, and wipe from front to back. Going from front to back helps avoid spreading faeces into your baby's labia. You do not need to clean inside the labia
- You might notice a discharge that looks a little like egg white. This is normal and it does not need to be removed
- Occasionally, you might find a small spotting of blood; this is usually a response to maternal hormones and you should not be alarmed. If you are concerned, speak to your child and family health nurse or doctor
- Do not use talcum powder as this can cause irritation.

DRY SKIN

Babies often have patches of dry, flaky skin. These areas of dry skin can be barely noticeable or there may be large areas of very noticeable dry and flaky skin. A non-perfumed skin moisturiser will improve the look of your baby's skin. Apply immediately after their bath to improve hydration. If the skin is very dry, apply several times during the day.

NAPPY CHANGING

Nappy changing is one of the very necessary and regularly repeated tasks of being a parent. Babies will have approximately 2,500 nappy changes in their first 12 months of life. As with all parenting tasks, this is a great opportunity to have a playful time with your baby, especially as they start to be more aware of their surroundings and enjoy being without a nappy. Talking to your baby, explaining what you are doing, and keeping your movements smooth and slow may help if your baby does not like having their nappy changed.

Keeping your baby safe always has to be top priority, so never leave them unattended on a change table or other surface, even just for a minute. Before starting to change your baby's nappy, make sure you have all the necessary equipment within arms' reach. This will include:
- A changing pad, table or towel.
- A container or plastic bag for the dirty nappy.
- A clean nappy, either disposable or cloth.
- A washcloth and some warm water or baby wipes.
- A baby cream – this might be a barrier cream or a moisturising cream depending on the condition of your baby's bottom.

To change the nappy:
- Lay your baby on the changing mat or table.
- Remove the dirty nappy. If your baby is dirty you can use a clean section of the nappy to remove some of the poo. Fold the dirty nappy into a tight bundle to stop spillage and place into a bag (see Chapter 3 on how to dispose of or wash nappies).

- Taking the nappy off might result in your baby weeing, so be prepared.
- Gently cleanse your baby's bottom, using either a baby wipe or a moist washer from the front to back.
- Hold your baby's legs with your fingers between their ankles and lift slightly, so their bottom lifts off the change mat or table. This will allow you to easily clean their bottom.
- Apply a smear of protective cream onto your baby's bottom to protect against nappy rash.
- Open a new disposable nappy or folded cloth nappy and place on your baby. Avoid covering their belly button (umbilicus) in newborns or making the nappy too tight.

See Chapter 3 for information about cloth and disposable nappies and change tables.

CARE OF UMBILICAL CORD

Before the cord falls off:
- Wash your hands before touching the cord.
- Make sure you dry gently but well after you bathe your baby.
- Avoid covering the cord with the nappy or plastic pants. If covered, it will become moist and increase the risk of infection.
- If the cord gets some poo or wee on it, gently wash off with soap and water and dry well.

Caring for the umbilicus once the cord has fallen off:
- No special care is needed.
- Just like your own umbilicus, it will occasionally get fluff in it. Use a moist washer and gently wipe. Avoid poking into the umbilicus – you are likely to cause it to bleed.
- If it appears inflamed, it is important to check with your doctor or child and family health nurse.

CUTTING NAILS

Baby fingernails and toenails grow quickly. The nails can become rough and jagged. As your very young baby does not have good control of their movements, they are likely to scratch themselves. You can use mittens, but this is a very short-term solution. There are also some risks associated with the use of mittens – if there are any loose threads they can wrap around your baby's fingers or toes, cutting off the blood supply.

Cutting a baby's finger or toenails can be a very challenging task for most parents. This is where knowing about your baby's states of consciousness can be very useful – until you are competent at cutting nails, a good time is when your baby is in a quiet sleep (non-rapid eye movement) state. In this state your baby will be very still (see Chapter 5). As you become more competent and your baby's nails harden, a good time to cut their nails is just after a bath.

Having your partner or a friend hold your baby while you cut their nails is another workable option.

You can use a small emery board, baby nail clippers or scissors (small and blunt ended). Take care not to snip the top or sides of your baby's finger as this is very easy to do.

- Hold your baby's fist or foot, put out one finger or toe.
- Cut one fingernail or toenail at a time.
- With fingernails, round off the nail, so they have no sharp edges.
- Toenails should be cut straight across the top of the toenail to avoid an ingrown toenail developing.

As your baby becomes older, you can cut their nails while they are sitting securely in a chair with a safety harness, or being held by your partner or a friend. You may need to have a toy on hand to distract them.

If you remain nervous or unsure of how to go about this task, your child and family health nurse will provide you with guidance.

EXTREMES OF WEATHER

Keeping your baby cool in summer is not always easy, especially during a heat wave. Dress your baby in a singlet and nappy. The singlet helps absorb any sweat and stops them becoming uncomfortable. On very hot days, find the coolest place in the house for your baby. If using an air conditioner or fan – keep your baby out of the draft as babies can lose heat and chill very rapidly. A bath using lukewarm water will be enjoyed by your baby. If your baby is breastfeeding, they may demand some extra feeds during the day. If they are fed with an infant formula, you can offer a small amount of boiled, cooled water between feeds. On very hot days your baby might be sleepier than normal or irritable.

In winter, babies need to be kept warm but not overheated. Dressing your baby in layers of clothing will help you easily regulate their temperature. Babies rapidly lose heat through their heads, so a beanie or hat is essential. Hands and feet need to be kept covered if going outside. Jumpsuits are a great idea in cold weather, as they often have built-in mittens and you can put socks on under the jumpsuit.

SUN PROTECTION

It goes without saying that protecting your baby from the sun is necessary at all times. Always avoid exposing your baby to direct sunlight. Use a sun hat for their head (that protects face, ears and neck), and dress your baby in loose closely woven clothing that covers arms and legs. Apply 30+ SPF sun protection lotion on exposed areas of skin 15 to 20 minutes before going out into the sun. Reapply every two hours.

Some babies have a minor reaction to some sun protection lotions – if this happens with your baby stop using it. Avoid taking your baby out into direct sun (especially during the middle of the day) as much as possible. Use shade screens in the car, on their pram or stroller.

KEEPING SAFE AROUND WATER

Australian babies are often exposed to water. They are taken into pools, rivers and surf from an early age. Whether in the backyard, at the beach or a public pool, babies love playing in water. A major rule when babies and young children are near or in water is the need for constant and vigilant adult supervision. There is an ever-present danger of babies drowning even in very small amounts of water. Learning first aid, especially cardiopulmonary resuscitation (CPR) is a key skill for parents, especially if they live near water or own a pool. Activities and behaviours to help ensure their safety include:

- Empty water out of wading pools and position where they cannot collect water from the rain. Remember to check for water collection in and around your property.
- Make sure nappy buckets have tight fitting lids and keep off the floor.
- Always empty the bath. Never leave water in the bath.
- Make sure pool fences and gates are in good condition and are never left propped open.
- Keep fish bowls and aquariums covered and out of reach.
- Secure covers over the pool when not in use.
- Cover birdbaths and fishponds with wire mesh or empty them until your child is school age.
- Do not use inflatable swimming aids.
- Always take your baby to patrolled beaches and only swim between the flags.

There are some hygiene rules that will make swimming with babies much more enjoyable for everyone in the same water. These include:
- Making sure your baby's bottom is clean before going into the water.
- Use a swim nappy when your baby is in the water.
- If a poo accident occurs in the pool everyone should get out immediately. If you are at a public pool, it is important to tell the pool attendants.
- Change nappies away from the pool so contamination of the water does not occur. If it's a wading pool at home, you will need to empty the pool, clean with disinfectant and leave in the sun.
- Don't take your baby into a pool or other public swimming area if they have diarrhoea and/or are vomiting.
- Don't allow your baby to drink the pool water.
- If your baby is prone to ear infections take care to avoid getting water in their ears.

Babies should not be taken into a spa as the germ risk for their immature immune system is great. The water is often also too hot for babies as they do not have the ability to regulate their body temperature.

NO MORE DUMMIES

Even though using a dummy will not be a lifelong habit, there comes a time when you need your baby to stop using one. Sucking on a dummy is a very pleasurable experience for a baby – the sucking helps soothe them and it also helps regulate their emotions. When stopping the use of a dummy you may need to provide additional emotional support that includes extra cuddles and lots of distraction. The following tips may be of help:

- Choose your timing. If you are stressed or going through a difficult period of change or if your baby is unwell, this will not be the time to try and get rid of the dummy.
- Start to restrict the dummy use, maybe only use at sleep times.
- Don't allow your baby to crawl or walk around with the dummy in their mouth.
- Some parents go 'cold turkey' and throw out all the dummies so there is no going back.
- Encourage everyone who cares for your baby to be consistent and provide extra cuddles if your baby becomes upset.
- Try not to go back to using the dummy.

See Chapter 3 for more information about dummies.

CHAPTER SUMMARY

- Learning to provide the basic care for your baby in the first few months can be daunting. If you lack confidence, ask your child and family health nurse for advice and support.
- Doing the day-to-day tasks (feeding, bathing, changing nappies) with your baby is a great opportunity for your baby to develop a positive and secure relationship with you.
- Even though most babies are robust and resilient, safety when handling them should be a major priority for parents.
- Never leave your baby unattended in or near water.

Part Two

INFANT DEVELOPMENT AND GROWTH

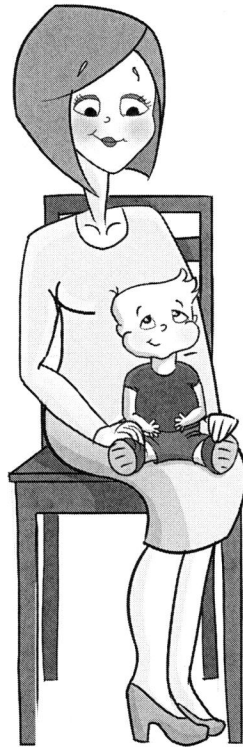

Chapter Five
SLEEP AND EARLY BRAIN DEVELOPMENT

A WHOLE NEW WORLD of knowledge about early brain development and child development is opening up for parents, scientists, health professionals, educators and even politicians. Thanks to research and the development of new technologies such as PET (positron emission tomography) and MRI (magnetic resonance imaging) scans, we are now able to think in new and innovative ways about the needs and care of young children.

In many instances, it has also confirmed what parents and some professionals already knew about their infants. For example, mothers have been saying that their newborn infants could see and were smiling at them, while others were discounting this experience as just 'wind'. We now know that babies can see (with some limitations), and they prefer their parent's voice, face and smell. If you respond positively to a smile, your baby will rapidly learn and want to repeat the smile. Babies who do not have parents who smile at them tend to be more reluctant to smile. Having Mum or Dad's attention is a huge reward and incentive for a baby, so, just keep on smiling!

The early years of a child's life are when the brain sets down the blueprint for their future health, the ability to regulate emotions and behaviour, and learn new things. During pregnancy your baby's brain development is influenced by your diet, behaviour and other lifestyle factors. The best possible environment for your unborn baby is one that is also healthy for the mother. This may include stopping smoking and avoiding second-hand smoke, improving your eating habits, avoiding certain drugs and alcohol, improving your sleep patterns, getting fit through exercise and learning to relax. All these activities directly impact on the growth and development of the baby's brain.

We now know there are sensitive times or windows of opportunity when the infant's brain is primed to learn special skills. For example, infants are born with the ability to make a diverse range of sounds so that they will be able to talk. They also benefit from having regular and early exposure to speakers of another language during their first 12 months of life. Research shows this can make it much easier for your child to learn a second language later in life.

A baby needs exposure to simple everyday skills and experiences to start to learn, so that they can go on to manage more complex and difficult skills and experiences. For example, having a Dad who regularly reads or tells stories (even at a very young age) is far better for an infant's development than being placed in front of the television to be entertained. They may become quiet in front of the television, but that is usually because the noise, colour and rapid movement can easily overwhelm their immature neurological system. We now know babies are born with multiple and complex abilities, the most important of these are that they are brilliantly intelligent learners in interaction with those that love and care for them. Parents who are devoted teachers give their children a huge advantage in the learning stakes.

LEARNING TO REGULATE BEHAVIOUR AND FEELINGS

All children need to learn to self-regulate their behaviour and feelings.

Self-regulation means being able to achieve functional goals, such as being able to interact well with others, settling to sleep and staying still long enough to focus on a task. It varies from child to child as it depends on the infant's temperament, state of health and many other factors. Supporting your baby to manage their emotions as part of their relationship and interaction with you and others is an important step in the development of a secure relationship.

Some babies are able to self-soothe from birth by sucking their fingers, while other babies calm by turning their head to the side and focusing on someone or perhaps on a light coming through the window. They might also settle easily when picked up by a parent. Other babies have not learnt skills to calm them. This variability may be due to a baby's genetic make-up or their environment and experiences. By the time a child commences school, self-regulation needs to be well established. Without this ability, the young child will have difficulty learning, or making friends, as their impulsive behaviour can be scary and disruptive for other children. This is why parents and other key adults in their lives are so important as babies cannot learn to organise their emotions and behaviour without ongoing support and modelling of behaviours.

The message is that babies, if provided with appropriate, timely and sensitive attention from their parents, will start to learn to self-regulate. They will look to you when they are in a new or strange situation, when they are excited or overwhelmed by their environment, to help them calm down or regulate their emotions. Every time you respond to your baby and try to soothe them by using touch, sound, movement and a whole range of other methods you are helping them self-regulate.

As your baby gets older, they will require less physical contact and may only require a smile from you, a gentle touch or a reassuring word to relax and start to enjoy a new experience or go back to sleep. Creating a relationship where emotions can be shared from the beginning provides a solid emotional foundation for your baby.

BABIES' TEMPERAMENTS

Your baby's 'temperament' is the personality that your baby has been born with. All babies are different. Some are easy going and quickly adapt to new people and situations while others can be difficult or challenging to manage and easily unsettled meeting new people or being in a new environment. A third group of babies takes time to warm to new situations or people, however they do start to enjoy themselves after repeating the experience a few times. This group of babies may find going to childcare a challenge at first. To help your baby adjust to this, let the staff know it might take some time for baby to settle in and suggest they provide a gradual introduction to the other children at the centre.

It's important that you're aware of your baby's temperament and personality. For example, if your baby is slow to warm up, it is worthwhile asking family and friends to approach baby gently. If your baby is easily upset by noise, try and avoid noisy situations and reassure your baby with lots of cuddles.

INFANT CUES

We know that babies can communicate their needs from a very early age using infant cues or signals as their language. As a parent, you are already an expert in the use of cues as you use them all the time to communicate your needs to others. By recognising your baby's cues, you will become familiar with their needs, too. That means you will go beyond relying only on their cry to understand that they might be upset or distressed. If your baby is premature or unwell, their cues may not be as distinct or easy to read. As a parent, the ability to understand and react to your baby's cues is a learnt skill. It does take time and practice.

There are two groups of cues – *engagement* and *disengagement* cues.

Engaging cues signal *I want to interact with you*. It is not hard to interpret these cues, as they are so obvious: smiling, holding arms out, feeding sounds, and so on.

Disengaging cues signal *I've had enough* or *I need a break from what is happening*. There are far more disengaging cues than engaging cues.

Babies don't have to work as hard to get parents to have fun with them (engage) than they do to get help (disengage). Importantly cues are neither good nor bad; they are just a form of communication.

How do you understand cues from your baby? There are both subtle (harder to read) cues and very potent (easy to read) cues.

The subtle cues: usually occur first to flag either a beginning interest (face bright, raising head or eyes wide and bright) or an early indication that the baby is soon going to need assistance or time out (fast breathing, hiccups, looking away or yawning).

The potent cues: tell you that they need assistance (fussiness, pulling away or crying) or attention from their parent (smooth movements of legs or arms or looking at your face).

Cues that are grouped together communicate a specific need, such as tiredness. Tired cues (signs) are the individual signals your baby gives to let you know they are getting tired and need to sleep. These may include facial grimacing, yawning, grizzling, frowning, sucking, staring, minimal movement or activity, turning head away, jerky movements or becoming more active, clenching fists, rubbing eyes, and squirming crying/fussiness.

The more you are aware of the subtle engagement and disengagement cues, the more settled your baby will be as there is no need for their demands to escalate. If you don't always read the cues correctly the first time, move quickly to better the situation. For example, stop what you are doing and give your baby a break. If you are playing a game with your baby and they look away, this is a signal they need a break from being over stimulated, or they may have seen something of more interest.

Stopping what you are doing and allowing them to take the lead will provide a space for your baby to recover without the baby needing to cry or become fussy. If you score a smile, take it to mean that your baby is ready to re-engage with you and the activity they'd been enjoying. These moments of connection are one of the major baselines of any relationship.

WHAT HAPPENS WHEN BABY SLEEPS?

Your infant sleeps a great deal in the early months so it's important to understand the various stages of sleep. There are two states of sleep, one transition state and three awake states. Each of the sleep states has specific functions, ranging from being very heavily asleep to a *quiet sleep* state, moving onto an *active sleep* phase or a rapid eye movement stage (REM). With many newborns you can often see their eyes flickering underneath their eyelids when they are in the active or rapid eye movement state. The baby then moves into a drowsy (transitional) state. They will either fall back to sleep or wake up. This is a stage when if you leave your baby alone or gently speak to them they would fall back to sleep.

In the *awake state* of *quiet alert* the infant is primed for learning – they have bright eyes and are observant. In an *active alert state*, the infant is excited, but often can easily tip over into *crying*. And of course, we all know what crying sounds like – though, if you listen carefully, an infant's cry can range from a grizzle to a very distressed, seemingly inconsolable cry. A baby's cry provides lots of useful information about what the infant needs.

Sleep states	Awake states
Quiet sleep Active sleep	Drowsy Quiet alert Active alert Crying

As well as being able to see visual characteristics in your baby's states, there are physiological changes occurring. These include changes in heart rate, muscle tone and blood flow. Each state has a predictable pattern that contributes to parents understanding of what action maybe needed. For example, trying to get your baby to feed when they are in a quiet sleep state will probably not be successful.

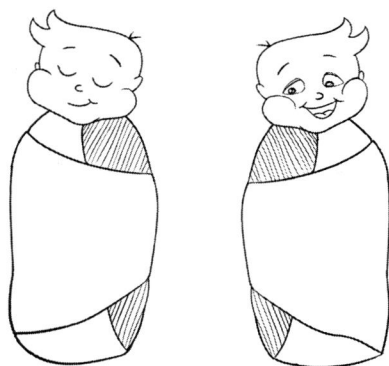

When your baby is in a **Quiet Sleep** state:
- Their body will be very still; they may have an occasional startle or twitch.
- Their face will be still but they may make an occasional sucking movement.
- Their breathing will be regular and smooth.
- Baby will be difficult to arouse as their threshold for any form of stimulus is very high. This means if you have to move your baby, this is the time to do it, as they are unlikely to wake. If they do rouse, they are likely to go straight back to sleep.

When your baby is in an **Active Sleep** state:
- Their body will make some movements.
- They will have rapid eye movements (REM).
- Breathing will be irregular.
- They may smile, or briefly make fussing or crying sounds.
- They are far more responsive to stimuli such as hunger, a wet nappy and handling.

When your baby is in a **Drowsy** state:
- Activity is variable, with occasional startled responses.
- Movements are usually smooth.
- Face usually remains still, with occasional movement.
- Eyes will occasionally open and close, with a heavy-lidded or slit-like appearance.
- Breathing pattern is irregular.
- They will react to sensory stimuli, but it may be delayed. A change in state to quiet alert, active alert or crying often occurs if they are stimulated.

When your baby is in a **Quiet Alert** state:
- Activity is minimal.
- Eyes are bright and wide.
- Face has an attentive appearance.
- Regular breathing pattern.
- Most attentive to the environment and will focus attention on anything of interest.
- Spend increasing amounts of time in this state.
- Providing something for your baby to look at, suck or listen to will help your baby maintain this state for longer periods.
- An excellent time to feed your baby.
- An important time for learning as your baby is at their most receptive.

When your baby is in an **Active Alert** state:
- Activity is variable, with mild startles occurring.
- Movements are smooth.

- Eyes are open, with a dull, glazed look.
- May have some facial movements, though often their face appears still.
- Irregular breathing pattern.
- Response to sensory stimulation is often delayed. When stimulated may change to quiet alert or crying.
- May have periods of becoming fussy and increasingly more sensitive to stimuli such as hunger, fatigue, noise or over handling.
- May become more and more active and excited, quickly switching to a crying state.

When your baby is in a **Crying** state:
- Increased movement.
- Skin colour becomes darker or changes to red.
- Has a facial grimace.
- Breathing pattern is more irregular than in any other state.
- Crying is a sign of reaching their limit. If distressed, being able to self-soothe is very difficult. Babies need an adult to help them return to a more settled state. At Tresillian we encourage parents to pick their baby up and cuddle them until they are calm then attempt to re-settle.

Parents often wonder why it takes so long to settle their baby from crying to being asleep, but the infant has to move down three states before they are asleep. This is no different than for adults, it takes time to wind down from an excited state to being able to sleep. The catchcry is *repetition* to help infants move down states, and *variety* to move up states. This is called 'state modulation'.

Having this knowledge about your baby's consciousness states (sleep and awake) often provides parents with insight into their infant's behaviour. It also contributes to making a decision about what action to take to help your baby regulate their emotions.

Much of the information about infant states and cues has been informed by: Spietz, A., Johnson-Crowley, N., Sumner, G., & Barnard, K., (2008), *Keys to Caregiving*, NCAST-AVENUW, Seattle.

SLEEP AND WAKE CYCLES

When babies are born they have reasonably short sleep and wake cycles. As your baby becomes older and their neurologic and biological systems start to mature, the cycles start to lengthen. That means they are awake or asleep for longer periods and transitions between these periods become smoother.

Babies are born with the **potential ability** to move through their various states (awake and asleep times) independently and smoothly. One complicating factor however, is that they cannot control/slow the release of their stress hormones once triggered. When they become upset, this hormone is released, contributing to the stress for the baby. All of this is normal. It is the parent's job to help soothe the baby and so dampen the stress hormones effects and move them through to the next state. This is also the beginning of feeling safe and developing trusting relationships for the infant. This period is strongest in the first three months and parents work hard to regulate and soothe their babies, so babies can learn this skill.

Babies at birth do not have a *circadian rhythm* (awareness of day and night) or *ultradian rhythm* (awareness of how to move from being awake and transitioning to sleep). The work of parenting and interacting with your baby in the first three months is to achieve these two circadian and ultradian rhythms. This is done through how and when parents choose to play, talk and soothe their babies. It is called 'achieving state regulation' for the baby.

To get to sleep or wake up, your baby's body needs to undergo many changes. For example, their heart rate and breathing slows or fastens and their brain activity and muscle tone changes. Sometimes babies need to be held until their bodies are still before they can be placed in their cots for sleep. Try to remember this when your baby is having a difficult time trying to go to sleep.

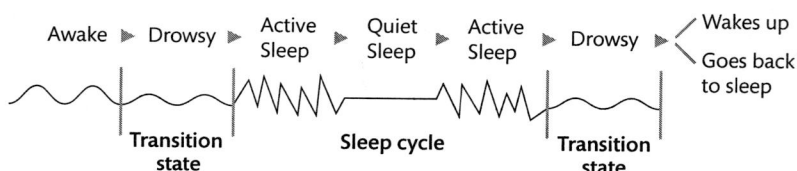

Awake ▶ Drowsy ▶ Active Sleep ▶ Quiet Sleep ▶ Active Sleep ▶ Drowsy ▶ Wakes up / Goes back to sleep

Transition state — Sleep cycle — Transition state

During a sleep cycle your baby will move through active sleep to quiet sleep and then back to active sleep. A newborn baby's sleep cycle (active sleep to quiet sleep and then back to active sleep) is very short. By four months each of these sleep cycles lasts between 45 to 50 minutes. At the end of a cycle they will move back into another sleep cycle or to a drowsy state of consciousness. This drowsy state is a transitional state, they may wake or even go back to sleep again, if left undisturbed. The sleep cycle of a newborn can appear quite long as they combine several sleep cycles, with short periods of being awake. The mismatch comes with adults who have a 90-minute cycle. So having a baby in the house causes a disruption of their parents' sleeping pattern.

By two weeks of age, sleep combining several cycles will last for around four hours. For some babies they start to be very unsettled and seem to sleep for very short periods and are easily woken. By three months, some rare babies can sleep up to eight hours as they combine several sleep cycles, however this is not usual, especially if your baby is breastfed. By the end of the first year, most babies sleep for extended periods at night and only have one or two (ideally) sleep periods during the day. On average, a baby (two to 12 months) sleeps from 9 to 12 hours at night and two to four-and-a-half hours during the day. However there are lots of individual variations.

The shift to being awake signals the end of the sleep cycle. Babies move from the drowsy state to quiet alert state. These states are crucial for your baby's emotional, social and physical development and your baby needs to have lots of positive interaction with you as you talk, sing and touch them.

Parenting a newborn baby feels and often is a bit chaotic. Your baby will seem to fall asleep for short naps some days, while on other days they will have much longer periods of sleep, often up to four hours. Their awake periods can be equally as disorganised, with some days seeming an never-ending day of attending to your baby's demands for attention and trying to calm them so they can go back to sleep.

Awake cycles vary in length, and as your baby gets older the cycles become longer. In the first weeks, the awake cycles can be very short before your baby will start to fall asleep again. This means that your baby is more likely to have short sleep and awake periods. When they get a little older, these periods start to consolidate, getting longer in duration. By 12 months of age many babies, but not all, are starting to have nine to 12 hours sleep at night. Daytime sleeps will usually be reduced to two naps, with some babies only needing one.

Between three to four months, babies will start to wake because they have had enough sleep not because they are hungry. You will notice a change in how they wake up; there is not the intense 'I am hungry' cry but a more exploratory calling out, or even some quiet activity in the cot without you being aware they are awake. This is when you can introduce another play period into their feed, play, sleep pattern (feed, play, sleep, play).

The times provided here are averages of when babies sleep and wake. There are lots of variations. Remember that your baby is still learning to regulate their physical and neurological systems and their body has not yet fully synchronised to light and dark as your adult body has. It may take them several weeks and some babies take several months to start to get into a daily rhythm.

SLEEP AND SETTLING

'Sleeping like a baby' is often used to describe an undisturbed and lengthy night's sleep. Obviously people using this statement have never been the parent of a baby! Babies need lots of attention through the night, especially during the early months. The capacity or size of their stomach is very limited (a simple measure is the size of a golf ball), and it needs regular filling. As your baby grows their stomach is able to hold more milk. At six months, you can start to offer your baby solid foods. This will help them sleep for longer periods and not wake because they are hungry.

At first your baby's stomach only contains either breastmilk or infant formula that gets emptied on a regular basis. They become uncomfortable because as the milk passes through their system they wet or poo their nappy. This nappy then gets uncomfortable as it is damp and gets cold. If your baby starts to wake they can have problems regulating their physiological (physical) system to enable them to go back to sleep. When this happens, your baby will often need help from you to get back to sleep. A benefit of attending to your baby's calls for help is that they will develop a sense of security knowing you will provide comfort when needed. Ensuring that your baby's needs are met will support your baby's developing ability to sleep for increasingly longer periods. That means more sleep for you, too.

As your baby passes through the different states of consciousness (sleep and wakefulness) from quiet sleep to active sleep, as described earlier in this chapter, there is an increased likelihood they will be disturbed and start to wake. There is a natural shift between sleep cycles, however, babies are often developmentally able to transition back to sleep, so they don't need help from their parents every time they are in a drowsy state to go back to sleep.

What might wake your baby?

- Hunger
- Having a dirty or wet nappy
- They are lying in an uncomfortable position
- They have a pain in their stomach or bowel
- Startling, as they have not been wrapped
- They want comfort from the people they most love.

Many parents find the way to work out how their baby might be feeling is to pay attention to their own or their partner's emotions, behaviours and needs. For example, think about how you or your partner behave when you're tired – this will help to learn your baby's cues. You might rub your eyes, tug at your ear or a piece of hair and your movements might get a bit jerky and clumsy. You might get a bit grumpy, or if you are really tired, get angry at small things that happen. Babies' behaviour is also a reflection of their feelings and emotions and becomes more varied as they get older.

The difficulty for a baby is when their distressed behaviour and cues are not recognised. A baby's behaviour becomes even more obvious as they become very upset and distressed. Unfortunately, this often results in the baby being more difficult to soothe. They will need far more help and time to return to a drowsy state before they can move into active and then quiet sleep.

ACTIVITY

To assist you to have a greater awareness of your baby's behaviour think about the following statements. You might find it useful to talk to your partner about the statements or write them down:

1. When my baby is ready to sleep I notice that they e.g. start to yawn:
2. When my baby is asleep I notice that they e.g. have periods where they are very still:
3. When my baby is upset and crying the things that work to calm them down are e.g. picking up and cuddling.

SAFE SLEEP ENVIRONMENT AND POSITIONS

There has been significant and important research into baby's sleep environments and sleep positions. The application of these research findings have made a dramatic difference to the statistics for sudden and unexplained infant deaths over the past 20-plus years.

It is recommended that you *do not* share a bed with your baby as it increases the risk of SIDS (Sudden Infant Death Syndrome) and fatal sleep accidents. An adult bed and bed coverings are not suitable for babies and young children as they put a baby at risk of overheating and suffocation. There is also a risk of an adult rolling over on their baby. This type of accident is heightened if the adult has been drinking or taking prescription or non prescription medication, or extremely tired or sleep deprived. It is much safer to sleep with your baby in their bassinet or cot beside your bed.

For more information on safe sleep environments see Chapter 3.

CRYING

Crying is one of the most difficult and heart-wrenching noises to tolerate as a parent. Hearing your baby distressed will make most parents feel totally helpless and some parents can even feel physical pain. Crying is a distress cue that communicates to you that your baby needs help, so it is not surprising that parents have real difficulty not responding to their baby when they cry. The research tells us that babies who are responded to when they are distressed are more likely to develop a secure relationship with their parent or parents.

Regardless of culture, most babies' periods of crying peaks at six weeks. Crying then starts to decrease, though for some babies it takes much longer for them to reach a peak in crying. By three months, babies typically cry for one hour a day.

Some babies are more sensitive to changes in their environment (e.g. they don't like being undressed, having their nappy changed or not being wrapped), or to the mood of the people handling them (e.g. if their mum or dad are feeling anxious or upset). Babies that are overly sensitive to their environment can be more difficult to soothe or slower to calm and settle. If your baby is more sensitive, then they will need even more help from you to learn how to calm and settle. Even though being with a crying baby is exhausting and frustrating (as you hold, touch and gently talk to them), it sends a powerful message that they are not alone and you will give them your support.

All babies cry, but some babies cry more than others. This is often called **colic**. It is usually crying that:
- Lasts at least three hours a day
- Happens at least three days a week
- Continues from three weeks to three months
- Begins and ends for no obvious reason.

If your baby starts to cry in an uncontrollable, highly distressed manner (especially if this is not their regular behaviour), take your baby to your local doctor or hospital where they can be examined. This will reassure you there is not a serious medical condition. It's also a good idea to ask for advice if for any reason your baby's unsettled behaviour is concerning or causing you distress. Visiting your child and family health nurse is a useful place to start to gain support and information. In some instances, a referral to other services or health professionals may be suggested or needed. For example, many parents are referred to organisations such as Tresillian Family Care Centres. Tresillian offer a range of services for families needing help and support with their baby.

SOOTHING YOUR BABY

When we talk about settling a baby, it is frequently linked to trying to get baby to sleep. This is often where parents get caught into thinking it is their responsibility to get their baby to sleep. This is not your responsibility as a parent – you cannot make a baby go to sleep or even calm down. Think about your role as soothing your baby by providing comfort and a sense of security.

Your role is to help your baby to settle by responding to their cues for assistance and providing a clear message that it is time to calm down. You can do this by rocking, gentle touch, soothing singing or music. In this role you are providing your baby with support to learn how to self-regulate. Learning to self-regulate to go to sleep takes time, and some babies will take much longer and need more support from their parents than others to master this important skill. We know parents who are able to read their baby's subtle disengagement cues find it easier to get in early to remove or reduce stimulation, or reassure their baby (see Infant Cues). This stops baby's mood escalating to a highly distressed state before their parents act to help them.

There are lots of strategies you can use to help your baby calm and settle. If you have tuned into your baby's cues for sleep, you may have noticed those already mentioned, such as whining, yawning, jerking movements of the limbs, clenching fists, fretting, facial grimacing, pulling at the ears, rubbing eyes and/or increased or decreased physical activity.

What you can do:
- *Check your baby is comfortable:* change their nappy, provide a feed if hungry.
- *Help your baby transition through the different states of wakefulness:* provide repetitive, slow and rhythmical movements (rocking) and noise (softly played music, singing or talking) to help calm your baby. Unfortunately this can take from minutes to hours on some days. Remember your baby is still learning how to self-soothe and self-regulate their emotions.

- *When wrapping, ensure your baby is able to get their hands to their mouth*: babies will often suck their thumb, fingers or hand as a way to self-soothe. Using a dummy can also be calming for your baby. If you are breastfeeding it is best to avoid a dummy until your breastmilk supply has been well established (see Chapter 10).
- *Provide a soothing bath or massage.*
- *Playing music is also very helpful to relax both your baby and you.*
- These strategies are most effective if you introduce your baby to them when they are in a calm state so they develop an association with massage, bathing or music and being calm. When pregnant, many parents start to play a favourite gentle piece of music when they are relaxing. We know that babies recognise noises they have been exposed to *in utero*, especially if their mother is calm and relaxed at the time. This is likely to be far more effective than using these strategies for the first time when your baby is upset as it can often make the situation worse.
- *A change of scenery*: take baby to another room, out in the garden or for a walk to help calm them. For older babies, sitting down and reading a favourite book will distract them and act to calm them down. Remember not to get too excited when reading the book if you are trying to soothe your baby, talk in a gentle voice.

SOOTHING AND SETTLING STRATEGIES

Most babies will take time to settle; consistency with your choice of strategies to help soothe your baby or to help them settle to sleep is really important in helping your baby learn to self-regulate and establish good sleep habits.

SETTLING IN ARMS (THE EARLY WEEKS)
Hold your baby in your arms until they fall asleep. Start with minimal input using your voice, face and hands. As you watch and understand your baby's response to your actions, you will learn what is working and what is not helpful. You can use gentle rhythmic patting, rocking,

stroking, talking, or softly singing prior to putting your baby into the cot asleep. If your baby wakes after a sleep cycle you may need to resettle (as above) to ensure adequate sleep.

HANDS-ON SETTLING

When you see your baby's cues (signs), prepare your baby for sleep using these suggestions:

1. Check your baby's nappy.
2. Wrap your baby in a light cotton sheet (optional) – taking care not to overheat (see Wrapping your baby).
3. Talk quietly and cuddle your baby to encourage a state of calm.
4. Position your baby on their back in the cot awake (calm/drowsy). Ensure cot sides are up and secure.
5. Comfort your baby by gentle ssshhh sounds, gentle rhythmic patting or rocking, or stroking. Stay with your baby until they are calm or fall asleep.
6. If your baby remains distressed you may need to pick your baby up for a cuddle until calm. Once calm repeat steps 4–5.

PARENTAL PRESENCE (OVER SIX MONTHS)

You may prefer this option if your baby is over six months of age and has not been separated from you at sleep time.

- Use the first five steps above (hands-on settling).
- Once calm, lie down or sit beside the cot within sight of your baby, pretending to be asleep.
- If your baby remains awake, give a little cough or quietly 'ssshhh time to sleep', signalling you are still in the room.
- If your baby becomes distressed, respond with the minimal action required to calm your baby and then repeat steps 4–5.
- Stay in the room until your baby is asleep during the day and sleep in the same room as your baby throughout the night.
- This continues for at least one week or until your baby has three consecutive nights of relatively uninterrupted sleep.
- You can now begin to leave the room before your baby is asleep.

A variation to this method is gradual withdrawal:
- Use the first five steps of hands-on settling.
- Once your baby is calm, remain in close proximity so they can see you, e.g. sit on a chair beside the bassinet or cot. This will allow your baby to fall asleep.
- Over time, the distance between you and your baby is gradually increased. Your baby will gradually gain confidence and skills in self-soothing and settling.

COMFORT SETTLING (OVER SIX MONTHS)

Comfort settling provides your baby with reassurance and support while also providing an opportunity for your baby to discover their own way of going to sleep.
- Use the first five steps above (hands-on settling)
- As your baby calms, move away from the cot or leave the room
- Listen to your baby's level of distress (intensity of cry)
- If your baby remains distressed, calm your baby again and move away or leave the room
- You may have to repeat this several times before the baby responds
- If your baby does not respond, pick your baby up and cuddle them until they are calm, then either:
  - reattempt comfort settling
  - use hands-on settling until baby is asleep
  - get baby up and try again later.

The length of time it takes to calm your baby will lessen as your baby learns to self-settle.

WRAPPING YOUR BABY

For very young babies wrapping is said to provide a sense of security. Just remember when your baby was *in utero* they were very contained, but had some movement. In the first three to four months, when your baby is in the active sleep state they are often very active and they startle easily. Wrapping can help contain their *moro* or startle reflex that often wakes a baby.

When wrapping there are several precautions:
- Use a light cotton or gauze wrap to avoid overheating your baby
- Dress your baby in light clothing
- Make sure the wrap cannot cover your baby's face or head
- Make sure the wrap is not tight or restrictive around your baby's hips and legs.

Some parents wrap their baby with hands tucked in a fold of the wrap. Others wrap the baby so they can use their hands to self-soothe by sucking a thumb or fist (this is the preferred method).

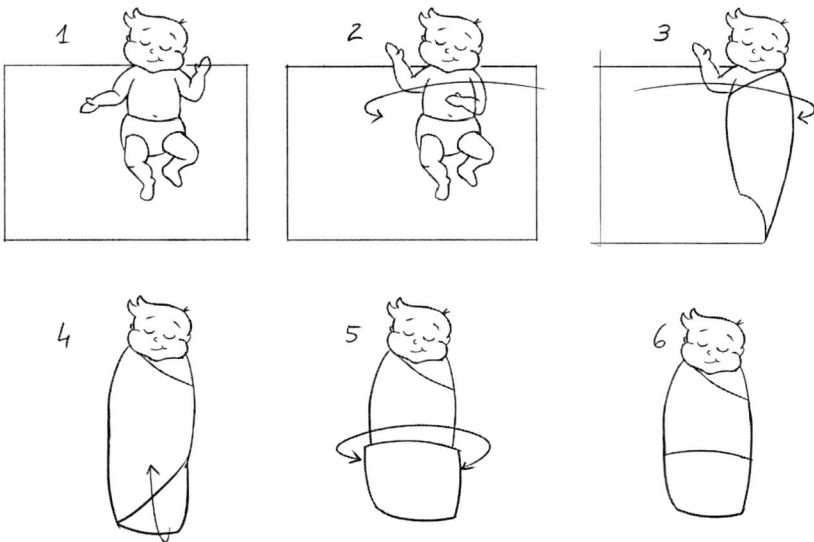

MASSAGE

Massage is an ancient and effective method of settling a baby. There are many claims for the benefits of baby massage. Benefits for pre-term babies include weight gain, improved activity levels and reduced hospital stay. Benefits for full-term babies include enhanced parent and infant relationship, reduced cortisol (stress hormone), improved sleep rhythms, reduction of colic symptoms and improved food digestion as a result of increased secretion of insulin and gastrin.

Massage provides an opportunity for parents to slow down and be with their baby and will allow you to increase your sensitivity to your baby's body, their likes and dislikes. Some babies take time to learn to enjoy being massaged, while other babies just don't like having their clothes removed.

The first time you massage your baby:

- Choose a time when you are both calm (when your baby is in a quiet alert state) – this will allow a connection with being calm and being massaged.
- If your baby doesn't like having their clothes off, start slowing by massaging their legs and arms without uncovering their body.
- If you have been playing music to calm your baby, this may also help to make a connection between being calm and being massaged.
- Explain to your baby what you are going to do. At first you might find this a little strange, but it will help you slow down.

To massage your baby:

- Make sure the room is warm and there are no drafts that will cause your baby to lose body heat.
- Slowly undress your baby and place on an old towel.
- Using a slightly warmed vegetable oil (e.g. olive oil) that is not highly perfumed will assist in the massage of your baby – rub this into your hands.
- Use long smooth strokes on arms, legs and chest.
- Your baby's tummy is sensitive so be very gentle using circular, clockwise strokes. Avoid this area if the belly button has not completely healed.

- Use your fingertips to massage your baby's face, stroking from the middle of the forehead, down the outside of their cheeks. Massage the scalp in small circles using your fingertips.
- Turn your baby onto their tummy and use long smooth strokes from their head to toe.

Always use respectful touch, and if your baby is upset or showing signs of discomfort, looking away or showing other disengagement cues, stop. Talking to your baby in a soothing voice and telling them what you are doing can calm your baby. For massage to be enjoyable and successful, you need to be relaxed and enjoying this time with your baby. Be aware of your baby's subtle cues or signals that they are no longer enjoying being massaged. It is important to stop before your baby becomes upset or distressed. Finishing the massage with a relaxed and happy baby is the main aim of massaging your baby.

WHEN NOTHING WORKS!

Unfortunately, some days your baby will find it very difficult to settle. No matter what you try, it does not work. If you start to feel tired, frustrated, upset or anxious, it is very likely that your baby will also remain upset and very unsettled. This can be difficult and overwhelming for both you and your baby.

Much of what Tresillian suggests parents do to support their babies is not difficult, but it is about being mindful of your baby and how they might be feeling. It is about learning to view the world from your baby's experience. It is also essential to be mindful as a parent, about how you are feeling.

When you are having a challenging day with your baby:
- It is important that you stop what you are doing.
- Put your baby in a safe place.
- Now take a moment to recognise if you are feeling anxious, frustrated, upset and/or angry.
- If you are, try to take a few minutes to relax or reach a calm state before picking up your baby again.

Some parents, to regain their composure, find it is useful to:

- Do a quick relaxation exercise.
- Sit quietly with a cup of tea or coffee (even if it's just for a minute!).
- Pick up the phone and call a friend.

If your baby is very unsettled for a prolonged period, call on friends and family for help. Ideally, someone will be able to take over the soothing of your baby for a few hours. Extended unsettled periods can be very dangerous for babies, as when parents become exhausted they may do things that are totally out of character, such as handling the baby more roughly than intended or shaking the baby out of sheer frustration. We know that this will cause severe brain injury to a baby and some babies do die from their injuries.

If you do not have anyone that can come to assist you, carefully place the baby in their bed. Ring a parenting helpline for advice and support. If this is happening during business hours, contact your child and family health nurse; they may be able to see you in their centre that day.

Other strategies are:

- Taking your baby for a walk in their pram.
- Having a shower to help you relax.
- Having a bath with your baby, so you both relax, often works wonderfully well. Be careful you don't fall asleep in the bath. So you can get in and out of the bath safely, have your partner hand you your baby after you get into the bath, and take your baby before you try to get out of the bath.

NOTE: Do not take your baby for a drive in the car if you are feeling tired, frustrated or angry.

On a positive note, be assured that your baby will eventually settle.

The reality is that along with enjoyable and satisfactory interactions, your baby will experience more unsettled episodes in the future. Try and work towards building a supportive network of friends and family who can support you through these difficult times.

A QUICK RELAXATION TECHNIQUE

You can do this either sitting in a comfortable chair or while standing:
- Breathe out with a long sigh, drop your shoulders as you sigh.
- Relax your face, unclenching your jaw. Be aware of your facial muscles, eyes and forehead and try to relax them.
- Focus on your breathing, keeping your breaths quiet, slow and rhythmic.
- Repeat this relaxation technique again and as often as you feel is necessary.

CHAPTER SUMMARY

- If you respond positively to your baby they will gain a sense of security.
- There are sensitive times when your baby's brain is primed to learn special skills.
- Talking, singing and reading to your baby is one of the most important and positive thing you can do for your baby.
- Babies need exposure to simple everyday skills and experiences to start to learn.
- Infant engagement and disengagement cues are the way your baby signals their need for interaction with you or the need for a short break for the activity they are involved in. They also signal hunger and a need to sleep through a clustering of cues.
- If disengagement cues are identified, stop what you are doing and allow your baby to take the lead. This will often provide a space for your baby to recover without needing to cry or become fussy.
- The length of time it takes to settle your baby will lessen as they learn to self-settle – this can be a slow process and every baby is different.
- It is important that your baby's sleep environment is safe.
- Always sleep your baby on their back.
- Babies cry as a sign of distress and that they need you to support and comfort them.

Chapter Six

BUILDING YOUR RELATIONSHIP
WITH YOUR BABY

ONE OF THE MOST important relationships a baby will have is with their parents or main carer. This relationship provides the template for all future relationships. This special relationship is built up through everyday interactions and is embedded in our every action. All relationships are the invisible threads within our life and through nurturing from early on a positive start to life can be achieved.

Strong ties with your baby may have started even before conception. As children, we often daydream about becoming parents and imagine how we will love and nurture our baby. A strong sense of connection or bond may have started to develop with your unborn baby well before you knew you were pregnant.

To develop a secure relationship with your baby takes time as you learn how to respond sensitively to their ever-changing physical and emotional needs. This is especially true when your baby is distressed or upset – baby trusts you to come and soothe them. This is the fastest way that they gain a sense of safety and trust. Importantly, your baby also contributes to the development of the relationship with you by giving you their absolute trust, but they need lots of support and opportunities to enable them to be responsive to your behaviour.

Some parents believe that being responsive to the baby's needs, such as providing cuddles and carrying their baby, will result in the baby becoming spoilt. In fact, we know that the opposite occurs – rather than being spoilt, the baby starts to develop a sense of trust, feeling secure in knowing that when they are upset, their mother or father will be there to help them. This is an essential lesson for babies as it helps them to forge a strong and secure connection with their parents.

Your baby needs to know:

- They are valued and loved.
- That what they say is worth hearing and you will respond to their attempts at communicating with you.
- You care about them.
- You enjoy and delight in *being with* them.
- Their world is a secure and predictable place so they feel safe to explore.
- Their world is a fun place.

PROVIDING A SECURE BASE

One of your roles as a parent is to be a reliable source of comfort for your baby. When your baby is distressed, frightened or in need, they need to know you will be there to help them overcome their distress or fear. You are their secure base. Providing a secure base for your baby will:

- Nourish them physically and emotionally.
- Provide comfort when they are distressed.

- Reassure them if frightened.
- Develop their self-confidence (belief in themselves).

It will also allow your baby to trust others as they venture out to include other people in their world. They will feel safe knowing there is somewhere to return to when they are in need of comfort or assistance and that they will be welcomed back by you as their parent. As a general rule, your role as a parent is to be available physically and emotionally, and be ready to respond *when called upon*. Encourage your baby and soothe by using calming and reassuring words and tone of voice. Intervene and take charge only when clearly necessary.

Other factors to help you and your baby develop a secure base include:

- Having a regular physical closeness, especially in times of need when upset, scared or distressed. Being physically held often calms a baby. This is not always possible, and as your baby grows it may not be the first action you take. Physical closeness can also be achieved by a gentle touch, making eye contact with your baby and smiling reassuringly. Talking or singing can also help to calm your baby.
- Understanding your baby's temperament and what your baby needs enables them to feel a sense of support and comfort, e.g. some babies cry to be picked up while others cry to be put to bed.
- Being able to identify and respond to your baby's cues (see Chapter 5).
- Helping your baby gain a sense of competence by acknowledging and showing delight in their achievements.
- Allowing your baby to practise their developing knowledge and skills by creating opportunities and activities that will reinforce that knowledge and skill.
- Providing a sense of predictability. For example, having a basic routine or responding to their distress quickly and appropriately.

PARENTING BEHAVIOURS

Here are five parenting behaviours that will make a huge difference in how well you develop a relationship with your baby.

1. *Be sensitive.* Being sensitive to your baby's needs is a pivotal part of being a confident and successful parent. Sensitivity is about being able to watch, listen and then respond appropriately and quickly to your baby's cues (behaviours and vocalisations). Fortunately most mothers are attuned to do this as baby is their main focus of attention.

   To be sensitive you need to be both physically *and* emotionally available to your baby. Being emotionally available is at times difficult, especially if you are feeling fatigued, unsupported, lonely, distressed or experiencing anxiety or depression. When feeling exhausted or upset, parents can perceive that their baby is trying to make their lives difficult, so remember to take up those offers of support and help from your family and friends.

   For some parents being sensitive to their baby's needs seems to come naturally, while for others it is something they have to learn about and make a conscious effort with. With practice, your sensitivity to your baby will grow and become an automatic response. A useful skill is to try to imagine what your baby might be experiencing. This is an important step in developing parental insight and providing answers so you know how to act when you are feeling overwhelmed with a crying baby.

   For example, ask yourself:
   - What would be causing me to be so distressed if I were a baby?
   - How might it feel if I was cuddled by the person I loved most in the world?
   - What might make me feel better if I was feeling so upset?

   Asking these questions allows you to start to explore your baby's experience and the associated emotions they may be feeling.

2. *Be responsive.* How do you respond to your baby appropriately? This might mean when your baby laughs, you laugh or smile back; when they cry you pick them up and make soothing noises; when

they make noises you start to have a conversation with them or when they just want some fun you sing to them; or if they put their hand on your arm you play simple finger games.

Your baby will reward you by being responsive in return. They will normally communicate their feelings to you through physical cues and respond to your attempts to calm, soothe or play with them. Not all babies respond the same way – it can be very difficult for premature or unwell babies to be responsive.

The important thing is to take every opportunity to respond and talk to your baby.

3. *Be visible.* Position your baby so that you can see your baby's attempts to communicate with you. They need to be able to visibly see you and check that what they are experiencing is okay. Your facial expressions, soothing words or touch give your baby visual and physical feedback. Make sure your baby is able to check with you for reassurance regularly. If they are in a forward-facing pram or stroller, regularly stop and talk while showing your face to your baby.

This is how infants learn to self-regulate their behaviour. They are not only learning to control their emotions but all their bodily systems. It is important to position your baby so you can easily make eye-to-eye contact. Interestingly, breastfeeding ideally positions your baby. It allows eye contact to be made, especially if you turn your head slightly to the arm that is cuddling your baby (most mothers do this naturally). It is also the perfect focal distance of about 22 cm for your infant to be able to clearly see your face. By two to three months of age your baby will be able to focus on lots of objects in different parts of a room. This is when they start to connect what they are seeing with what they are hearing, tasting and feeling.

Remember, you are their most loved object. Your baby will often have extended periods where they gaze at you. This provides a wonderful opportunity to just be in the moment with your baby, gently stroking their head or arms, playing gently with their fingers and softly talking. These are truly magical moments.

4. *Talking.* Helping your baby develop a rich and large vocabulary is one of the most significant gifts you can provide for their future education and life. Having a well-developed vocabulary by the time your baby goes to school will assist them to be social and ready for school. If they have words to talk about their feelings or ask for help, they will not need to be aggressive to get help from their teachers or friends. Talking also helps develop a sense of creativity and their place in the world as they sing songs, tell stories and share their everyday experiences.

Reading and talking in descriptive and expressive language is the way to support the development of language skills. DVDs or television are not a substitute for lots of interaction from adults. Using descriptive language is value adding to any interaction you have with your baby. Instead of saying 'look at the ball', expand your description of the ball: 'Look at the round red ball. Can you feel how smooth it feels?'

At first this might seem a bit strange or awkward talking like this to your baby, but with practice, it becomes much easier and more natural.

Take this even further and provide words for emotions: 'You look so sad at the moment' or 'I just love your smile; you must be feeling so happy'. It is never too early to start to talk to your baby in this way.

Babies love books, so from your baby's very early months reading is an important activity. At first it might be talking about the pictures in the book or making up your own story about the pictures. Remember to position your baby so they can see your face and your expressions and joy, as you read the book. Even with the event of eBooks, paper-based books remain extremely important for children as they provide opportunities not available with digital books.

Turning pages helps to improve children's fine motor skills. Paper-based books also provide less distractions than those associated with eBooks, so they assist in extending a child's concentration. EBooks will also be of great interest to your baby – they expand the possibilities for interaction and provide other valuable experiences. By the time they are 12 months they will be very proficient at swiping their finger across the screen to change the screen content.

5. *Your facial, verbal and bodily expressions.* Your facial expressions and body language often display how you are feeling. As mentioned earlier babies use another's facial, verbal and bodily expressions to regulate their responses to novel, new or frightening experiences or situations. Importantly, babies need to see their parent's face to fully use the messages being provided when they are in strange or new situations. This need to see parents has implications for the baby equipment you purchase. For example, consider buying a pram or stroller that faces *towards* you rather than away. This provides your baby with the ability to easily check your expression and for you to provide soothing words in situations where there is lots of noise and movement.

CONNECTING WITH YOUR BABY

Staying in tune with your baby will build your relationship with them. By noticing little things about their facial expressions, their body language and emotions you will feel more connected to your baby and understand what they are trying to tell you. It will also enhance those special moments where you feel deeply connected with your baby.

For example:

- At birth or shortly after birth some babies have a short period where they will lay in your arms looking at you with an intense wide-eyed stare.
- When they are feeding and grasp your finger and look into your eyes.
- When you receive your first recognisable smile.
- When they follow you around the room with their eyes.
- Watching them while they are asleep.
- At four months when they give you a big toothless grin.
- Having an intense conversation with you. Making sounds, leaving spaces for you to talk and respond.

These are just some of the joyous moments that provide the glue for your relationship with your baby.

ROUTINES

Baby routines over the years have gained a lot of bad press. Routines are frequently discussed as rigidly adhering to a timetable of activities. For many parents having their baby in a routine has been a lifesaver. Importantly, babies seem to respond well to having a routine, especially if the routine is mostly baby-led or follows your baby's emerging daily pattern and developmental needs. A routine provides reassurance that all is well in your baby's world. They know that when they get up in the morning there will be food, they can have a play and then it's time for another sleep or a bath and so on. Their world becomes a predictable place as there is a pattern to their day.

Routines that work usually have some degree of flexibility to allow for the intrusion of daily life. They are not rigid, but rather provide a predictable flow to the day. Having a routine also helps parents start to read their baby's cues as they can easily link them with what comes next in the routine. Unfortunately, sometimes the routine needs to be broken. There are common events that can cause routines to be disrupted.

The first is when happy events occur, like family visits, parties, and other social events or holidays. These events can challenge the maintenance of a routine. Rather than not participate, reassure yourself that when you get home you will start the routine again.

The second circumstance is when a parent returns to the paid workforce. There are lots of new activities to get used to for both baby and parent. Having a routine is very important for babies and their parents in the paid workforce. See Chapter 17 for further information.

The third circumstance is when your baby reaches a new developmental stage, e.g. they want to practise a new skill like rolling or standing. They become more alert and aware of their world, and sleep and awake periods become longer.

The final circumstance where routines can be disrupted is if you or your baby become unwell. Once again, rather than trying to maintain a routine, it is better to go into survival mode until you or your baby are well again.

Many babies, if they have a general pattern or flow to their day, will easily return to the routine after short disruptions. It may take up to a week, but the important thing is that you try to remain consistent with your baby.

Your baby is strongly influenced by the environment, daily activities and routines. A predictable routine (sequence of activities) including a wind down period (for example, meal, bath, cleaning teeth, story time, cuddle and kiss, and into the cot/bed) helps your child establish good sleep patterns.

The feed, sleep, play routine (for younger babies) or feed, play, sleep, play routine (for older babies) is the core structure of a baby's day.

As your baby matures, daytime play increases and night patterns continue but without playtime. Your baby is unique, therefore their need for sleep and the time of waking varies. Some days things will go smoothly, but illness, disruption to the family environment and/or extra busy days can all affect your baby's routine. It takes time for your baby to develop a predictable routine. Being consistent and patient are the key characteristics that babies need to help form and maintain a routine.

The following routines are a guide only as your baby's needs and tired cues (signs) for sleep may vary from the examples below.

DAILY ROUTINE – BIRTH TO THREE MONTHS

The first three months is when routines start to be formed. The early weeks are usually a little chaotic as parents learn about their baby's likes and dislikes. This is a time when some babies are usually the most unsettled, often crying for what seems like very long periods of time. Babies can require two to three night-time feeds. The period between 4 to 6 pm can be when they are extremely unsettled, crying for extended periods of time. Some parents feel as if they are on a treadmill of feeding, trying to settle their baby, having a baby who sleeps for very short periods and then wakes crying ready for their next feed. Believe it or not, this is the start of a routine developing and it will become easier as awake and sleep times consolidate and become longer (see Chapter 5). Tresillian recommends the following pattern for babies from birth to three months:

Birth to three months	
Early Morning	• Milk feed • Will often return to sleep or get up to start the day
Sleep	
Breakfast time	• Milk feed • May return to sleep • Or have some gentle play time, e.g. singing, music, tummy time, showing and talking about toys
Sleep	
Mid morning Awake time 1½ to 2 hrs	• Milk feed • Gentle play
Sleep	
Lunchtime Awake time 1½ to 2 hrs	• Milk feed • Gentle play
Sleep	
Mid afternoon Awake time 1½ to 2 hrs	• Milk feed • Gentle play
Sleep May only require a short nap	
Evening	• Milk feed • Bath • Quiet time • Cuddle
Settle for night SLEEP Two to three milk feeds may be needed overnight	

THREE MONTHS TO SIX MONTHS

Babies become more predictable in their routine by three to four months. It is not until three to six months that most babies are capable of sleeping for longer periods through the night (approximately six hours). They generally settle well overnight but may still need one to three milk feeds. Awake time is becoming longer. Time spent playing with and talking to your baby is very important for their development. Some ideas for interacting during awake/play time include:

- Tummy time (floor play)
- Using rattles and soft toys
- Taking baby for a walk in the pram
- Telling stories using soft books, learning to turn the pages
- Having a relaxing bath time or baby massage
- Singing songs or playing music
- Visiting friends
- Having lots of conversations with your baby.

Sleep times can vary, with some babies having three longer sleeps per day and others needing only short naps. If your baby is generally alert and happy, your baby is probably getting enough sleep. Remember to help your baby transition from play to sleep and have a period of activities that are calming, e.g. calm and soft talking, music or singing, and cuddles.

When your baby is awake try to interact with them. Babies love:

- Supervised tummy time (floor play)
- Playing music and singing songs
- Reading stories or singing nursery rhymes

- Playing finger or toe games
- Providing toys that move, make sounds, are colourful and vary in texture
- Giving lots of cuddles
- Visiting friends/your local park/join a playgroup.

Tresillian recommends the following pattern for babies aged three to six months:

Three to six months	
Early Morning	• Milk feed • May return to sleep • Or have some play time
Sleep	
Mid morning Awake time 1½ to 2 hrs	• Milk feed • Play
Sleep	
Lunchtime Awake time 1½ to 2 hrs	• Milk feed • Play
Sleep	
Mid afternoon Awake time 1½ to 2 hrs	• Milk feed • Play
Sleep May only require a short nap	
Evening	• Milk feed • Bath • Quiet time • Cuddle
Settle for night SLEEP One to two milk feeds may be needed overnight	

NOTE: As your baby becomes more mobile, it is important to ensure your home and play areas are safe.

SIX TO 12 MONTHS

By 6–8 months your baby's routine is starting to change. This is often a time when your baby is more active during the day. By eight months many babies only need two daytime sleeps, while other babies still need three sleeps per day. Base your routine on your baby's cues/needs for sleep. If your baby is generally alert and happy your baby is probably getting enough sleep. They may be less hungry when they wake and enjoy a short period of play before being fed.

By six months your baby can start solids. It is also a good time to begin feeding your baby cooled boiled water from a cup. Some ideas for interacting during your baby's awake time include:

- Floor play
- Music/singing
- Story time/nursery rhymes
- Finger/toe games
- Toys that move, make sound, colourful and vary in texture
- Cuddles
- Baby massage
- Water play, especially at bath time.

For babies aged from six to eight months, Tresillian recommends the following pattern:

Six to eight months	
Early morning Awake time 2–3 hrs	• Milk feed • May return to sleep • Or have some play time
Sleep	
Mid morning Awake time 2–3 hrs	• Play • Milk feed (can be followed by solid foods) • Play
Sleep	
Lunchtime Awake time 2–3 hrs	• Play • Milk feed (can be followed by solid foods) • Play
Sleep	
Mid Afternoon Awake time 2–3 hrs	• Milk feed (can be followed by solid foods) • Bath • Quiet time • Cuddle
Sleep Some babies may no longer require four sleeps during the day	
Evening	
Settle for night SLEEP Optional milk feed overnight	

By eight months your baby may have moved to just two daytime sleeps. If your baby wakes early or you need your baby to go to bed later, an additional sleep may be needed. At this age babies may still be night waking or even start to night wake – this can be related to separation anxiety (a developmental stage for this age). Babies at this age also like to practise new skills such as pulling to stand, crawling and talking. If this happens provide your baby with reassurance and try to resettle with minimal fuss.

Some ideas for interacting during playtime include:
- Playing music, singing and dancing
- Providing moving toys/dolls/teddies
- Reading stories and using cloth books
- Singing nursery rhymes
- Playing stacking games
- Playing with toys that move, make sound, colourful and vary in texture
- Playing with posting games – putting colourful shapes into a container with a special lid that has a matching shape hole
- Using pulling and pushing toys
- Visiting friends, local parks and play groups.

For older babies aged eight to 14 months, Tresillian suggests the following pattern:

Eight to 14 months	
Morning Awake time 3–4 hrs	• Breakfast • Milk feed • Play time
Sleep	
Mid morning (If awake) Lunchtime Awake time 2–3 hrs	• Water with a snack • Play • Lunch • Milk feed • Play
Sleep	
Mid Afternoon Awake time 2–3 hrs	• Water with a snack • Play
Evening	• Dinner • Milk feed • Bath • Quiet time • Cuddle
Settle for night SLEEP Optional milk feed overnight	

NOTE: As your baby gets older they will progress to only one sleep per day – watch your baby to see when they give you cues (signs) they are tired. The morning sleep will progressively get later in the day until it becomes a middle of the day or early afternoon sleep. Your baby is now more mobile so it is very important to ensure your home environment is a safe environment. Now is the time to install childproof locks and other home safety devices.

CHAPTER SUMMARY

- The relationship between a baby and parent provides the template for all future relationships.
- An important parenting role is to be a reliable source of comfort for their baby.
- Parents need to be physically and emotionally available for their baby.
- Babies respond well to having a routine or pattern to their day as routines make their world more predictable, but routines need to be flexible and baby-led whenever possible.
- Babies love books and to be read to from a very young age.
- A parent's role is supporting their baby to develop complex skills by helping them settle to sleep and enjoy their awake times.

Chapter Seven
YOUR BABY'S DEVELOPMENT

IN THE FIRST 12 MONTHS of life your baby will grow and develop at an amazing speed. It's hard for the parents to keep up with so many changes, let alone the baby having to adapt to these developmental experiences.

All babies go through a sequence of rapid and predictable developmental changes in their first year of life – from being very dependent on their parents to developing integrated skills that enable them to actively and meaningfully interact with the outside world. Parents are often amazed at how rapidly their babies gain new and complex skills. 'Development' is used to describe the sequence of physical, emotional and social changes a baby is expected to achieve.

On the other hand, 'milestones' is a term used to describe the developmental expectation at specific time periods, for example, sitting on their own or crawling.

Things you should know about your baby's development:

- Babies develop in a predictable sequence. They gain head control before they can sit, for example.
- Babies develop at varying rates. Some babies walk at 10 months while others take a couple of months longer.
- Babies need to be allowed opportunities to achieve milestones. One way to do this is to place them on their tummy so they can learn to crawl.
- Babies need opportunities to practise new tasks, such as learning to use a spoon or drink from a cup.
- If you are worried about your baby's development you need to raise it with your child and family health nurse or your doctor.

BABY'S DEVELOPING KNOWLEDGE AND SKILLS

Many parents worry about their baby not developing at the same rate as those at mothers' groups or their own friends' babies. Rest assured that babies are programmed to develop in a specific sequence. This is nature's way of providing them with a safeguard to minimise situations where they will be placed in danger.

There are **two** sequences that take place to help your baby develop.

The first sequence is *cephalocaudal* (Latin for 'head to tail'). It starts with the ability to gradually control their head and keep it upright. It ends with the ability to walk, jump, skip and run. A baby has to learn to gain head support, roll over, then to sit up unsupported. They learn to crawl and pull themselves to stand as they cruise around furniture gaining the skill of balance. Then baby finally starts to take their first tentative unsupported steps.

The second sequence is *proximodistal* (the literal meaning is from 'near to far'), where the movements start from the centre and move out to their arms. For example, the baby starts with very gross movements of grasping. They then refine these arm movements, down to fine movements of fingers, allowing your baby to pick up small items from the floor at around nine months of age.

If you are aware of these sequences you can prepare for the next step in your baby's development. This might mean moving precious items out of the reach of curious little hands; making sure you sweep the floor on a more regular basis or moving laundry chemicals off the floor onto high shelves.

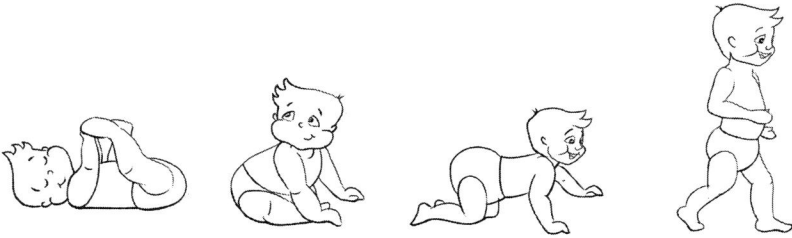

REFLEXES

Babies are born with a set of reflexes. These reflexes act to protect your baby. Some are transient, disappearing after a few months, while other reflexes are permanent, staying with your baby for life. Some reflexes will start later in your baby's first year. Reflexes protect us from harm and assist us to react to such things as painful stimuli, e.g. a surface that might burn, or expanding and contracting the pupil in our eye as a reaction to bright or dim light.

Some reflexes go from being involuntary to a learnt behaviour. Weak or absent reflexes, or reflexes that remain after the expected time they should have faded, might indicate a problem in your baby's development and should be checked by your child and family health nurse or doctor.

Remember that some reflexes go from being involuntary (automatic) to voluntary (being able to control). The ability to suck is an important reflex that starts *in utero*. At birth, a baby has to be able to coordinate their sucking action, swallowing and breathing. This is a very complex behaviour that at first some babies struggle to achieve. Sucking becomes less reflexive and more voluntary and purposeful as they become successful with feeding.

The rooting reflex is essential as it helps your baby locate the breast or teat. If you gently stroke their cheek, they will turn their head towards your hand. At first it is not a very refined movement as they will move their head from side to side. By three weeks they will very quickly locate the source of their next feed.

During the first weeks, the *moro* reflex is a more dramatic reflex. If an unexpected movement or noise startles your baby, or their head moves suddenly or falls backwards, they will react by throwing out their arms and legs and extending their neck. They will then rapidly bring their arms together. They may become distressed and cry loudly. This is a good reflex to avoid triggering. One of the reasons to lightly wrap a young baby is to control this reflex, which can wake them.

A reflex that often amazes parents is the ability of a newborn baby to step and walk. By holding your baby securely under their arms and placing their foot on the underside of a ledge the baby will step up onto the top of the ledge or table. If you then hold your baby in the same way and let their soles touch a flat firm surface they will start to walk. This reflex disappears after a couple of months to become a learnt skill at the end of the first year.

A very engaging reflex for parents is when you place your finger in the palm of your baby's hand and they grasp your finger. At first this is an automatic reflex, but quickly becomes a learnt behaviour, enabling them to grasp and release objects as they become more mobile.

The following table provides some of the reflexes your baby will have during their first year. Some are permanent lifelong reflexes, others are temporary.

Reflex	Stimulus	Response	Reflex disappears/stays
Eye blink	Shine bright light at eyes or clap hands loudly	Quickly closes eyelids	Permanent
Sucking	Place a clean finger in your baby's mouth	Rhythmical sucking	Replaced by voluntary sucking after 4 months
Moro reflex (primitive reflex)	Your doctor or nurse will make a loud sound, or let baby 'drop' slightly and suddenly	Baby extends legs, arms and fingers. Their back will arch and the head will drop backwards	Fades by 4 months, gone by 6 months
Walking (primitive reflex)	Hold baby under the arms with their feet touching a flat surface	Baby will make stepping-like movements, their feet will alternate as in walking	Fades by 8 weeks
Rooting	Stroke your baby's cheek with a finger or nipple	Baby will turn their head toward the touch, open their mouth and make sucking movements	Fades by 6 months
Tongue thrust	Touch your baby's lips with a spoon	Tongue will poke out	Gone by 6 months
Tonic neck reflex (primitive reflex)	While your baby is awake and on their back turn their head to one side	Fencing position assumed by your baby. Arm on the side the head is turned towards, will extend	Fades by 4 months
Grasping (primitive reflex)	Using your finger stroke the palm of your baby's hand	Fingers will close around your finger, making a strong fist	Fades by 4–5 months
Babinski (foot) (primitive reflex)	Stroke the sole of your baby's foot from toes toward the heel	Toes will fan out	Fades by 8–12 months
Gag and cough	Milk flows too fast	Baby will gag, cough	Permanent
Sideward protective reflex	When sitting and falling to the side	Infant puts arms out to save if tilted off balance	Starts from 6 months
Forward protective reflex	When sitting or standing and falling forward	Arms and hands extend forwards	Starts at 7 months
Backward protective reflex	When sitting and falling backward	Both arms extend backwards when pushed backwards	Starts at 9 months

Sheridan M, 2008, *From birth to five years: Children's developmental progress*, ACER Press, Melbourne.

HABITUATION

From birth, humans have the ability to gradually reduce their response to repetitive stimuli; this is called *habituation*. For example, if you live under a flight path, you use this skill all the time. Very quickly you get used to the noise of airplanes as they land or take off and after a while don't notice it at all. That is, until a visitor makes a comment about the noise and you are rapidly drawn back into hearing the airplane sounds.

Babies show this habituation by a decline in looking and heart and respiration rate. When a new stimulus occurs, there is a change in the environment or a sudden noise, the baby's responsiveness returns – this is called *recovery*. As your baby develops, they will habituate and recover more quickly. This indicates that they are processing information much more efficiently.

Researchers who are involved in research about infants and their responses to the world use habituation and recovery as an important and reliable research tool. They now know from using habituation and recovery that fetuses learn *in utero*. If a fetus is regularly played the same music *in utero*, once the baby is born they will more quickly habituate to that music than a baby who has not heard the music before. This is useful knowledge, as by playing calming music to your baby when *in utero* or shortly after birth (when they are settled), they will start to habituate to it. When they become upset or unsettled, if you put the same music on, they are more likely to stop and calm as they are used to habituating to that music.

PHYSICAL SKILLS DEVELOPMENT

Physical development progresses in two ways, through cephalocaudal and proximodistal development as discussed above. The development of physical skills is usually divided into two discrete areas – *gross motor* and *fine motor*.

Gross motor includes the development of head balance, sitting, crawling, standing, posture, walking, running, jumping and skipping. Gross motor development has a sequence. For example, a full term baby at birth has some ability to momentarily hold their head erect. You will find when you gently pull your newborn baby from a lying to a sitting position that their head will lag behind (drop backwards). By three months, they will be able to hold up their head. By four months, when lying on their front, they will be able to lift their head and front portion of their chest approximately 90 degrees above the flat surface they are on and bear their weight on their forearms. From four to six months, head control is well established. To sit requires head control and the ability to straighten their back.

The following table provides a summary of other gross motor milestones including rolling over, sitting and learning to walk.

Age	Milestones
Birth	• No or minimal head control. • When held in a sitting position, their back is curved and head will fall forward.
Around one month	• When lying on their back, keeps head to one side. • Moves arms and legs in large jerky movements.
Around three months	• Has good head control. • Hands loosely open. • Needs shoulders supported when being bathed or dressed. • Lying on their front, they can lift head and front portion of their chest to a 90 degree angle, taking their weight on the forearms. • Can start to sit for short periods of time in a well supported sitting position. • When held in a standing position on a firm surface, sags at the knees.
Around six months	• Will roll from abdomen to back around 5–6 months. • Will roll from back to abdomen around 6–7 months. • Head control well established. • Will sit with support, head and back are straight. Able to turn head from side to side to look around. • Has increasing coordination of their hands (from four to six months).
Around nine months	• Pulls self to a sitting position. Can sit alone unsupported. They will begin to explore their surroundings in this position. • Will adjust body posture when leaning forward to pick up or play with a toy, without losing their balance. • Can bear all their weight on their legs when held to standing and steps purposefully on alternate feet. • Will roll, wriggle on abdomen or crawl across the floor, to get what they want. • Can pull to standing and stand holding furniture. • When being carried by an adult, supports self in an upright position and turns head to look around.
Around 12 months	• Sits on the floor for long periods. • Easily goes from lying down to sitting position. • Crawls on hands and knees, may crawl up stairs. • Pulls to stand, holding onto furniture and able to sit down again. • Walks while holding onto furniture, or if two hands are held. • May walk with one hand held or alone without support.

Fine motor is the development of the ability to accomplish fine tasks. At first larger gross movements are refined to become much finer movements. This includes uncoordinated movement of arms to more purposeful movements of arms and hands. Fine motor tasks usually require the ability to pick up small objects like food using a pincer grip, and being able to use a pencil effectively requires a well-developed pincer grip (thumb and forefinger come together).

This next table summarises the progression from gross to fine motor skills development.

Age	Milestones
Around one month	• Hands are predominantly closed.
Around three months	• Hands are mostly open. • Waves arms symmetrically. • Shows a desire to grasp an object. • If a rattle is placed in their hand, they will actively hold onto it. • Grasp is no longer a reflex, it is now a voluntary action.
Around six months	• Voluntarily grasps onto an object. • Increased manipulation skills – holds a bottle, grasp their feet and put them in their mouth, and they can hold a rusk. • Can transfer an object from one hand to the other.
Around nine months	• Palmar grip is gradually replaced by a crude pincer grip. • Pincer grip sufficiently developed to enable a raisin and other finger food to be successfully picked up. • Deliberately lets go of an object. • Offers an object to another person. • Enjoys banging objects. • Explores moving parts of a toy. • Holds an object in each hand.
Around 12 months	• Pincer grip is refined and very functional. • Puts objects in a container and then enjoys removing them. • Tries to build a tower of two blocks, but often just misses the placement of the block.

DEVELOPMENT OF VISION, HEARING AND LANGUAGE

In the first year of life, vision, hearing and language development are fundamental areas of skills development that impacts on so many other areas of your baby's development. Language, fine motor skills and cognitive development are all reliant, in some part, on the development of hearing and vision ability. Seek medical opinion if you are concerned about your baby's lack of response to noise or their ability to see (for further information see Chapter 15).

WHAT CAN YOUR BABY SEE?

Even though babies are able to see at birth, there is significant improvement in their vision during the first 12 months. We know that babies have a visual preference for looking at human faces.

At six weeks they begin showing interest in a picture of a face with eyes rather than no eyes; at 10 weeks a greater response is gained from a picture of a face with eyes and eyebrows; at 20 weeks a face that also includes a mouth is necessary; at six months baby can easily distinguish a familiar from a strange face.

Importantly, contributors to this vision development include *binocularity* or the ability for both eyes to work together to create one cerebral picture. This begins to develop at six weeks and is well established by four months. By the age of seven to nine months, depth perception (*stereopsis*) is starting to be established as an important safety mechanism. For example, this depth perception will assist with negotiating stairs or stacking blocks one on top of the other.

Age	Milestones
At birth	• Close their eyes to sudden light. • May focus on a slowly moving object 22 to 30 cm away in a range of 45 degrees. • Will gaze at a face or object within 22 to 30 cm. • Head and eye movements are not integrated (doll's eye reflex – eyes lag behind if head is rotated to one side).

Age	Milestones
Around one month	• Tear glands begin to function from two to four weeks. • Pupils react well to light. • Watches parent intently when spoken to. • Gaze caught and held by a bright dangling object gently moved in their line of vision. • Gazes at an object that is slowly moved towards and away from their face. • Turns to a diffuse light source, e.g. a lamp.
Around three months	• Visually very alert, particularly preoccupied by human faces. • Follows adult movement. • Binocular vision (using both eyes together) begins at six weeks. • Convergence of vision (coming together) on near objects starting at six weeks. • Doll's eye reflex disappears (it is not normal for it to be present after three months). • Defensive blink reflex may take up to six to eight weeks to be well established. By 12 weeks blink reflex clearly shown. • Hand regard when lying on the back – watches movement of their own hands, engages in finger play, pressing palms of hands together, and opening and closing their hands.
Around six months	• Eyes move in unison. • Follows adult movement across the room with purposeful alertness. • Change position to see an object. • Able to rescue a dropped toy when falls within visual field. • Has a preference for more complex visual stimuli. • Starting to develop hand-eye coordination.
Around nine months	• Visually very attentive to people, objects and what is happening in their environment. • Can focus on very small objects. • Depth perception developing (ability to work out the position of an object to another within their visual field). • Begins to point at more distant objects and people. • Will watch people, activities or animals within three or four metres with interest for several minutes.
Around 12 months	• Can follow rapidly moving objects. • Recognises familiar people approaching from a distance. • Shows interest in pictures. • Drops and throws toys and objects deliberately, watches with interest as they fall to the floor. • Looks in the correct place if object falls out of sight.

WHAT CAN YOUR BABY HEAR?

Hearing also develops over the first year. Hearing is an essential ability, to enable language to develop at an appropriate developmental rate.

Age	Milestones
At birth	• Startle or *moro* reflex will be activated in response to a loud noise. • Responds to the sound of a human voice more readily than any other sound. • Becomes quieter in response to gentle soft singing or heartbeat.
At one month	• Startled by sudden noises; reactions include stiffening, blinking, extending limbs and crying. • Movements momentarily 'frozen' in response to a new noise, cannot locate the source of the noise, but may move head towards the source of the noise. • Stops whimpering to the sound of a soothing human voice.
Around three months	• Head turns to the side of a sound made at the level of the ear, may wrinkle their brow. • Turns head to locate sound and looks in the direction of the sound. • Quietens or smiles to the sound of a familiar voice before being touched. • Quietens to a gentle noise (rattle or bell) made out of sight.
Around six months	• Sound is located by head to the side and looking up or down. • Turns immediately to a familiar voice across the room. • Listens to voice even if their parent is not in view.
Around nine months	• Attentive to everyday sounds. • Turns head in an curving arc to locate sound. • Turns head directly towards sound.
Around 12 months	• Locates sounds from any direction well. • Immediately responds to own name. • Starting to control and adjust their own response to sound, e.g. listening for a sound to start again. • Recognises familiar tunes by trying to join in.

WHEN WILL MY BABY TALK?

Regardless of place of birth or culture, all babies:
- Coo before they babble
- Understand language before they can speak
- Start to speak their first words around 12 months of age.

Babies have an amazing capacity to learn languages. They recognise familiar voices and listen intently from an early age, especially to their parents' voices. Babies are also attracted to higher-pitched voices. Interestingly, most adults intuitively start to talk motherese (or parentese) without realising they are doing this. A higher-pitched sing song voice, combined with short and simple sentences are regularly used by parents. Babies prefer motherese to regular grown-up voice tones. It has been identified that motherese helps babies learn language through the high pitch, elongated vowels, exaggerated facial expressions and short, simple sentences. For example, 'you are sooo pretty and so cuuute'.

Babies often make speech-like noises. Long before your baby can speak, they are learning the rules that govern language. Cooing commences at around two months of age and consists of vowel-like sounds; cooing has a pleasant 'oo' quality. While babbling starts at around six months of age; your baby will repeat consonant-vowel combinations – 'babababababab' or 'dadadadada'. Sometimes mothers get upset as their baby seems to be favouring their father by first saying 'dadada.'

Cooing and babbling are thought to be an essential component of your baby learning how to talk as they practise moving their lips, tongue, jaw, mouth and making sounds. By four to six months, you will often find your baby happily talking to themselves. This is the time to join in and have a conversation with your baby. Give meaning to your baby's babbles and coos – 'you sound so happy today', 'I just love it when you talk to me'.

Avoid talking over them, wait for a pause in their babbling, just as in an adult conversation. Leave spaces for them to respond. This can be one of those very special moments with your baby. This is a time to just *be in the moment* with your baby.

Babies, regardless of their birthplace or culture, start to babble at approximately 4-to-6 months. Even babies who are deaf from birth start to babble at this time, producing a similar range of sounds. If babies don't hear talking they are likely to stop babbling, so make sure you talk to your baby frequently and with lots of descriptive words from birth.

By the second half of the first year, babies start to understand word meanings. They will turn to their mother when the word mummy is spoken. Your baby will also have an increased awareness of what they want and need. They will start to point, crawl or gesture towards the things they want.

Your baby may stumble upon words like 'mama' or 'bye-bye'. Through your reinforcement, your baby will start to repeat, especially if you act pleased and excited. Using picture books will assist in reinforcing words and relationships.

Around 12 months of age, babies start to use their first words with clear meaning. At this stage they comprehend more words than you probably realise. Differences in language development start to be identified at around 18 months.

Learning more than one language is a real gift for children growing up in a global world. It will provide so many more education and employment opportunities. We now know that babies are able to manage multiple languages. When babies first start to babble, they make lots of different sounds, including some that are not part of the language they are hearing. By nine or 10 months their repertoire of babbling sounds start to narrow to the set of sounds they regularly hear in their everyday environment. The other sounds are then dropped.

This knowledge about the repertoire of sounds babies instinctively make highlights the importance of reinforcing these sounds, so they are not lost. Parents are now encouraged to expose their babies to more than one language in their first year so their babies will simultaneously learn these languages. If babies do not have this opportunity they may find it more difficult learning a second language later in life.

Some parents are very committed to teaching their baby sign language. This is especially true if they, as adults, are dependent on signing to communicate or their baby has been diagnosed with a hearing problem. It has been demonstrated that babies can learn the signs for simple objects and tasks, e.g. sleep, play and eat. It is believed that this reduces the baby's frustration as its cognitive development is greater than language development. As with most learning it requires parents to be persistent and willing to provide lots of repetition to reinforce your baby's learning. More information is commercially available on the internet and publications, however make sure the providers of the program have appropriate qualifications and experience before signing up.

Approximate age	Milestones
From birth	• Cries to indicate distress and need for assistance from parents and others.
Around one month	• When content they will utter little guttural noises. • Will coo and make pre-speech lip and tongue movements in response to parent's talk from soon after birth. • Cries lustily when uncomfortable or hungry.
Around three months	• Smiles at the sound of your voice. • Coos and makes other pleasant vowel sounds. • Shows delight by making sounds when spoken, as well as integrating smiles, eye contact and hand gestures. • Begins to imitate some sounds. • Turns head toward the direction of sound. • Cries when annoyed or uncomfortable. • Starts to show excitement at the sound of pleasurable experiences, e.g. approaching voices, footsteps and running bathwater.

Approximate age	Milestones
Around six months	• Starting to happily babble tunefully to self and others. • Laughs, chuckles and squeals aloud during play. • Has a very large repertoire of sounds, beyond those they regularly hear. • Responds to own name (around five months). • Begins to respond to 'no'. • Distinguishes emotions by tone of voice. • Responds to sound by making sounds. • Uses voice to express joy and displeasure. • Babbles chains of consonants. • Starts to include sounds from spoken language. • Starts to comprehend commonly used words.
Around nine months	• Repertoire of sounds starts to narrow. • Deliberate in their vocalisations as means of communication to show friendliness or annoyance. • Babbles loudly and tunefully in long and repetitive ways. • Enjoys having conversations with others. • Reacts by looking around to questions, e.g. 'where is Mummy/Daddy?'. • Responds when name is called. • Responds to 'no' (around 10 months). • Tries to imitate words and sounds, e.g. coughing, makes raspberries, and clicking sounds.
Around 12 months	• Pays increasing attention to speech. • Responds to simple verbal responses. • Uses simple gestures, such as waving bye-bye and shaking head for 'no'. • Says 'Mama' and 'Dada' (around 12 to 14 months). • Shows behaviours that demonstrate the linking of words to actions, e.g. 'give it to Mummy'.

Early investigation is necessary if you have any concerns that your baby is not reaching these milestones. The earlier intervention is commenced the better the outcomes for your baby will be in most instances.

BABY'S COGNITIVE, SOCIAL AND EMOTIONAL DEVELOPMENT

Cognitive development is the ability to process information, understand and learn. Many of the activities and experience of the first 12 months provide the foundation for future educational success. By 12 months of age, babies are a long way from reaching cognitive maturity but, as discussed in Chapter 5, experience is vital for brain and cognitive development. Cognitive development is closely linked with social and emotional development.

Your baby's social and emotional development begins the day they are born. Basically, this means your baby is learning a sense of self through different experiences and interactions. Research tells us that babies practise managing their feelings, emotions and social roles from the very beginning and that's how they are able to trust those closest to them and have a sense of belonging and acceptance.

There are lots of products, toys, books and music you can purchase (some at great cost), that make claims to enhance your baby's intelligence or social and emotional development. We also know that extraordinary amounts of intellectual stimulation have minimal impact on the cognitive development of normal infants. What infants need is exposure to the world they live in through a wide range of social, emotional and physical experiences that are appropriate to their developmental stage. They need lots of descriptive explanations of their world, opportunities to experiment with new skills and ideas, and to feel secure in the knowledge that you are there to help them if they become frustrated with a task, upset or distressed.

An important developmental achievement is *object permanence*. It means the ability to understand that even if you cannot see something, it still exists. At first babies do not show any sign of searching for a toy if it falls out of their cot or that has disappeared under a blanket. By 6–8 months, they will look over the side of the cot to find the dropped toy or food. They may even start a game of throwing the toy out of the cot, so you can rescue it again and again. You will usually tire of the game before they do! By 8–12 months, they will actively search for a missing toy, persisting until they find it. By 12 months, most babies understand that just because they cannot see an object, it does still exist – they have developed object permanence.

Social and emotional milestones do vary from baby to baby, but here's a guide as to what you can expect in the first 12 months:

Age	Milestones
Birth	• At this stage, baby does not have the ability to integrate information from several senses. • Provides cues of engagement and disengagement, e.g. distress cues, clustered cues for hunger and satiation. • Starts to establish interaction with parents through eye contact, imitative and spontaneous facial gestures.
Around one month	• Practises endlessly – sucking, listening, looking, grasping. Starting to coordinate different sensations, e.g. baby will look towards a sound and suck. • Becoming more alert and responsive – social smile and vocalisations becoming obvious. • Eye-to-eye contact deliberately maintained and terminated. • Still unable to link body actions to results outside their body.
Around three months	• Eager anticipation of breast or bottle feed. • Beginning to react to normal routines, e.g. smiles, increased body movement. • Enjoys bath and caring routines. • Responds with pleasure to friendly and familiar handling. • Enjoys being spoken to in motherese, playful tickling and singing.
Around six months	• Shows delight with rough and tumble play. • Anticipates and reacts appropriately to often-repeated games and songs. • Becomes absorbed in looking at toys or objects. May seem oblivious to parent's attempts to engage in an interaction. • Still friendly with strangers but starting to show some reluctance to engage with the stranger when approached too quickly, especially if familiar adult is out of sight. • Becomes more cautious of strangers from about seven months. • May start to grasp for spoon when being feed solids.

Age	Milestones
Around nine months	• Very interested in feeding self, wants to hold the spoon. Explores the food in the bowl with their fingers. • Offers food to familiar people. • Delights in babbling with a mouth full of food. • Will find a toy they see being hidden under a pillow. • Enjoys dropping objects over the side of their cot or feeding chair and having them retrieved by an adult. • Plays peek-a-boo. • Imitates hand clapping. • Still takes everything into their mouth.
Around 12 months	• Baby goes after what they want, combining understanding with a task, e.g. moves a pillow to get a toy. Understanding of object permanence is becoming well developed. • Uses their mouth less often to explore objects. • Likes to see and hear familiar people. • Waves goodbye spontaneously and on request. • Plays pat-a-cake spontaneously and on request. • Enjoys playing with both adults and toys. • Manipulates toys especially if they make a sound. Will repeat actions to make toy produce the sound. • Gives toy to an adult both spontaneously and on request. • Starts to demonstrate an understanding of objects use, e.g. spoon and bowl, hairbrush and toothbrush. • Enjoys eating with the family during meal times.

IMITATION

Babies are wonderful imitators. From birth babies have a primitive ability to imitate, so they can learn through copying others' behaviours including facial expressions and noises. For example, a very young baby is able to imitate someone poking out their tongue or pulling a face.

Researchers have identified specialised brain cells called *mirror neurons* that are thought to underlie these imitation abilities. It's believed that these mirror neurons can assist in the development of complex social abilities, including empathy and understanding others' intentions. Over the first two years of life, your baby's capacity to imitate will significantly expand.

Babies use imitation as a means of exploring their social world and learning social behaviours. They get to know people by matching their emotional states. Your baby is achieving significant learning about their self as they notice similarities between their own actions and those of others.

Imitation is a wonderful tool for parents, but it also places a significant responsibility on you, as a parent, to model the behaviour you want from your child as they develop into adulthood.

SEPARATION ANXIETY AND STRANGER FEAR

Beginning around seven months of age, babies start to develop separation anxiety and stranger fear. These behaviours are normal and expected. Your baby may become clingy and not want to be held by others or they may protest when you try to leave them in childcare or with a babysitter.

Babies use their parent's face as a form of social referencing. They will look to the parent to see how they are reacting. If Mum or Dad appear concerned or anxious, the baby will react in an anxious or upset way. If Mum or Dad provide a reassuring smile, the baby will be likely to settle and be happier to be in the presence of the stranger.

A number of factors can influence the intensity of your baby's protest:

- Stranger's gender, size and age – it can help if the person tries to make themselves smaller, e.g. reduces eye contact with the baby, sits rather than stands, comes down to baby's level if in a pram.
- Avoid overwhelming your baby with a loud, sudden or intrusive approach. This causes babies distress. It is important to follow your baby's lead.
- Baby's proximity to parent – being close to or held by their parent is important.

If your baby becomes unsettled and upset around people, encourage the person to:
1. Talk softly.
2. Meet the baby at eye level (to appear smaller).
3. Maintain a safe distance.
4. Avoid sudden intrusive gestures (such as holding out arms or smiling broadly).
5. Use shorter periods of eye contact and mirror baby's facial expressions.

A common time for separation anxiety during the second half of your baby's first year is bedtime. This can be a trying time for parents. See Chapter 5 for more information on managing sleep related problems.

Parents are often given advice not to encourage their baby's clinging behaviour as they will spoil the baby and encourage the behaviour to continue. This behaviour is normal, healthy and desirable as it assists your baby to develop emotionally. During this period babies need additional support and the sense of security their parents provide. If your baby is reassured by your presence, they will learn that you and others are reliable and safe to be their carers. They will also learn a most important lesson – that you will be there if they need your support.

DEVELOPMENTAL CONCERNS

Some babies are slower to develop or reach their developmental milestones than others. We know there are many variations in the timing of developmental achievements. Some babies are walking before their first birthday, while others don't start to walk until some time after their first birthday.

Developmental achievement is governed by lots of things beyond genetics. For example, if your baby is not given tummy time on a regular basis, then they may not learn to crawl when expected. If you respond to your baby's attempts at having an early conversation with you, they are more likely to be more talkative and develop a larger vocabulary.

Despite parents providing a rich developmental environment, some babies do not achieve each developmental stage within the desired time period. This can be both worrying and frustrating for parents. You may even have well-meaning family and friends telling you not to worry as they knew of a baby "who didn't walk until they were much older and now they are an elite sports person!"

Importantly, if your baby is not meeting their developmental milestones, or you are at all concerned, you need to have your baby assessed by your child and family health nurse or doctor. We now know from research into child development and early brain development that early intervention is vital as it can significantly change the life course for many babies. It is much easier to intervene when problems are starting to occur, rather than many years later when the problems have become major and your baby's brain has less ability to change.

Ask for a medical assessment if your baby:
- Does not look at you.
- Does not seem to see things, there is something about their eyes that bothers you, or their pupils are cloudy or white.
- Does not consistently respond to sound.
- Has an unusual cry – a high pitched cry or squeal.
- Is crying more than three hours per day every day, especially after three to four months of age.
- Is not interested in what is going on around them.
- Does not move or use both arms and legs.
- Cannot hold their head up by the age of three to four months.
- Is not sitting well by 10 months.
- Does not want to bear their own weight by 12 months.
- Or anything else that concerns you about your baby.

CHAPTER SUMMARY

- Babies grow and develop new skills at a rapid rate during the first 12 months of life.
- Development occurs in a predictable sequence.
- Babies need opportunities to develop and practise new skills.
- Parents need to anticipate the development of new skills to ensure they are able to keep their baby safe.
- Visiting the child and family health nurse or doctor for regular developmental checks is important to enable early intervention to be put in place if your baby needs some additional developmental support.

Chapter Eight
SUPPORTING YOUR BABY'S DEVELOPMENT

YOUR BABY IS RELYING on you to introduce them to different life experiences. You can do this by looking for everyday opportunities to extend their learning. Often as parents we miss opportunities because we are looking at the world through adult eyes. This is a very different view of the world from how your baby might experience it.

For example, it is a great experience for your baby to be taken for a walk around the garden facing outwards in a pouch to look at, smell and feel the flowers. You hold their hand and you are totally in the moment with your baby. You go about talking, touching and reassuring them and joining in with your baby's exploration of the garden. Creating a relationship where feelings can be shared provides a solid emotional foundation for your infant.

This is a very different experience than being taken to the shopping centre in an outward facing pouch. Where you might be preoccupied with shopping or talking on your phone, the baby is being bombarded with lots of noisy activities, and with people and objects looming into them. They could be waving their arms in an excited manner and this action is often interpreted by parents as having a good time and excitement, but as you have learnt in Chapter 5, it is more likely a cue that they are becoming distressed and need to disengage from the experience.

Your baby needs you to help regulate their emotions. As they are facing outwards they are unable to rest their head against your chest to block out some of the stimulus and regulate their emotions and they cannot gain reassurance that you are there because they cannot see, smell or touch you. If it is for an extended period they are unable to fall asleep, or if they do, it is probably not restful sleep due to the positioning of their body.

Your baby's development will provide lots of opportunities to assist them to learn about their world and to develop many necessary skills. A major skill for parents is to know when to leave your baby alone to work out a situation or achieve a task without interference, and when they need you to intervene and help.

Having your timing right about when to intervene can be difficult. Sometimes with the best intentions, parents get it wrong and they either intervene too early or not early enough. Where possible try and recognise when you have made a mistake and rectify it. It is in the 'not always getting it right' and then 'trying to repair the situation' that capacity building and emotional resilience is developed for both you and your baby.

PLAY

Play is a very important part of baby's development as it helps develop their physical, cognitive, social, emotional and communication skills. It also helps them feel confident, competent, safe and happy. Playing with your baby is therefore more than just having fun, it is the vehicle to support your baby's development, in which they learn about their bodies, their world, and cause and effect.

Importantly, when playing with you, your baby will enjoy being the centre of attention. Your baby will enjoy being delighted in by you as their parent and being told they are clever, beautiful and so much fun.

Babies can and do play on their own; but for babies and parents, play is about the sharing of a mutually pleasurable experience. How often do you play with your baby and don't even know it?

Parents often do not recognise many of the interactions they have with their baby during the day as subtle forms of play. A common time is when you play a simple finger or action game to distract your baby if they are getting fidgety or starting to cry; or during feeding when your baby reaches out to touch and explore your face or clothing.

We now know that babies from birth can imitate. It takes patience but you can slowly get your baby to mirror your expressions – you can teach your baby to poke out their tongue or pull a face. Your baby does not need lots of toys, as having you as their playmate is more than enough.

Play activities need to be simple. Very young babies enjoy play that involves gentle touch and singing. Babies love the sound of their parents' singing – enjoy this time as a singer and having your baby as your biggest fan. Make up songs or sing along with the radio. Follow your baby's movement and mimic the sounds they make.

As your baby grows you can become more adventurous with play activities. They start to enjoy movement, especially dancing around the room in your arms, gently moving as you rock them, or gently swooping them through the air. Remember to never use sharp shaking movements with your baby as this can result in damage to their very fragile brain.

Opportunities to play will happen throughout the day. These can include during a feed, at bath time or when changing your baby's nappy. As your baby grows you will be rewarded with spontaneous and regular smiles, giggles and laughter. A wonderful moment is when your baby starts to anticipate the games you regularly play and starts to initiate these games with you.

As you play, think about the cues your baby is providing you. Your baby, as discussed in Chapter 5, will provide lots of information about their needs. Do you need to slow down? Do you need to give your baby a short break in the activity? Is your baby's attention focused on something else in the room? Is your baby about to go from active alert to crying? Is your baby ready to start playing again? Learning to follow your baby's lead will result in interesting and fun times for both of you.

FLOOR PLAY

Provide your baby with floor play, especially by placing them on their tummy. You can start to give your baby time on their tummy during their early weeks. Perhaps start by laying your baby on your chest while lying down (remember not to fall asleep). This will help them to develop head control, body strength and assist with their ability to learn to crawl. Most importantly, you must stay with your baby and remain alert when they are on their tummy as they are at risk of SIDS.

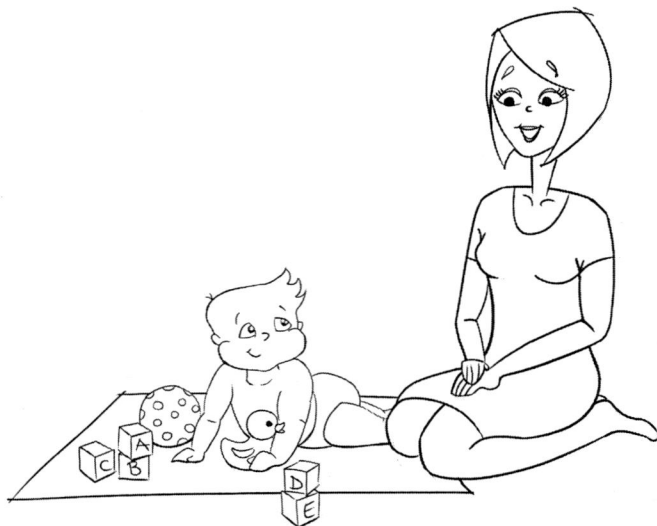

Tummy time:

- Place your baby on their tummy on a rug on the floor.
- Place a small brightly coloured toy in front of your baby about a hand span away so they can see it.
- Remember to stay with your baby.
- Some babies don't like to be on their tummy and will protest. Start with a few minutes and gradually increase the time. Talk to them to reassure, especially if this is the first few times on their tummy.
- It can help for you to also get down to floor level. Your baby will be reassured if they can see your face.

Whenever you place your baby on the floor, make sure you check for any dangers. The best way to do this is to get down on the floor and see what might attract your baby's attention and be dangerous. This is especially important once they start to move and explore. At around 7–9 months their pincer grip will start to develop and they are able to easily pick up very small items from the floor.

Other things to ensure their safety include:

- Making sure any pets are not in the room when your baby is on the floor.
- Bookcases are anchored to the wall.
- Tablecloths are not within reach.
- Remove any cords or heavy objects that can fall on them, e.g. an iron on an ironing board.
- Precious ornaments are out of reach.
- Stairs, heaters and fans are not accessible.

READING TO YOUR BABY

It is never too early to begin reading to your baby. Babies love books. Parents often start with thick-paged picture books. These provide opportunities to tell stories using descriptive language (see Chapter 7) and pointing to pictures so your baby will start to copy this behaviour. By four months, you can start to teach your baby to turn the pages of the book. Remember to position your baby so they can see your face as you read to them. Your facial expressions will add to your baby's enjoyment.

Your local library will have a great range of baby books you can borrow, although your baby will usually develop a preference for a couple of books. Rereading the same books contributes to a predictable life and events for your baby.

As the use of eBook readers increase, many parents use these with their babies. Importantly, your baby will develop useful skills while reading eBooks, but they may miss other important skills such as developing the fine motor skills of turning pages. As with most things in life, a balance is needed.

TOYS

Babies learn and grow rapidly in their first year and toys can help to stimulate their development. They do not need lots of toys. Even with this knowledge, it is sometimes hard to resist the amazing array of colourful and engaging toys. Many toys are also promoted with claims of educational benefits. Just remember that when deciding on the toys you will purchase, many will be developmentally appropriate for your baby for only a short time. Also, a toy on its own will have limited value. The important element is your active involvement in your baby's play – encouraging, turn taking, following their lead and repositioning the toy or your baby.

When buying or being given toys check they are safe. Make sure that:
- It has no small pieces as they are a potential choking hazard.
- Paint must be non-toxic as babies use their mouths to explore and learn.
- It has smooth edges and is not likely to cut or injury your baby.
- Any moving parts are firmly attached and unable to be removed.
- It has no parts that can trap small fingers or pinch skin.

Your local council or library will often have a toy library where you can borrow age appropriate toys. This provides a wonderful opportunity for your baby to be exposed to a range of interesting toys without the cost of buying them.

MUSIC

Music and singing are key elements to support your baby's development. Music has the capacity to soothe babies. It is fun and stimulates one of your baby's important senses – hearing. Music therapy is regularly used for pre-term babies and their parents in neonatal intensive care units. Listening and playing music is soothing as it helps babies and parents relax. It also builds a connection between a parent and their baby. Playing music and making music with your baby is a very positive and enjoyable activity for both babies and parents. For example, if your baby is six months old and sitting in a high chair, try banging lightly on the chair tray, pause and watch to see what your baby does. If they imitate and bang on the tray and pause, it is now your turn to bang again. Babies really enjoy simple turn taking activities that make noise.

As your baby grows, they enjoy making music by banging on a saucepan with a wooden spoon or banging on a toy drum. Start to sing nursery rhymes and do the actions. Move to the rhythm of the music while holding your baby.

There is lots of music that is suitable for babies available on CDs or as downloads. Ask friends and family members with young children what type of music their babies enjoyed. They may even lend you the music for a little while. Your local library will also have a selection of CDs that may be appropriate to use with your baby.

DIGITAL TECHNOLOGIES AND BABIES

Your baby is a digital native. They have been born into a world that is full of digital technologies – television, computers, tablets, digital music devices, mobile phones, DVDs, the internet, Skype and computer games. The temptation is to make sure your baby has lots of exposure so that they have every advantage possible for their future life.

Babies are very attracted to the rapidly changing colours and bright lights of many digital devices, however, it is strongly advised by child development experts that parents avoid or limit exposing their babies to television, computers, tablets, mobile devices and Playstations.

There is no evidence that television or digital devices will assist or enhance your baby's learning. Interacting with people is the best way to enhance a baby's learning. It is very difficult for a baby to gain visual information from a screen. Digital devices also distract babies from important investigations of their environment and other play activities. Using the television as a form of babysitting or a distraction to keep your baby occupied can also result in a habit being formed.

If you decide to allow your baby to watch television or play with a digital device as they grow ensure that:

- It is for a short periods only
- Programs or digital activities are appropriate to the age of your baby
- You are with them
- You talk to them about what is happening.

Now is also a good time to review your own usage of technology. If you tend to spend a lot of time on your mobile phone or computer, consider leaving it to when baby is asleep.

ACTIVITIES AND BABIES

There are lots of enjoyable activities you can do with your baby. Remember you are their favourite and most educational plaything. Being willing to take the time to follow your baby's lead will provide you with many new experiences and insights into your baby's world. Activities that give your baby a sense of their body; provide links between cause and effect; encourage physical skills development and provide a rich environment of language and music are all ideal.

Give your baby lots of floor time to practise their newly developed control over arm, leg, chest, and head movements. This should include time on their tummy. Your baby needs to learn to enjoy that position and discover they can push against the floor, strengthening the muscles in their upper body. Encouraging them to push their feet against your hands will strengthen leg muscles.

Babies develop their inborn learning ability through play, so provide your baby with lots of interesting and varied playthings. Many ordinary objects are perfect for stimulating learning. These include small empty boxes, food, and even the bathwater! Of course, safety should always remain a constant priority with everything you do with your baby.

Remember babies differ greatly in their emotional characteristics. For example, some babies are more reactive and more easily frustrated than others. These differences will start to show as your baby grows and develops and they try to achieve new tasks and are exposed to new experiences. Some babies will be wary with new toys, while others start to explore and play with the new toy immediately. Importantly, identifying and accepting these differences in babies will assist you to provide the best learning and fun experiences for your baby.

The following activities are examples of how you can interact with your baby. Be creative and most importantly enjoy yourself!

Age	Activities
Newborn to around 3 months	• Show your face to your baby. Hold your baby about a hand span away from your face. Allow your baby to just stare at your face as babies delight in looking at their parent's face. • You can pull some faces and see if your baby imitates your expressions. Take your time doing this as it does take a little while for the expression to be captured by your baby. • Your newborn will enjoy looking at and following bright coloured rattles and toys. Remember to hold them about a hand span away and if you are moving them do it slowly and across a 45 degree arc . • Babies enjoy looking at toys and objects with contrasting colours – red, black and white. They like objects that have faces on them or checks and stripes. • Talk to your baby using descriptive language – describe their world to them. • Start to read and look at books. • Start to play music when your baby is calm and softly sing to them. • Play with their fingers and toes, gently stroke their arms and legs – the sensations you create help your baby make important connections between the limbs and their brain. • Let them experience different textures – put them on the grass, lay on some velvet or the carpet. • Start tummy time – place a bright object in front of your baby to attract their attention. • Babies really enjoy floating in water, but make sure you have a secure hold on them to keep safe. • Regularly change the position of your baby so they get to see different parts of the room. • Gently pull to sitting. • Gently hold your baby in a standing position. • Take your baby for a walk in the garden or park and allow them to touch and smell some flowers and herbs. • Name your baby's different emotions and how they might be feeling.

Age	Activities
Around 3 months	Continue doing many of the activities you have been doing with your baby. You may increase the complexity of many of the activities but also include: • Read and look at books together. Remember to use descriptive language. You can make up new stories using the same book. • Start to have conversations with your baby by following their lead when they start to coo. • If they are looking at something in the room, describe what you think they are seeing. • Give toys to feel and handle that have different textures. • Sing nursery rhymes and start to do the actions. • Start to teach them to hold a rattle. • Bath time is starting to be lots of fun for your baby. • Put bright coloured socks on your baby's feet to encourage them to look at their feet. • When you move away from your baby keep a link by talking and singing to your baby. • Help your baby roll from front to back or back to front.
Around 6 months	Continue doing many of the activities you have been doing with your baby. You may increase the complexity of many of the activities but also include: • Provide opportunities to crawl by placing them on their tummy – put a bright coloured toy just out of their reach. Sometimes allowing them to use your hands to push their feet against will help them move. Give lots of verbal encouragement. • When eating allow them to feel the texture of their food with their hands. Give your baby a spoon to play with while you feed them. • Bath time is now great fun as your baby learns to sit on their own, they will become very adventurous. • Babies love mirrors and will happily touch the baby in the mirror. • Play simple games like peek-a-boo, this little piggy, and round and round the garden. • Move out of sight and call your baby's name. Then come back into sight saying "here I am". Now find another place and hide again. • To help practise balancing and sitting alone, prop your baby up using soft cushions or a 'boomerang' pillow. You can even sit your baby safely in a laundry basket supported with cushions (watch they don't tip backwards).

Age	Activities
Around 9 months	Continue doing many of the activities you have been doing with your baby. You may increase the complexity of many of the activities, but also include: • Once your baby has started to crawl make a simple obstacle course. • Make bath time fun with some simple bath toys and containers. • Give your baby small pieces of food to pick up and eat, e.g. sultanas, blueberries, grapes, pieces of melon, apple or pear. • Invite other parents with similar aged babies to come and play. • Wave bye-bye or blow a kiss when leaving a room. • Hide a toy and encourage your baby to find it. • Give your baby a saucepan and a wooden spoon to make music. • Give a block for each hand and show how to bang together • Pulling toys, e.g. a car on a string. • They will enjoy posting different shaped objects into a lid with corresponding holes. • They enjoy tipping out objects from a container or the washing basket. • Will have favourite toys, e.g. teddy bear. • When your baby babbles, repeat the sound after them. • Clap when your baby does something exciting or successful. They will start to clap as well. • Roll a soft ball to your baby and get them to roll it back to you. • Help your baby to explore new toys. Show her/him how the toy can be turned, rolled or shaken.

Age	Activities
Around 12 months	Continue doing many of the activities you have been doing with your baby. You may increase the complexity of many of the activities, but also include: • Play 'hide and seek' with objects of different sizes. • Make lots of animal noises when reading a book or if you see an animal. • They will be very busy investigating objects left in reach. • They will have favourite books and want them read again and again. • They will enjoy trying to build a tower of blocks even though rarely successful. • They will have favourite songs and move rhythmically in response to the music. • Enjoy water play especially in summer, pouring water from one container to another. • Can hold a crayon and scribble. • Babies love tearing and scrunching paper. • Put sultanas in a container with a hole and allow your baby to shake the container to see if they can get the sultanas out of the container. • Using a mirror make funny faces and encourage your baby to join in. • Encourage your baby to talk to their father, grandparents or other close friends or relatives on the phone. • If you have not started a bedtime ritual now is a good time to start. • Use homemade puppets to 'talk' to your child. • Babies love crawling in and out of boxes. • Make your own 'touch and feel' book from odds and ends around the house. Include materials of different textures, such as cardboard, sandpaper, bubble-wrap and cotton wool.

When considering how to play with your baby it is helpful to think about the developmentally appropriate activities your baby can do (refer to the developmental charts in Chapter 7). These developmental tasks and milestones provide you with clues about what your baby needs to practise. Once they have achieved these tasks or milestones move on to slightly harder tasks.

CHAPTER SUMMARY

- Babies rely on their parents to provide new experiences and opportunities to learn and practise new skills.
- Play is the way babies learn.
- For very young babies play is often subtle, e.g. playing with their fingers, massage or gently singing to them.
- Parents need to be aware of their baby's cues during play periods as they can become overwhelmed and sometimes just need a couple of minutes or even seconds downtime to recover.
- Babies need to have regular opportunities to play while lying on their tummy, but you need to stay with them.
- Parents and everyday items (as long as they are safe for your baby to have) make wonderful playthings. Babies especially love having the full attention of their parents.
- Babies learn about relationships and emotions from their parents.
- Babies learn from their parents' modelling how to repair situations when things don't turn out as expected or go wrong.

Part Three

INFANT FEEDING AND NUTRITION

Chapter Nine
FOOD FOR YOU AND YOUR BABY

HAVING PARENTS WHO eat a healthy diet with a wide range of foods will influence a baby's future eating habits. You may need to rethink the way you cook your food and the type of food you regularly eat. The busy lifestyles of parents can make it easy to eat lots of processed convenience foods rather than a healthy balanced diet that does not contain added fat, sugar, salt or artificial flavouring and colouring.

Remember, it's never too late to change your eating habits.

PREGNANCY

The food you eat during pregnancy has a direct impact on your baby's health now and into the future. This is especially so if you are underweight, overweight or obese. Rather than going on a fad diet to lose or gain weight, it is more important to talk to your doctor and ask for a referral to a dietician. A dietician will ensure any changes in your diet do not compromise your health or the health of your growing baby.

When you are pregnant:

- Eat to satisfy your appetite and have a varied and nutritionally rich diet.
- Drink enough fluids to maintain a sufficient level of hydration.
- Make water your main source of fluid.
- Avoid soft drinks, energy drinks or drinks with caffeine.
- If you are eating a balanced nutritious diet, there is no need for additional supplements unless advised by your doctor or midwife.
- Limit your intake of fruit juice (especially if commercially processed) as it can dramatically increase your kilojoule intake. It is much better to eat a piece of fruit as it contains fibre that is important for healthy digestion.
- If using prescribed medication, herbal medicines or over the counter medication, it is essential to check the safety of the medication with your doctor or pharmacist or in some states there are telephone advisory services (your child and family health nurse will provide you with the telephone number).
- Do not drink alcohol, as it passes through the placenta to your baby.

If you are experiencing morning sickness, it is important to discuss this with your doctor or midwife. They will help you develop a plan to maintain an adequate nutritional intake. This may include smaller, more frequent meals or snacks.

A HEALTHY FAMILY DIET

Whether you are breastfeeding or bottle feeding your baby, try to eat a nutritious diet. Caring for a baby can place parents' bodies under considerable stress due to fatigue, sleepless nights and the additional physical work of caring for a baby.

It is not uncommon for new parents to miss meals or survive on convenience foods with a low nutritional value. This type of eating pattern can further compound feelings of fatigue.

Regardless of whether you are breast or bottle feeding, ensure you:
- Have three meals a day.
- Eat a range of foods that include fruit, vegetables, protein, grains, legumes and natural oils.
- Eat foods that are high in calcium, such as milk, cheese, and yoghurt (a great snack food). Other ways to get calcium is from the bones of tinned fish (tuna, salmon and sardines), almonds, tofu, legumes, tahini and hummus. There are small amounts of calcium in green vegetables. Some soya products and breads also have added calcium.

If you are breastfeeding, the same principles apply as when you are pregnant with a few additional ones:
- There is no need to drink excessive fluids as it does not increase breastmilk volume.
- Have a drink of water to quench your thirst every time you feed your baby.
- Make water your main source of fluid.
- Alcohol and nicotine pass freely into breastmilk. Nicotine can also change the flavour of your breastmilk.

Research is now clearly demonstrating that cigarette smoking can affect and negatively impact on your breastmilk supply. There is also evidence that cigarette smoking can cause baby to have an upset tummy (gastro-intestinal problems). If you cannot quit smoking, it is important that you do not smoke at least an hour before you are going to breastfeed your baby – this may reduce the level of nicotine in your breastmilk. No one should smoke in the same room or in close proximity to your baby.

It is strongly advised that you do not drink alcohol during pregnancy or if you are breastfeeding. If you do drink alcohol limit it to one glass and have it after you feed. Alcohol levels in breastmilk approximate that of the mother's alcohol blood levels. However, due to the baby's immature stage of kidney and liver development, it can take a lot longer to metabolise the alcohol and rid it from their body.

MORE THAN JUST FEEDING

Feeding times are more than just providing food to your baby. Regarding feeding times as an important and valid time to be with your baby is really worthwhile for your relationship and is especially important if you are bottle feeding, as it is so easy to hand this task over to others. At Tresillian, we would encourage you not to hand your baby over to others to feed, except for your partner, who also needs to develop a very special relationship with their baby.

When you are feeding, hold your baby so they can see your face and eyes. By looking at you, babies learn about emotions and get to know and love you. Talk or sing gently to them during the feed, play games with their fingers, and gently stroke their face, arms and legs. Watch out for disengagement cues or behaviours that tell you they need a moment or two without stimulus or a break from feeding. These disengagement cues can be a turning or pulling away from you, a raised hand that looks like a halt sign, or a closing of their eyes (see Chapter 5).

Reduce distraction by turning off the television or mobile phone. Babies need short periods of your undivided attention. Put on some soothing music so you can both relax. This is very helpful if you are breastfeeding.

The period when you can have such a quiet and intimate time with your baby is short-lived. The first year will disappear and you will have an active toddler who will want to continually test their independence. So, enjoy this feeding time!

KNOWING WHEN YOUR BABY IS HUNGRY

Babies clearly show when they are starting to get hungry, when they really need to be fed right now, and when they are desperate to be fed. As discussed in Chapter 5, babies use a cluster of cues to tell you they are hungry, or that they have had enough food. Watch for the following:

Early hunger cues
• Smacking or licking lips. • Opening and closing mouth. • Sucking on lips, hands, fingers, toes or clothing.
Feed me now cues include all of the above and:
• Fussing or breathing fast. • Nuzzling around on the chest of whoever is holding your baby. • Trying to get into a suitable position for breastfeeding, either by lying back or pulling your clothes. • Fidgeting or squirming around a lot. • Clenching fingers or making a tight fist over the chest or tummy.
Desperate to be fed cues include all of the above and:
• Moving head from side to side . • Crying.

KNOWING WHEN YOUR BABY HAS FINISHED A FEED

Knowing when your baby has had enough to drink or eat is not difficult. When your baby's hunger is starting to be satisfied, or they are no longer hungry they will:

- Spontaneously release the breast, bottle or spoon.
- When older they turn their head or pull away from the breast, bottle or spoon.
- Have a small amount of milk in their mouth at the end of a milk feed.
- Have a relaxed body with hands open or splayed and extended legs.
- No longer use hunger cues – hunger cues include crying, body tense, agitation, fist to mouth.

- Be asleep or in a contented state.
- Have the hiccups but are calm and relaxed.

An easy way to tune into your baby is to think about how you feel when you've had enough food.

WHAT TO EXPECT FROM YOUR BABY AT FEEDING TIME

Age	Behaviours
Birth	• Feels hunger and cries for food • Expresses satisfaction by falling asleep • Sucking, rooting and swallowing reflexes • Has a strong tongue extrusion reflex
3 to 4 months	• Automatic poking out of their tongue (tongue extrusion reflex) beginning to lessen • Beginning eye-hand coordination
4 to 5 months	• Drooling begins • Can bring lips together on the rim of a cup, but still very messy and lots of fluid will be spilt
5 to 6 months	• Begin to offer solids at approximately 6 months • Starting to use fingers to help feed self • Starting to play with food • Starting to enjoy being part of family meals • Teething starting
6 to 7 months	• Starting to chew and bite
7 to 9 months	• Refuses food by keeping mouth and lips closed • Holds a spoon and plays with it during their feed • May be able to drink with a straw • Drinks from a cup with assistance
9 to 12 months	• Picks up finger foods and feeds self • Drinks from a cup; will spill some of the fluid • Uses a spoon with much spilling • Will pick up small foods from tray using finger and thumb (pincer grip) • Likes to play with their food and make a mess • Likes to eat with the family

Whatever method you choose to feed your baby, it is important to think about feeding as more than just another meal time for your baby. Feeding is also an opportunity to nourish the relationship you have with your baby, teaching your baby new things about their world; and once your baby is eating solid foods, sit them in the high chair at the table so they're able to socialise and interact with the rest of the family.

Get into the habit of washing your hands before handling food or breastfeeding, and wipe down your baby's hands. Poor hygiene as a result of not washing hands is clearly identified as a major risk factor for infants and young children

BREASTFEEDING

Breastfeeding is without doubt the best food for your baby. The current recommendations encourage mothers to fully breastfeed their baby for the first six months of life. This means that your baby is not given any other type of milk, juice or solid food during this first six-month period. Even boiled water is not necessary. The World Health Organization (WHO) recommends that mothers continue to breastfeed up until their baby is two years old, with the gradual addition of solids after six months of age.

INFANT FORMULA FEEDING

For mothers who are unable to breastfeed there are safe alternatives. These infant formulas will provide appropriate nutrition for your baby. Importantly, care needs to be taken during the infant formula preparation and storage to ensure it remains safe for your baby.

INTRODUCING WATER

Babies who are being breastfed do not need extra water until six months of age. Offer more frequent feeds if you are concerned about heat stress related to illness or extremely hot days. A formula-fed baby can be offered small amounts of cooled boiled water in addition to their normal quota of infant formula feeds on hot days or at times of potential heat stress (e.g. if they have a fever). Take care that you don't offer water too close to a normal feed time as it may reduce your baby's appetite.

For babies aged under 12 months, it is safe to offer them tap water so long as it has been boiled and cooled beforehand. Giving baby bottled water on a regular basis is not recommended as it does not usually contain fluoride and can compromise your baby's future dental health (if you are using bottled water this needs to be treated with the same precautions as tap water as it is not sterile).

MANAGING OTHER CHILDREN WHEN FEEDING YOUR BABY

Having a toddler or preschooler can add to the challenge of feeding your baby. Whether you are breastfeeding, bottle feeding or starting your baby on solid foods, try and focus on your baby as they feed. Feeding is an ideal time to develop the relationship with your baby, but active and impatient brothers or sisters don't always understand the need for patience while the baby is being fed.

A few ideas that might help:

- Arrange some special activities for your toddler or preschooler during your baby's feeding time such as drawing or building with playdough
- Give your toddler a snack to eat
- Keep aside some special toys or books that come out only when you are feeding your baby.

Toddlers and preschoolers thrive on one-on-one time with their parents, so promise a special time or activity after the feeding time but don't forget. If at all possible provide the special time or activity immediately after you finish the feeding your baby, that way, everybody is happy.

CHAPTER SUMMARY

- When you are feeding your baby, hold your baby so they can see your face.
- Watch out for disengagement cues that tell you your baby needs a moment's break from feeding.
- Try to avoid distractions when feeding your baby so you can give your baby your full attention.
- Pregnancy is an ideal time to look at your family's diet to make sure it is nutritionally balanced.

Chapter Ten
BREASTFEEDING

IT HAS LONG BEEN KNOWN that mothers who breastfeed and babies who are exclusively breastfed enjoy many long-term health benefits. These include the potential to reduce the risk of breast and ovarian cancer, and helping you to return to pre-pregnant weight faster along with many other health and lifestyle benefits. The benefits for breastfed babies include often having a lower cholesterol level and lower rates of obesity and type-1 and 2 diabetes in adulthood. The World Health Organization (WHO) and governments worldwide have invested a great deal of effort and money in promoting the advantages of breastfeeding babies and the need to support breastfeeding mothers for good reason.

The Australian government advises health workers to support the principles of the Baby Friendly Hospital Initiative (BFHI). These steps provide health professionals and others with the guidelines and actions they need to take to support mothers to successfully breastfeed.

BFHI 10 STEPS TO SUCCESSFUL BREASTFEEDING

1. Have a written breastfeeding policy that is routinely communicated to all health care staff.
2. Train all health care staff in skills necessary to implement this policy.
3. Inform all pregnant women about the benefits and management of breastfeeding.
4. Help mothers initiate breastfeeding within one hour of birth.
5. Show mothers how to breastfeed, and how to maintain lactation even if they are separated from their infants.
6. Give newborn infants no food or drink other than breastmilk, unless medically indicated.
7. Practise rooming-in (allow mothers and infants to remain together), 24 hours a day.
8. Encourage breastfeeding on demand.
9. Give no artificial teats or pacifiers (also called dummies or soothers) to breastfeeding infants.
10. Foster the establishment of breastfeeding support groups and refer mothers to them on discharge from hospital or clinic.

NHMRC 2012, *Infant feeding guidelines: information for health workers*, Australian Government, Canberra.

The experience of breastfeeding is unique, as no two mothers or babies are the same. It may take up to 6–8 weeks to be well established. Your baby needs to take a deep mouthful of the *areola* (the dark area around the nipple) as they latch on to breastfeed. This stimulates the suck reflex on the roof of your baby's mouth.

All mothers will experience increased nipple and areola sensitivity at the start of a breastfeed, while feeding is being established. It's important that you learn correct attachment as this will result in more comfortable feeding and a satisfied baby.

There are lots of professional and non-professional supports that you can contact to gain education, information and support. The first key professionals will be the midwives and child and family health nurses you have contact with during the antenatal period, early postpartum period and then during your baby's first year. Your local doctor may also have an interest in supporting the establishment of your lactation and helping you to problem-solve breastfeeding problems that can occur. In some hospitals and community health services you will also have access to a lactation consultant if you are experiencing breastfeeding problems.

Tresillian has a long history of providing support for breastfeeding mothers and their babies. Being able to ring a child and family health nurse working on the parent helpline is always reassuring for mothers (and fathers) if breastfeeding concerns or problems start to occur. More intensive support is also available through home visits, day visits or a residential stay at one of the Tresillian centres. The long established and reputable Australian Breastfeeding Association (ABA) also provides advice, education and encouragement for breastfeeding mothers.

INITIATION OF LACTATION

During your pregnancy, especially in the last couple of months, you may have noticed if your breast is squeezed it will excrete a small amount of thick, yellowish liquid. You might also have a light film form on your nipple. This is *colostrum*. Colostrum is an important first food for your baby and will continue for the first three to four days until your milk 'comes-in'.

Even though colostrum is produced in very small amounts, it is a high value food for your baby. Colostrum has a laxative effect and helps your baby open their bowels and this aids in the excretion of *meconium* (baby's first bowel motion) and excess *bilirubin* or the substance that makes babies jaundiced. So it can help prevent jaundice. The really important contribution colostrum makes is to your baby's immune system as it provides passive immunity and reduces the risk of infections. The concentration of immune factors in colostrum is much greater than in mature breastmilk, which is present when your breastmilk supply is established.

By the third or fourth day you will have started to produce *transitional* breastmilk as your milk goes from being colostrum to mature breastmilk. During the next couple of weeks it will become mature and start to increase in volume and appear more transparent in appearance. Sometimes your milk may have a slight bluish tinge. This is very normal in human breastmilk.

The composition of breastmilk changes during each feed. At the beginning of a feed your milk has a lower fat content, allowing your baby's thirst to be quenched. As the feed progresses the fat content increases. This enables your baby to have their hunger satisfied. If your baby is allowed to finish emptying the first breast they may not need or want the second breast at each feed.

Allowing your baby to breastfeed as soon as possible after birth is the very best way to stimulate *lactation*. Lactation is the process of producing breastmilk for your baby. Ideally, your baby should be offered a breastfeed within the first hour after birth. Unfortunately, as we don't live in an ideal world, this may not be possible for some mothers and babies due to medical or other circumstances. Remember that babies are resilient, so if you are not able to offer your baby a breastfeed in the first hour, begin as soon as possible after that.

If your baby is unable to breastfeed for an extended period due to prematurity, illness or some other reason, it is important that you ask for assistance to *express* your milk. Many mothers express for extended periods of time (days and even weeks) until their baby is ready to go to the breast. This does take perseverance and having lots of support and encouragement from family and friends can really help.

Lactation can take up to six weeks to be well established. During this time avoid:

- Using feeding bottles, as they require a different method of sucking than at the breast.
- Using a dummy or pacifier.

Breastmilk is produced using a 'demand and supply' principle. The more breastmilk your baby takes, the more breastmilk is produced. If your baby is offered the breast frequently during their first days and weeks, a very strong message is sent to your body to keep producing milk. To help establish your breastmilk supply, it is recommended to feed a minimum of eight times in 24 hours. But don't be surprised if your baby, on some days, demands more feeds. A baby's stomach is very small – about the size of a golf ball or a baby's clenched fist.

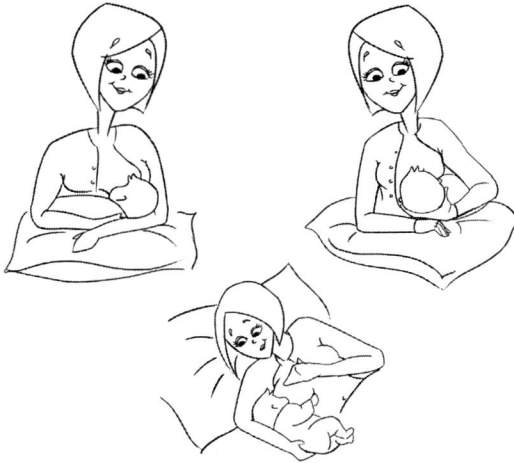

Benefits of breastfeeding for babies:
✓ Ideal food for babies as it satisfies both thirst and hunger.
✓ Provides all the nutrition a baby needs for their first six months.
✓ It's safe and contains antibodies that increases your baby's passive immunity and resistance to common diseases and infections.
✓ Breastmilk is readily available at little cost to the energy intake of the mother.
✓ Long-term effect of contributing to a lifetime of good health.
✓ Adults who were breastfed often have lower cholesterol and blood pressure, and lower rates of obesity and type-1 and type-2 diabetes.
✓ It helps develop a very special bond between mother and baby.

Benefits of breastfeeding for women:
✓ Can reduce the risk of breast and ovarian cancer.
✓ Helps women return to pre-pregnant weight faster.
✓ Lowers rates of obesity and osteoporosis.
✓ Help to stabilise blood sugar levels.
✓ Reduces workload and resources required.

LET DOWN REFLEX

The *let down reflex* for most mothers usually occurs within seconds of their baby attaching to their breast to feed. This is due to the release of *prolactin* and *oxytocin* when the baby sucks, stimulating the nerve endings around the nipple. Oxytocin is an essential hormone for breastfeeding. It enables your breast to push out or let down your milk. If you are stressed this can initially inhibit your let down reflex and can be a problem if expressing milk.

When breastfeeding, a mother can experience multiple milk let downs during the period of the feed or when expressing breastmilk. A mother can also experience a let down if they think about their baby or see another baby; even when the baby is not physically with the mother. So, if you need to express and you are not with your baby, have a picture of your baby there to help you with the release of breastmilk.

Some mothers report no noticeable sign or sensation of the let down reflex, whilst other mothers notice one or more of the following signs:

- Tingling or prickling 'pins and needles' in the breast
- Sudden feeling of fullness in the breasts
- Skin temperature increase
- Dripping or leaking of milk from the opposite breast while breastfeeding
- Feelings of wellbeing or relaxation
- An intense thirst or dry mouth
- Uterine contractions can occur in the immediate postpartum period due to the effect of oxytocin when letting down milk.

> **NOTE:** It may take you several days of observation after 'the milk comes in' to recognise these changes. If no signs are seen or felt, you can confirm a let down by watching for your baby to swallow or gulp at the start of a feed. Also, your breast will get lighter and softer.

CARING FOR YOUR BREASTS

All women need to care for their breasts at all times. It is important to know what your breasts feel like so you can identify problems early, so regularly checking your breasts for lumps is essential. This is your greatest defence against breast cancer.

The problem with pregnancy and lactation is that your breasts change. Lumps you may have been concerned about can be a common occurrence in lactation. Lumps should be present for a short period only. If you do find a lump or lumps it is important to monitor that the lump does disappear. Lumps in lactating breasts may be a sign of a blocked milk duct, which if unresolved, may develop into *mastitis* (inflammation and possible infection of the breast).

SIZE OF YOUR BREASTS

If your breasts have developed normally through puberty and pregnancy, the size of your breasts has no impact on your ability to produce breastmilk or breastfeeding. Some mothers with large breasts may need to take a little more care when positioning their baby for feeding.

With large breasts, feeding can pose some challenges, but these are easily managed. You might like to:

- Feed your baby using a cradle hold, football hold or lying down on your side
- Use a pillow to help support your baby so it is more comfortable for you.

Regardless of the feeding position you use, it is essential while feeding to ensure your baby is positioned to encourage effective sucking. If baby is positioned well, their chin will be touching the breast while their nose will be clear; and you will not need to use your finger to keep the breast away from your baby's nose to enable them to breathe.

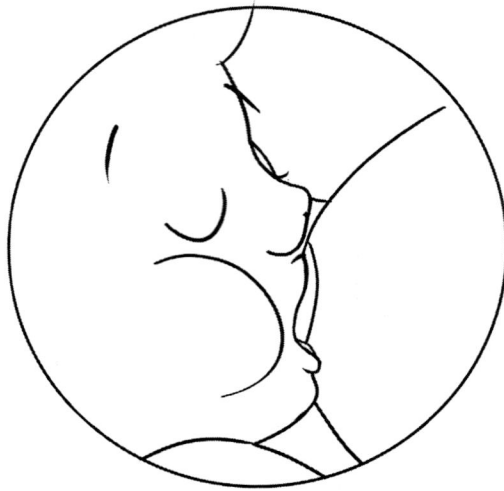

NIPPLES

Nipples are designed for breastfeeding, despite variations in shape and size. For a small number of women nipple variations such as non-protractile or inverted nipples can present difficulties when initiating breastfeeding. Very large nipples, previous breast or nipple surgery, or nipple piercing, can also cause difficulties and each case needs to be individually assessed and managed.

Discuss your concerns with your doctor, midwife, child and family health nurse or lactation consultant.

BREASTFEEDING BRA

A well-fitting, supportive bra will add to your comfort, whether you have small or large breasts. Bras for breastfeeding over the past decades have become much more attractive and there are many more styles to choose from. You might find it helpful to have the bra professionally fitted to ensure it is supportive but not restrictive. Most large department stores have a bra fitting service.

Your bra should have:
- No areas of constriction or pressure
- Wide straps that provide adequate support

- Easy to open to gain access to your breast for feeding – remember you will also be juggling a baby
- Made from natural fibres – these are often cooler than synthetic fabrics
- Room for breast fullness once you start to lactate.

Start with two feeding bras during pregnancy. Three bras are ideal once you start to breastfeed – one to wear, one in the laundry, and one as a backup.

Having a well-fitted and comfortable bra can provide you with much needed support. It really is a matter of personal preference whether you use a maternity bra or a regular bra. However, the advantage of a maternity bra is the ability to easily open the bra for breastfeeding.

- There is no one right time to start wearing a maternity bra. You might find in the early weeks of pregnancy that you very quickly grow out of your non-pregnant bra.
- Many of the hormonal and growth changes to your breast will have occurred by 16 weeks. Purchasing a new bra usually occurs at this point in your pregnancy.
- Get your bra professionally fitted to make sure that it will remain comfortable and supportive. This is usually a free service provided by specially trained sales staff
- Bras with an underwire are not recommended as your breast size regularly changes during the day when you are breastfeeding and milk is produced and removed by your baby. There is a risk that the underwire will place pressure on your breast that my lead to a blocked milk duct. If you do prefer a bra with an underwire, make sure it is designed to be flexible and will change shape with your changing breast shape.
- It is recommended to hand wash your bras using a mild soap, rinse well and dry in the sun if possible to prevent an environment for candida (thrush) to multiply.
- Some women find it more comfortable to wear a bra to bed at night to support their breasts. However, this is not necessary and often in the early weeks it is best avoided in order to allow free leakage of excess milk overnight, between feeds.

BREAST PADS

Breast pads provide an extra protection if you leak milk between feeds. Breast pads are either reusable or disposable. There are many commercial brands to choose from. Importantly, ensure the pads you use don't cause moisture and heat to build up on your nipples. Both heat and moisture provide the ideal ground for infections to develop, especially candida. The end result can be very sore and easily damaged nipples. If using disposables pads, avoid ones with plastic backing.

FEEDING PROCESS

Time spent feeding will vary from feed to feed and with each baby. As a guide, when breastfeeding is being established, a feed may take up to an hour, but as your baby matures the duration of the breastfeeds decreases. When your baby is feeding, a suck-pause-swallow-and-breathe cycle occurs. Initially your baby will suck vigorously then slow down to a pattern of a few sucks followed by a pause. This cycle usually continues for the length of the feed, but will become slower and more drawn out. Your baby might pull off the breast or become very sleepy. This does not always mean the feed has finished.

If you feel that your baby needs to feed for longer, try waking your baby to continue feeding by:
- Unwrapping your baby or changing their nappy.
- Allowing a minute or two for your baby to burp, though they do not always need to burp.
- Both breasts should be offered at each feed, but the first breast needs to be well drained before your baby is offered the second breast. A change in breast fullness indicates transfer of milk (or that the side is drained) in the early weeks. This feeling of fullness may change at each feed as the milk volume in your breasts is changing in response to your baby's needs.
- Alternate the starting breast at each feed, e.g. start with the right breast for one feed, then the left breast for the next feed.

- Your baby may or may not feed from the second breast at each feed. This will depend upon appetite and stage of development or growth.
- Feeding time from the second breast may be of a shorter duration but will assist in maintaining a good milk supply.
- Babies need adequate sleep to feed well and if too tired will not be able to feed effectively. Allow your baby to have a short sleep and then re-offer the breast.
- All babies will have different feeding and sleeping patterns, e.g. some can feed more often at one time of the day and have less feeds and a longer sleep at another.
- It can be normal for a newborn to feed at intervals of two to five hour.
- In the early months your baby needs a minimum of 6–8 feeds in 24 hours.

POSITIONING AND ATTACHING AT THE BREAST

- Ensure you are positioned comfortably with your back well supported.
- Allow your breast to fall naturally.
- Unwrap your baby to allow easy handling, skin contact and avoid overheating.
- Ensure your baby is well supported behind the shoulders and your baby's body is facing you with baby flexed and held close. Baby's head should be free with the top lip in line with the nipple.
- Your baby should be slightly lower than the breast with their lower arm brought around under your breast.
- Your baby's chin is touching or tucked into the breast.
- Support the breast with your free hand with your fingers well back from the nipple/areola, aim your nipple towards your baby's nose.
- A wide mouth gape is encouraged by allowing your baby to feel the underside of the nipple on their top lip.

- As your baby's mouth gapes widely, bring quickly to the breast with the nipple now pointing towards the roof of the mouth with your baby's chin coming to the breast first.

SIGNS OF GOOD ATTACHMENT

- It is usual to experience some nipple sensitivity (discomfort) when you start the feed, however this should ease after a minute or two.
- Your baby will have taken not only the nipple but also a large amount of the areola (dark area around the nipple) into the mouth, forming the nipple into a teat shape with their tongue. After an initial short burst of sucking, the rhythm should be slow and rhythmical with deep jaw movements and intermittent pauses.
- Pauses are a normal part of the feed and these become more frequent as the feed progresses.
- Noticeable changes in your baby's sucking/swallowing pattern is the most consistent sign of milk transfer; audible swallows may also be heard at the commencement of breastfeeding.
- If your baby has been properly attached, your nipple may be lengthened, but will look normal – your nipple should not be squashed or pinched.
- If your baby's cheeks are being sucked in or there is audible clicking, your baby may not be attached correctly; detach by placing a clean finger between your baby's lips to break the suction. Correctly reattach as described above.

DETACHING BABY FROM THE BREAST

To detach your baby from the breast:
- Place your clean finger in the corner of your baby's mouth between the lips to break the suction and protect your nipple as the infant detaches.

KNOWING YOUR BABY IS GETTING ENOUGH BREASTMILK

Uncertainty about the amount of breastmilk your baby is having can be very concerning. It can also be counterproductive as the more you worry the more anxious you become, and this can impact on your let down reflex. Breastfeeding as with many aspects of parenting is a bit of a confidence trick. You need to tell yourself and the world that you "can breastfeed your baby". Babies cry for lots of reasons, not only because they are hungry. It is normal for babies up to six months of age to have fussy periods. These periods can be connected with your baby's growth spurts. At these times they may need to have some extra feeds during the day. These extra feeds will also help to increase your breastmilk supply to meet the changing needs of your baby.

Babies, just like adults, need extra fluid on hot days, especially when they have been outside or travelling in the car. The best way to provide this extra fluid is by giving extra breastfeeds during the day.

If you are concerned, don't hesitate to get some advice from a health professional such as your child and family health nurse, doctor, a lactation consultant, or contact Tresillian or the Australian Breastfeeding Association.

To reassure yourself that you have an adequate milk supply, check that your baby is:

- Being breastfed frequently (expect at least eight feeds in 24 hours during the early days).
- Having lots of very wet nappies. Their urine should not have a strong smell and it will usually look pale in colour. You will need to change your baby at least five to six times per day. If your baby is having other fluids or solid foods, wet nappies may not be an accurate guide.
- Having one or two loose bowel motions per day. As your baby gets older the number of bowel motions will decrease and it is not uncommon for breastfed babies to go for extended periods without a bowel motion. Sometimes it can be up to five or seven days. This is because breastmilk is so fully utilised and has very little waste product.

- Having some periods during the day when they are settled, alert, active and happy.
- Gaining the right amount of weight, as they will also be growing in length and head circumference.

Often a reaction to an unsettled baby or one who hasn't gained a great deal of weight over a couple of weeks is to question an adequate breastmilk supply. The mother is then bombarded with advice and suggestions that sometimes includes giving the baby a bottle. From our experience at Tresillian, putting a baby on the bottle does not always solve the problem of an unsettled baby. In some instances, new and different problems start to occur.

If you do have concerns about your baby's health, growth or development it is essential to ask your local doctor or child and family health nurse to assess your baby. Continuing to breastfeed should always be considered the first option with strategies put in place to support this.

EXPRESSING BREASTMILK

'Expressing' refers to the removal of milk from your breasts. When is it necessary to express your breastmilk? Expressing is used to:
- Initiate lactation if your newborn baby cannot go to the breast due to prematurity or illness.
- Make your breast feel more comfortable after your baby has fed or if you are weaning.
- Increase your breastmilk supply.
- Freeze and store milk, so your baby can have breastmilk when you take time out, go to work or if you are going to be unable to feed due to separation or hospitalisation.

There are three ways to express breastmilk. Follow this sequence:
- Start with hand expressing to achieve the first let down.
- Then use a hand pump.
- Lastly, use an electric pump.

It is advisable to express somewhere warm and where you can ensure privacy and can relax. This will aid your let down of breastmilk.

Ask the midwife while in hospital or the child and family health nurse to show you how to hand-express or help you use the hand or electric breast pump for the first time.

If your baby is premature or unwell and unable at this stage to be breastfed, you might find it worth investing in or hiring an electric breast pump. Using an electric pump will be less tiring than hand expressing or using a hand pump.

HAND-EXPRESSING

Hand-expressing can be a messy activity until you become more practised. You may benefit from using a wide brim sterile bowl or collecting container to catch the flow of milk.

The equipment you will need:
- A sterilised plastic, or glass or ceramic bowl with a wide opening.

The basic steps for hand-expressing are:
- Always start by washing your hands with soap and warm water.
- Gently massage your breasts. Start from the top of your breast and stroke towards your nipple. Don't forget to massage the underside of your breast. Repeat this several times to ensure the whole breast is massaged. This will help improve your let down reflex. If you intend storing the expressed breastmilk do not use oil to massage your breast. It may contaminate the expressed breastmilk.
- Place a sterile bowl or plastic container under your breast, rest it between your legs or on a low table, this will leave both your hands free. A clean towel is useful to catch any spills or for wiping slippery, wet fingers.
- It may be helpful to support your breast with one hand if you have large or heavy breasts.
- Place your thumb and finger directly opposite each other, either side of the areola and well back from your nipple.

- Gently compress your areola inward towards the centre of the breast until you feel the bulk of the breast. Expressing should not be painful. If it is, you are pressing too hard or in the wrong place and risk bruising your breast.
- Gently press finger and thumb towards each other using a rhythmic rolling movement. This will compress the ducts and milk will flow out of your nipple. Until your let down reflex is activated there may only be a few drops of breastmilk. Following the let down, you should get sprays from the nipple with each squeeze.
- Once the milk flow slows, change the position of your fingers to a different part of the breast behind the nipple and press again – this helps express more milk and empty all sections of the breast. Change hands if your fingers get tired.
- Repeat the process on the other breast.
- If you need more milk, change from breast to breast, or wait and try again later.

EXPRESSING WITH A HAND-HELD PUMP

Hand-held breast pumps consist of a shaped breast piece to fit over your nipple and areola attached to a bottle or container to collect the breastmilk. There are many varieties available and it can get confusing; some have a piston-type hand piece while others a handle bar that you squeeze. Your child and family health nurse will be able to discuss the advantages and disadvantages of the various types commercially available.

Just as with hand-expressing, the first step when getting ready to express with a hand pump is to ensure privacy – relax and make yourself comfortable. Gentle massage as described previously is a good idea too.

Before starting, make sure all the equipment that will come in contact with the breastmilk has been sterilised. Always start by washing your hands with soap and warm water.

When you're ready to start:

- As with hand-expressing, gently massaging your breast first to help activate your let down reflex. Once your milk lets down and starts to flow you can switch to the hand pump.
- Place the breast piece of the pump directly over your breast or nipple.
- Squeeze the pump handle gently and rhythmically – you might see only drops of milk until your let down happens, and then it'll spray into the pump container.
- If it is painful stop and check the positioning of the pump before starting again. It may need to be repositioned so it is centred over your nipple.
- Pump until your milk flow slows down.
- To switch breasts, release the suction by gently easing your breast away from the wall of the breast piece.

EXPRESSING WITH AN ELECTRIC PUMP (SINGLE OR DOUBLE PUMPING)

Electric breast pumps do most of the hard work for you when expressing. They will rhythmically create a negative suction so the breastmilk will flow. Expressing via a double electric pump (both breasts pumped at the same time) can save time and increase your prolactin, the milk making hormone, thus increasing supply and the amount of milk expressed.

As with expressing by hand or by hand-help pump, you need to ensure privacy, be comfortable and relaxed.

Before starting make sure all the equipment that will come in contact with the breastmilk has been sterilised. Always start by washing your hands with soap and warm water.

When you are ready to start:

- As with hand-expressing, gently massaging your breast first will help activate your let down reflex.
- Place the breast piece of the pump centrally over your nipple.
- Start with the suction on the low setting and gradually increase it to a level that is comfortable for you. Stronger suction does

not draw out more milk as it is dependent on how long and how effectively the breast is drained.

- Pump until your milk flow slows down.
- When you have finished release the suction by gently easing your breast away from the wall of the breast piece.
- Switch to the second breast and repeat the process.

You can buy or hire electric breast pumps from the Australian Breastfeeding Association, medical equipment suppliers and most chemists. You will need to buy your own pump kit to attach to the electric pump.

STORING, DEFROSTING AND TRANSPORTING EXPRESSED BREASTMILK

You can't always be with your baby and when breastfeeding there may be occasions when you will not be available to put your baby to the breast. These could include: needing to attend a social occasion, getting held up in traffic or having to return to the paid workforce.

To be prepared for these situations you will need to express (see expressing breastmilk). You will need to know how to store and defrost breastmilk. You will also need to know how to safely transport breastmilk. Like all milk, the quality and safety of breastmilk needs to be preserved by correct cooling and storage to prevent nutrient degradation and any risk of contamination that may make a baby unwell.

STORAGE OF BREASTMILK

Expressed breastmilk should be used as soon as possible after you have expressed. A decision you will have to make is what to store your milk in. Expressed breastmilk can be kept in either the refrigerator (if using in the short-term) or in the freezer (if needing to store for a longer period). If it is to be stored in the refrigerator for a few hours or days, you can use a sterilised feeding bottle that has a secure cap to stop contamination or spillage. If you are storing in a freezer, you can use plastic bottles or storage bags or covered ice block trays (with lids) for the storage of breastmilk.

Breastmilk	Room temperature (26°C or lower)	Refrigerator (5°C or lower)	Freezer
Freshly expressed into a container that has a lid	Store 6–8 hours if less than 26°C. If refrigeration is available store milk there at 5°C or less	Store no more than 72 hours (5°C or lower). Store in back of the refrigerator where it is the coldest.	Store for: Two weeks in freezer compartment of a single door fridge (–15°C). Three months in freezer section of fridge with separate door. 6–12 months in deep freeze (–20°C or lower).
Previously frozen – thawed in the fridge but not already warmed	Four hours or less (that is, next feed)	Store for 24 hours	Do not refreeze
Thawed outside fridge in warm water	Until the end of the feed (maximum of one hour)	Hold for four hours or until the next feed	Do not refreeze
Baby has started to feed	Only until the end of the feed, then throw away (maximum of one hour)	Discard	Discard

Reference: NHMRC 2012, *Infant feeding guidelines: information for health workers*, Australian Government, Canberra, p. 59.

THAWING

There are two methods to thaw milk. You can:

- Place the frozen expressed breastmilk in a container of warm water to rapidly thaw. Swirl milk gently before use. Expressed breastmilk thawed in this way must be used or discarded within four hours, even if refrigerated, or

- Place the frozen expressed breastmilk in the refrigerator to thaw. EBM (expressed breastmilk) thawed in this way must be used or discarded within 24 hours of removal from freezer. Expressed breastmilk fully thawed outside the refrigerator must be used or discarded within four hours.

TRANSPORTATION OF EXPRESSED BREASTMILK

Frozen expressed breastmilk should remain frozen during transportation. A foam cooler or Esky with ice blocks or bags of ice is the most convenient way to achieve this. Keep the foam cooler or Esky in a cool environment or air conditioning when possible. Transport fresh EBM in the same manner.

FEEDING IN PUBLIC

Mothers should feel encouraged and supported to feed their babies in public. A baby needs to be fed when they demand it and it is not always convenient. There is no law against feeding in public. In fact, it sends a very positive message that breastfeeding is a normal and accepted part of family and community life. Too few children know about breastfeeding or have never seen anyone breastfeed their baby.

Needless to say, some mothers do lack confidence or get embarrassed about feeding in public, especially in the early days when you are unable to do it in a relaxed manner that no one really notices. Feeding in public can also be a little more challenging when your baby reaches an age when they are interested in their surroundings and easily distracted.

Some suggestions to feel more comfortable when breastfeeding in public:
- Use your pram or stroller as a visual barrier.
- Use a light cotton wrap or shawl to place over your shoulder for privacy.
- Wear clothing that is buttoned down the front so you can reduce the exposure of your breast.

- Wear a light, loose shirt or top that provides your baby with easy access to your breast, whilst still providing you with privacy while breastfeeding.

Some shopping centres provide parenting rooms for feeding and changing babies. Unfortunately, these are sometimes found near the public toilets and are not very pleasant places to provide your baby with food.

As you become more confident and relaxed with breastfeeding, feeding your baby in public will become less of an issue.

WHY DO WOMEN GIVE UP BREASTFEEDING?

It is always surprising that with so much publicity about the value of breastfeeding that many women make the decision not to breastfeed or only breastfeed for a short period of time. Some of the reasons mothers choose not to breastfeed or don't continue to breastfeed after a couple of days, weeks or months include:

- A lack of adequate family and community support. A common statement is 'I didn't breastfeed you and you turned out okay!'
- Encountering breastfeeding difficulties such as nipple pain or engorgement.
- Feeling fearful about the responsibilities of motherhood.
- Being concerned the baby is not getting enough milk or not gaining enough weight.
- Feeling pressured to breastfeed without being provided with adequate support, education or opportunity to explore fears and uncertainty.
- Being provided with inaccurate information about breastfeeding.
- Being physically or emotionally unwell.

Before making the decision to wean it is important to explore your options with someone knowledgeable about breastfeeding.

BREASTFEEDING AND CAESAREAN SECTIONS

There is no reason why most women cannot breastfeed their babies after a caesarean section. If your caesarean is planned, your baby will probably be alert enough to breastfeed. If you required an emergency caesarean it is likely that both you and your baby will be a little stressed and fatigued. The type of anaesthetic you received will also impact on your baby's state of alertness.

Prior to going into the theatre, remind your doctor or midwife that you want to breastfeed your baby as soon as possible after surgery. If an epidural is being used, once your baby has been assessed as not needing any intervention, the staff may place the baby on your chest and assist you to breastfeed when ready.

The sooner your baby is able to breastfeed the better. If breastfeeding gets delayed beyond one or two hours don't be too concerned. As long as someone helps you to express as soon as you are feeling able, this will start to trigger the onset of lactation. If your baby is in the special care nursery it is really important someone takes you to see your baby as soon as you are feeling well enough to visit. Expressing in sight and proximity of your baby will help your let down of colostrum or breastmilk.

Feeding or expressing frequently every few hours is essential during the first few days and weeks. This will mean waking at night at least once or twice to feed or express. Even though you would prefer to sleep through the night, it is better to get up once or twice for your establishment of lactation and to prevent engorgement. Prolactin levels are higher overnight and this is often the most effective time to breastfeed or express to help increase your breastmilk supply.

The way your baby is positioned on the breast is very important as it will help establish effective breastfeeding and prevent nipple damage. The midwife will help you find a feeding position that is comfortable for you and that will help your baby attach and feed. When holding your baby make sure your baby's body is close to you with their chest to your chest, their chin tucked into your breast and nose tilted clear.

Suggested positions are:

- Lying on your side.
- Sitting with a pillow on your lap. This will support your baby, but protect your wound.
- Placing your baby in a twin position – under your arm with feet towards your back.

If you are unable to take your baby home the day you are discharged because they are still in the special care nursery, you will need to continue to express. This expressing needs to be 2–3 hourly during the day and 3–4 hourly overnight.

See above information on expressing, storage and transport of breastmilk.

BREASTFEEDING MORE THAN ONE BABY

Having more than one baby to breastfeed can be an initial challenge. However, many women successfully fully or partially breastfeed twins, triplets and even quadruplets. Arranging a well functioning support system of family and friends to assist you is paramount. This will be particularly important in the early days after birth.

Many parents find making contact with the Multiple Birth Association or the Australian Breastfeeding Association very helpful as they provide an opportunity to talk to other parents who have breastfed their babies. Parents who have already had the experiences of breastfeeding multiple babies can help to reassure you and provide lots of practical suggestions and tips to make the experience more manageable.

GOING HOME FROM HOSPITAL BEFORE YOUR BABY

Some babies just can't wait until their due date and come early, while others are unfortunately born with a medical problem that requires treatment. Whatever the reason for baby having to stay in hospital, this can be very upsetting and extremely tiring for parents. Providing colostrum or breastmilk will contribute to your baby's health and wellbeing. They will strengthen your baby's immune system and fight off infection, especially in the early days. Breastfeeding is a very positive thing you can do for you and your baby, even if it is only for a few days or weeks.

Making the decision to express after discharge will require some effort and planning. If you need to express for more than a few days, consider hiring an electric breast pump. You will also need to learn how to store and transport your expressed breastmilk. Importantly, make sure you feel confident expressing before you go home. If you experience any problems, the midwives or special care nurses will assist you when you visit.

Try to regularly visit your baby. Seeing and touching your baby helps you stay emotionally connected and will assist your breastmilk supply to become established. When you are expressing, have a picture of your baby to look at and a piece of clothing they have been wearing that you can smell. These will help boost your levels of prolactin and oxytocin, which will help you let down your milk more readily.

CHAPTER SUMMARY

- Tresillian has a long history of supporting mother's who breastfeed their baby.
- Breastmilk is the ideal food for babies.
- Colostrum is an excellent first food for babies.
- Mothers are advised to exclusively breastfeed their babies for the first six months of life, then continue to breastfeed with the addition of solid food.
- The size of a woman's breast does not influence the production of breastmilk.
- The let down reflex enables your breastmilk to start to flow and be available for your baby.
- It can take up to six weeks for your breastmilk supply to be well established.

Chapter Eleven
BREASTFEEDING PROBLEMS

IN YOUR BABY'S FIRST YEAR most mothers will encounter the occasional problem with their breastfeeding. They are usually inconvenient, but short-lived. In some instances, they will cause you some discomfort or pain and you will need medical or other professional help. Acting early at the first sign of discomfort, or when you have a feeling that things are not quite right with your breasts or baby's breastfeeding behaviour, will usually help resolve or lessen the impact of the problem.

DISCOMFORT WHEN BREASTFEEDING

Sometimes, when breastfeeding, you will experience some discomfort. Rather than continuing the feed, it is worth detaching your baby from the breast and then correctly reattaching to the breast to see if that improves your comfort level.

These are a few techniques and options that may help promote your breastfeeding comfort, whilst enabling your baby to effectively position and attach to the breast:

- Make sure you're comfortable, e.g. sitting in a supportive chair, pillows behind your back.
- Position your baby across your chest with your arm supporting their shoulders and back (feet pointing towards your body) or lie down on your side with the baby beside you. If necessary, a pillow can help support your baby at the height of your breasts.
- Gently compress the areola between the thumb and fingers – this will help your nipple protrude.
- Shape the nipple to match the direction of your baby's mouth by positioning your fingers behind the margin of the areola (dark area behind the nipple).
- Aim your nipple slightly upwards towards the roof of your baby's mouth.
- If you are concerned that your baby's nose is blocked by your breast, tuck your baby's buttocks and legs into their body, and place a supporting hand behind your baby's shoulders, ensuring your baby's chin is tilted into your breast.

CHECKLIST FOR CORRECT POSITIONING

Your baby will:
- Open their mouth wide with lower lip curled outwards
- Have their body facing front-on to your breast
- Tuck their chin into your breast
- Tuck their body well into your body
- Not cause you any nipple pain when they suck
- Have a rhythmical sucking pattern with occasional pauses.

NOT ENOUGH BREASTMILK

If your milk supply is insufficient for your baby's needs there are many ways to improve the situation. Before weaning your baby onto formula, try to increase your breastmilk supply first. Seek advice from your child and family health nurse, a lactation consultant, an early parenting organisation like Tresillian or the Australian Breastfeeding Association. They can provide you with support and information on breastfeeding.

INCREASING YOUR BREASTMILK SUPPLY

The key to increasing your breastmilk supply is to increase the number of times you feed your baby and therefore effectively drain your breasts of milk. The more milk that is removed, the more breastmilk is produced. Effective positioning and attachment is important for breast drainage and will increase your breastmilk supply.

Tips to increase your breastmilk:

Problem	Suggested action
Does your baby only feed for short periods?	Try to encourage your baby to stay longer at each breast or re-offer the first breast.
Is your baby going for long periods between feeds?	Reduce the time between feeds for a couple of days by offering the breast more frequently.
Are your nipples sore or tender?	Check if your baby is well positioned on the breast (you might need to have some specialist help with this). If your baby is not well positioned, they may not be able to stimulate a let down or effectively drain your breasts.
Do you get anxious or upset every time you have to breastfeed your baby?	If you are feeling anxious and upset this may be impacting on the let down reflex that allows the free flow of your breastmilk. If this is happening you may need to seek some assistance from your child and family health nurse or a lactation consultant. Before each feed take a few moments to do a short relaxation exercise (see quick relaxation exercise in Chapter 5).

Problem	Suggested action
Are you giving your baby extra top-up feeds with formula milk?	Unless advised by your doctor, slowly stop these extra feeds and increase the number of breastfeeds to meet your baby's needs.
Have you introduced the baby to solid foods too early (before six months)?	Return to offering breastfeeds only until six months. If your baby is over six months always breastfeed before offering your baby their solid foods.
Are you smoking?	Smoking can reduce your breastmilk production. Consider going onto a Quit program or reducing the number of cigarettes you smoke each day. Seek the support of your doctor or child and family health nurse.
Are you or have you been unwell or overly tired?	It might be time to see your local doctor about this, especially if it's impacting on your wellbeing and/or your breastmilk supply. In the meantime you can improve your diet – make sure you are eating healthy, nutritious food and drinking plenty of water. Try and increase the amount of rest you are having by having a sleep during the day, even a short period can be helpful. Ask for and accept help from family and friends with household tasks. Have some time out and do something that you enjoy to help you relax.
Is your baby unwell?	If your baby is unwell this may be impacting on their ability to suck vigorously and stay awake to gain adequate nutrition. You may need to provide them with shorter but more frequent feeds until they are healthy again. Do not delay, if your baby remains unwell make an appointment to see your local doctor (see Chapters 15 and 16).
Are you offering your baby a dummy or pacifier to extend the periods between feeds?	Feed your baby more frequent feeds rather than using the dummy or pacifier to delay feeds.
Are you taking medication either prescribed, over-the-counter, recreational or natural/herbal remedies?	Either discuss the safety of these medications with the person who prescribed them or talk to your local pharmacist for advice. Recreational drugs can also have a negative impact on your milk supply, your health and your baby's health and safety.

Problem	Suggested action
Are you having a change in your hormones?	This may be due to menstruation re-commencing, you may be ovulating again, you may have recently started a new contraceptive or you could be pregnant. In most instances (unless you are pregnant) the impact is short-lived and the taste of your breastmilk and baby's behaviour will return to normal in a couple of days. Importantly, if you are pregnant you can still continue to breastfeed.

WHEN BREASTFEEDING ISN'T WORKING

For some mothers, regardless of the effort and commitment, breastfeeding just does not seem to work out. Their production of breastmilk remains insufficient to adequately feed their baby. If nothing is working to increase your milk supply, now is the time to:

- Make an appointment to see your doctor. There could be an underlying medical problem that is preventing you succeeding with breastfeeding such as past trauma, illness or breast surgery.
- Ask your child and family health nurse or lactation consultant to assess your situation and observe a breastfeed.
- Consider asking for a referral (from either your doctor or child and family health nurse) to an early parenting centre such as Tresillian where experienced specialist nurses can advise and support you. Visit www.tresillian.net for information on the types of services available in your area.
- Breastfeeding support groups such as the Australian Breastfeeding Association have trained breastfeeding counsellors that can also be of great assistance at this time.

If you have tried everything and are still unable to fully breastfeed your baby, all is not lost. You may decide to combine breastfeeding and expressed breastmilk or infant formula. There are also many things you can do to ensure a special and strong bond occurs between you and your baby (see Chapter 12 on formula feeding).

TOO MUCH BREASTMILK

How do you know if you've got too much breastmilk? Your baby may appear to choke, gulp and bring up milk, or to 'fight the breast'. Breastfeeding in these situations can seem difficult. Usually this settles down after a few days. However, sometimes, depending on the cause it can take a little longer.

If you have a problem with producing too much milk, the following might help:

- If your baby is less than six weeks of age and your breasts are very full, you may need to express some milk prior to attaching your baby – this helps soften the nipple and areola, encourages a deeper latch and more effective drainage of the breast.
- If your baby is gulping or having difficulty coping with milk flow and pulls off, allow your breasts to leak then re-attach your baby once the flow of milk settles. This can be repeated as necessary if subsequent let downs cause your baby to pull off. If it persists, ask your doctor or child and family health nurse to exclude *tongue tie* as a cause. If your baby has a tongue tie and it is causing problems with feeding, you will be referred to a tongue tie clinic or paediatrician.
- Offer the second breast when your baby has drained the first side. Express a small amount from the second breast to repeat the process with your baby.
- Try feeding your baby in a different position, e.g. underarm or more elevated (sitting more upright than usual).
- If your breasts are still uncomfortably full at the end of a feed, express for comfort only and apply a cold compress for 15 to 20 minutes.

SORE NIPPLES

Tender nipples are a common problem for mothers during the first days of breastfeeding. If your nipples become sore or painful you need to seek help from your child and family health nurse, a lactation consultant, the Australian Breastfeeding Association, your doctor or an early parenting centre such as Tresillian. Frequently the cause of persistent sore nipples arises from incorrect positioning and attachment at the breast. This difficulty can be resolved with the assistance of a knowledgeable health professional.

When sore nipples develop it usually indicates that your baby is not well attached to the breast. They are sucking on your nipples only and need to be attached further onto your breast. After you have made sure your baby is attached correctly, there are some additional things you can try. These include:

- Feeding your baby before they become too hungry.
- Start feeding on the breast that has the least sore nipple.
- Trying to stimulate your let down reflex prior to putting your baby on the breast. Once breastmilk starts to flow nipple sensitivity may be reduced.
- If you are unable to feed because it is just too painful, make sure you express regularly in place of breastfeeding. This breastmilk can then be offered in a bottle or cup to your baby.
- Take some pain relief medication (check with your pharmacist to ensure it is safe for your baby) – this should be a temporary measure only. If the pain continues seek health professional advice.

If your nipples continue to be sore or you have shooting pain into your breasts, you will need to have your nipples checked for signs of an infection. Thrush (*Candida Albicans*) can also be a common problem and it causes significant pain and stops the nipple healing. It is very likely that both you and your baby will need some topical treatment (drops and gels) to treat a thrush infection. You may also need a course of treatment using antifungal tablets to treat the condition. Thrush is frequently passed back and forward from your baby to you, so in most cases you will both need concurrent treatment. If the condition is resistant to treatment, you may need to consider if either your partner or other member of the household may be carrying candida, e.g. in the form of tinea or a vaginal infection.

INVERTED NIPPLES

Inverted nipples can be identified by gently compressing your areola between your thumb and forefinger. A flat or normal nipple will protrude. A truly inverted nipple will retract.

If you have **inverted nipples** you may need professional assistance when breastfeeding your baby. There are things you can check and do:

- Make sure you know how to correctly attach your baby to your breast.
- Use your hand to cup your breast from underneath and shape the areola (coloured part of the breast around the nipple) between your thumb and fore finger to provide as much areola as possible for your baby to grasp.
- Prior to feeds express small amounts of breastmilk to soften the nipple and areola, allowing the nipple to extend and to be more compressable for baby to draw into their mouths.
- Drawing out your nipple is also possible by using a hand or electric pump for 1–2 minutes on low suction before the feed to aid attachment – always make sure you start with using the minimum suction setting and release the suction before removing from your breast to avoid the possibility of trauma to your nipples
- You could also try using a silicon nipple shield. This is a short-term aid to attaching and it may help your baby accept the breast and learn how to suck effectively.

FEEDING AIDS

Sometimes mothers need a little extra help breastfeeding. Useful devices include nipple shields and supply lines, however prolonged use of these devices can cause problems of their own that may interfere with the ease and enjoyment of breastfeeding or create dependence on the aid.

NIPPLE SHIELDS

Inappropriate or prolonged use of nipple shields may influence the infant's ability to attach directly to the nipple. A silicone nipple shield may be useful if the infant is unable to latch and feed effectively due to:
- Breast refusal, e.g. to encourage back from bottle to breast.
- Sucking difficulties that haven't improved with other interventions.
- Inverted/flat nipples.
- Extreme nipple sensitivity.

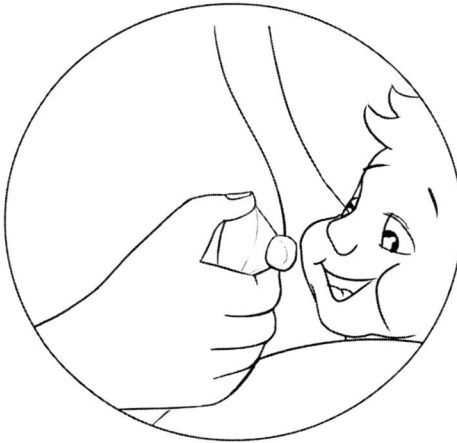

USING A NIPPLE SHIELD

If the use of a nipple shield has been suggested, explore with your midwife, child and family health nurse, lactation consultant or doctor the type and sizes available, and what the benefits and limitations are. You will need to know how to avoid nipple damage and how to maintain your milk supply.
- Wash your hands before handling the nipple shield.
- You may need to express a small amount of breastmilk onto the nipple shield, moistening the rim of the shield.
- Then turn up both sides of the brim with your thumb and finger placing the cone of the nipple shield centrally over the nipple.
- Using your finger and thumb compress the end of the shield and release to help draw the nipple up into the shield.

- Smooth out the sides of the shield to lay flat over the areola.
- Touch your baby's top lip with the nipple shield, wait for a wide-open mouth then bring infant quickly and deeply onto the breast, ensuring that your baby's lips are spread out over the breast and that correct positioning and attachment is achieved.
- Your baby's lips should be spread outwards over the base, not be pursed on the cone part of the nipple shield.
- Make sure the shield remains in place and does not slip up and down whilst your baby is breastfeeding.

NOTE: Nipple shields are not designed to be heat sterilised or disinfected in an antibacterial solution.

When cleaning the shield:
- Rinse in cold water
- Wash in warm soapy water
- Then rinse well
- Pat dry
- Store in a sealed container for future use.

BREAST REFUSAL

A baby may refuse the breast for a range of reasons. It may be that your baby:
- Is having problems attaching to the breast.
- Is feeling unwell, especially if they have a common cold.
- Is uncomfortable or in pain.
- Is finding your breastmilk flow has changed – it has become faster or slower to let down than usual.
- Is not getting enough breastmilk at the breast due to a diminished supply.
- Has developed a strong preference for one breast over the other breast.

- Is finding the taste of your breastmilk has changed. This can be due to something you have eaten, hormonal changes (your periods may have started again), or new medication.
- Is distracted (this is common for babies over four months of age). Try breastfeeding in a quiet place with minimal distractions.
- Is over stimulated or overtired.

Most of these causes of breast refusal will either go away without doing anything or can be sorted out with a few simple changes to your routine. None of these reasons for your baby refusing the breast require you to give up breastfeeding. However, if your baby persists in refusing a particular breast, ask your doctor for a breast check to rule out any abnormalities that may be causing your baby to refuse the breast.

The following strategies may help you to get your baby to return to breastfeeds again:
- Do not force your baby onto the breast.
- Trying a new feeding position may help, such as underarm or lying down.
- Expressing some breastmilk into your baby's mouth. This might encourage them to feed.
- Try to breastfeed your baby after a bath or massage when they are warm and relaxed.
- Start the flow of your breastmilk before trying to latch your baby onto your breast.
- Play some relaxing music.
- Avoid distractions of other people or excessive noise.
- If your baby has just refused a breastfeed and is becoming upset, calm them down and then use distraction by showing a toy, singing a gentle song or playing a simple finger game. Try breastfeeding again after a few minutes.
- Start to offer the feed as your baby wakes up or when they are sleepy.
- If refusal is still a problem, or your baby has developed a preference for bottle feeds, consider trying the temporary use of a nipple shield to encourage your baby back onto the breast then remove once refusal has been resolved.

BITING

Babies often start to bite on the breast when they are teething. The first bite is usually an accident and it can really hurt!

If your baby does bite, say 'no' calmly and firmly and remove your baby from the breast. If you react too strongly or loudly, your baby might think you're playing a game – or it might frighten them. Biting is usually a passing phase.

Babies might bite due to a slow let down or not enough milk after the initial let down of breastmilk. If the biting is a response to a slow let down then expressing a small amount of breastmilk to trigger your let down before you offer the breast will often remedy the situation. If there is not enough milk after the initial let down of breastmilk, see information in this chapter on how to increase your breastmilk supply.

BLOCKED MILK DUCTS

A blocked milk duct usually presents as a sore lump in your breast that is due to ineffective drainage and a build-up of milk. If treated quickly it will not cause you any adverse effects.

To reduce or eliminate the lump:
- A warm shower and massaging your breast under water will help break up the lump. This will also allow you to relax.
- A warm compress used before the feed will help to soften the lump – try a warmed (not hot) heat pack wrapped in a soft cloth or tea towel and held to your breast for a few minutes. Always check the temperature of the compress on the inside of your arm before applying to your breast to avoid a burn.
- Feed your baby frequently to help empty the affected breast.
- Give your baby the affected breast first when they are the most hungry.
- Using a circular motion up away from the nipple, gently massage the lump as you feed your baby.
- Check that your baby is positioned and attached correctly.
- Make sure your feeding position allows the milk to flow 'downhill' from the blockage to your nipple.

- Vary your feeding positions to make sure all sections of the breast are being emptied effectively and regularly.
- If your baby is unable to clear the blockage by feeding, try expressing by hand.
- Place an ice-pack (wrapped in a tea towel) or chilled cabbage leaf on your breast to relieve pain and inflammation after a feed.
- Check that your bra is not too tight as it may be restricting the milk flow.
- Try removing your bra during feeds. This will allow the milk to flow more easily.

If you can't clear the blockage within 12 to 24 hours, or you start to feel unwell (as if you're coming down with the flu), see your doctor – you might be developing a common infection in breastfeeding mothers, known as *mastitis*.

ENGORGEMENT

Engorgement is defined as a build-up of milk, blood and other fluids in the breast or surrounding tissue. It may temporarily affect milk flow or the ability of your baby to attach to your breast due to flattened nipples.

When engorged, breasts can become very hard, swollen and tender and nipples become flattened and taut. It can be very painful for the mother and make it difficult for a baby to attach to the breast due to breast distention and flattened nipples.

The following steps may assist in reducing the onset of engorgement:
- From birth regularly feed your baby on demand.
- Do not limit the time your baby spends at the breast.
- Allow your baby to drain the first breast well before offering the second breast.
- If your breasts become full and uncomfortable (especially at night) wake your baby and offer the breast.
- Make sure your baby is well positioned and attached correctly to the breast as this will assist in maximising the amount of breastmilk your baby is able to get from the breast and, in turn, decrease your engorgement and associated discomfort.

Many mothers will experience breast fullness that sometimes leads to engorgement around the time their 'milk comes in'. This is due to the rapid fluid increase into the breast for imminent production of breastmilk. The fluid may be what is known as 'interstitial' or 'between the breast tissue' and not simply breastmilk that is easily expressed. Until the engorgement settles, milk may not flow easily. In these situations it is important to ensure that the baby is attaching well and feeding effectively and that the length and frequency of feeds are being determined by the baby's needs.

Mothers who experience severe engorgement often find it helpful to use a breast pump to completely express the milk from their breasts. Also, applying cool or cold compresses intermittently throughout the day and taking pain relief medication or an anti-inflammatory medication may assist in reducing the engorgement and with drainage of the breast. If you are taking over-the-counter medications while you are having treatment for engorgement, it is important you speak to your pharmacist to ensure it is safe for your baby and if there are any safety precautions that should be followed.

When your breasts are engorged, breastfeeding and expressing breastmilk may be difficult. With engorgement the intracellular fluid can cause compression of the cell walls rather than the milk within the ducts.

There are many ways you can relieve painful, sore breasts. Follow the same instructions as for reducing blocked milk ducts.

MASTITIS

Having full breasts in the first few weeks of breastfeeding is often a normal occurrence as your lactation is becoming established. However, having inflamed, sore, red or swollen breasts, or feeling like you are getting the flu (chills, fevers, shivers, shakes, lethargy and generally feeling terrible) you may be developing or have mastitis. Mastitis can start with a blocked milk duct that has been leaking milk out into the surrounding breast tissue thereby setting up an inflammation process.

The treatment for mastitis is similar to that used for a blocked milk duct (see information in this chapter). Start by trying the suggested strategies for resolving a blocked milk duct. The main thing to remember is to continue to breastfeed your baby. You should also:

- Visit your doctor as soon as possible. The doctor will usually prescribe antibiotics to help relieve the inflammation and any infection that may be present. Importantly, continue to breastfeed.
- Keep breastfeeding as your baby is the most efficient expresser of breastmilk. If you stop breastfeeding you will have to express and you will not be as effective as your baby. There is a risk of developing a breast abscess if you stop breastfeeding suddenly or do not effectively treat mastitis.
- If for some reason you are unable to continue to breastfeed, you must express your breastmilk until you can resume breastfeeding. Offer your baby the expressed breastmilk. Breastmilk remains safe for your baby to drink even if you have an infection as the infection is located outside the breast ducts and will not normally enter your breastmilk.
- Drink adequate amounts of fluid. While you are feeling unwell it is easy to decrease your fluid intake, which will slow down your recovery.
- Get plenty of rest to help you recover quickly.

Be prepared for your milk supply to lessen while you are unwell and recovering. During the period you are experiencing mastitis there is a temporary increase in sodium levels and a decrease in lactose levels in your breastmilk. Until the inflammation and infection resolves, keep in mind your baby may fuss for a few days on the affected breast due to the salty taste of your breastmilk and the temporary decrease in milk volume. By feeding more frequently, your breastmilk supply will increase to meet the needs of your baby.

Mastitis can make you feel very unwell and unable to tackle routine daily tasks, so having the right treatment and calling on your friends and family to help will speed your recovery.

ECZEMA/DERMATITIS

Eczema and dermatitis are skin conditions that can also affect the nipples and breasts of the lactating mother. There are three main types:

- Atopic eczema – where the nipples are affected by more widespread skin disease.
- Irritant contact dermatitis – in response to an agent applied to the nipples.
- Allergic contact dermatitis – a delayed hypersensitivity reaction to an allergen in contact with the nipple/breast.

If you have or think you have eczema or dermatitis on your nipples it is important you seek medical assistance. Your doctor may prescribe a cream to apply sparingly on your nipples after each feed.

WHITE SPOT

A white spot that appears on the nipple can cause you considerable 'pin point' nipple pain. It is usually the result of a blocked nipple pore covered by a very fine layer of skin. This blockage of the nipple pore can inhibit drainage of the corresponding duct that may lead to inflammation, breast pain and mastitis.

If you have identified a white spot on your nipple and it is not accompanied by pain or a blocked duct, no treatment is required, providing the milk spot disappears spontaneously within a few days. However, if it is blocking a nipple pore or a duct you can try:

- Applying a moist compress or soaking your breast in a bowl of warm water for a few minutes before a feed; this may help soften and shed the layer of skin covering the white spot and allow you to roll the nipple and massage out the plug.
- Also, feeding your baby as soon as possible post-soaking will help to draw out the white spot and drain the duct.

After a few days if it has not disappeared ask for advice from your child and family health nurse, lactation consultant or doctor, especially if you have pain or feel that you have a blocked duct and inflammation or fever.

BREAST RASH

Extra breast care may be needed to avoid a rash occurring under your breast, especially in hot weather or if you develop a thrush infection:

- Wash and dry the area under your breasts with care. You may need to do this at each feed to ensure they remain comfortable, especially if you are developing a reddened area.
- If a rash occurs, use a soothing cream. Your pharmacist will be able to provide guidance.
- If the rash does not disappear or keeps reoccurring you may have a thrush infection and an anti-fungal cream may be necessary. Always wash your hands after handling your breasts, especially if you have a persistent rash.

CHAPTER SUMMARY

- Most breastfeeding problems are short-lived and easily managed.
- If you are experiencing a breastfeeding problem, seeking assistance early is essential.
- Engorgement is a build-up of milk, blood or other fluids in the breast or surrounding tissue. It is a temporary condition.
- It is extremely rare to have to stop breastfeeding because of a breast problem.
- Continuing to breastfeed is an effective way to empty your breasts and help resolve any breastfeeding problems.

Chapter Twelve
BOTTLE FEEDING

GOVERNMENTS AND HEALTH PROFESSIONALS work consistently to promote and increase breastfeeding as the method of choice for infant feeding and recommend it for at least the first six months of a baby's life. There is now no argument about the benefits of breastfeeding for both baby and mother.

In some instances, you may feel pressured to wean your baby onto a bottle. This could be due to your baby being unsettled and wakeful or not seeming to be gaining adequate weight. However, before you wean your baby onto formula milk, it's important to understand there is no guarantee that infant formula feeds will make baby more settled or sleep for longer. In many cases, the baby becomes more unsettled on infant formula.

If you need to or want to offer your baby either breastmilk or infant formula from a bottle, there are a couple of decisions to make:

- The type of infant formula you will use, if you are not going to use expressed breastmilk.
- The equipment needed, and how to sterilise this equipment.

You will also need to:

- Learn about safe preparation, storage and transportation of infant formula.

For some babies, taking a bottle is never a problem, but for other babies it can be extremely distressing. This is where your knowledge of your baby's cues can help you slow down and become more responsive to their needs (see Chapter 5). When your baby becomes distressed during a feed, always remember to ask yourself:

- What is my baby experiencing?
- What is my baby feeling?
- What am I experiencing?
- What am I feeling?

Babies often respond to our emotions and the tensions in our bodies. They are often much more attuned to us as parents than we are to them as babies.

THE MARKETING OF INFANT FORMULAS IN AUSTRALIA

In 1992 the Marketing in Australia of Infant Formulas (MAIF) agreement was developed as part of Australia's response to the World Health Organization (WHO) code on infant nutrition. The MAIF agreement is a self-regulatory code between manufacturers and importers of infant formula. The WHO code and MAIF agreement aim is to provide safe and adequate infant nutrition through the promotion of breastfeeding and ensuring breastmilk substitutes (infant formula) are properly used by supplying adequate information and appropriate marketing. These code requirements include:

- All infant formula labels and information state the benefits of breastfeeding and the health risks of substitutes.
- There is to be no promotion of breastmilk substitutes.
- No free samples of breastmilk substitutes are given to women, mothers or their families.
- There is no distribution of free or subsidised substitutes to health workers or facilities (e.g. hospitals).
- The demonstration of the preparation of infant formulas is only provided to a mother or family members who need to use a formula.

Infant formula:
- Does not contain antibodies that are found in breastmilk.
- If not properly prepared there are risks due to possible contamination of the infant formula powder, unsterilised equipment and unsafe water.
- Inadequate nutrition can occur from over-dilution of the infant formula.
- Significant health problems can occur if the infant formula is too concentrated.

WHAT TYPE OF INFANT FORMULA SHOULD I GIVE MY BABY?

- Most infant formulas are cow's milk based with added vitamins, minerals and different fats that babies need in order to grow and stay healthy. Infant formulas are modified to make them as close as possible to breastmilk. However, even though infant formula tries to resemble breastmilk, it is not identical.
- All infant formulas you buy in Australia are safe for your baby for the age group written on the tin. Most infant formulas have a similar composition and nutritional value. It comes as a powder, in liquid pre-prepared tetra packs, or as liquid in a tin that must be diluted strictly according to the instructions.

- If your baby is under 12 months of age they should be fed using an infant formula. Importantly, normal cow's milk is not suitable as it needs to be significantly altered before it is suitable for an infant. Cow's milk is much harder for your baby to digest and its high level of salt, protein and minerals make it very dangerous for their immature kidneys.
- Making the decision about what infant formula you should feed your baby can be confusing. There are so many different types on the supermarket and chemist shelves. There can also be a significant variation in cost. Being more expensive does not mean they are better for your baby.
- You may also be told about specialist infant formulas. These should only be used if recommended by your doctor or your baby's paediatrician.
- Soya and goat's milk infant formulas are available but not generally recommended. These can be more expensive than cow's milk based infant formulas. If you would like to use these, check with your doctor or child and family health nurse for a detailed review of your baby's and your individual situation and nutritional needs.

HOW MUCH INFANT FORMULA DOES MY BABY NEED?

The amount of infant formula an individual infant/child needs varies. A full-term healthy infant will need by day five, on average 150 mL per kg of body weight per day to meet their nutrient needs before the introduction of solids.

Time	Approximate amount
Day 1 to 4	Commence at 30–60 mL/kg/day and increase over the next few days
Day 5 to 3 months	150 mL/kg/day some babies, especially those who were pre-term, will require up to 180–200 mL/kg/day
3 to 6 months	120mL/kg/day

6 to 12 months	100mL/kg/day
	some babies may reduce to 90mL/kg/day
	babies of this age also take solid food

NHMRC 2012, *Infant feeding guidelines: information for health workers*, Australian Government, Canberra (p.79).

The best person to advise you on the amount of infant formula to feed your baby is your child and family health nurse. Six to eight wet nappies in 24 hours, regular soft formed bowel motions, consistent (but not excessive) weight gain, adequate length and head circumference growth and a thriving, active infant will all indicate that the infant's nutritional needs are being met.

If you need to offer expressed breastmilk in a bottle or cup your baby will require similar amounts of breastmilk.

CLEANING AND STERILISING FEEDING EQUIPMENT

- Most people talk about sterilising infant feeding equipment, but what is really occurring is that the equipment is being disinfected. Disinfection is not a sterilising process. Disinfection involves the inactivation of non-sporing organisms by the use of heat, water (thermal) or chemical means. Sterilisation, however, is a process that is used to render a product completely free of all forms of micro-organisms. Most people simply call it sterilisation, so for greater ease, we will continue to call it sterilising.

There are three types of processes that are commonly used by parents:
1. Immersion in an anti-bacterial solution
2. Electric steam sterilisers
3. Or using boiling water.

NOTE: At Tresillian we would recommend either the anti-bacterial solution method or using an electric steam steriliser – there is a significant risk of hot water and steam burn injuries when using boiling water.

What else needs to be sterilised prior to feeding? Anything that will come in contact with milk or goes into your baby's mouth. For example, any equipment used to contain or mix formula, bottles, teats, cups, and so on. Dummies or pacifiers also need to be sterilised as they go into your baby's mouth. If you are breastfeeding as well, sterilise the breast pump components that come in contact with the breast or breastmilk.

Nipple shields should be washed in warm soapy water and rinsed (see nipple shields in Chapter 11). If sterilised they will become cloudy and lose their structural shape. Also, anti-bacterial solutions (sodium hypochlorite solution) left on the nipple shield can increase the risk of nipple thrush by altering the skin's natural flora.

ANTI-BACTERIAL TABLET/SOLUTION METHOD

Before commencing, carefully read the anti-bacterial (sodium hypochlorite) solution prep-aration instructions. These should be clearly visible on the bottle. If you are still unsure about how to use the tablets or solution, you can check the details with your child and family health nurse or pharmacist. Most parents find the use of tablets much easier and safer than the use of solution.

Equipment needed
- Prepared anti-bacterial tablets or solution and a large container with a lid for the prepared solution
- Feeding equipment: at least six bottles, teats, or feeding cups to ensure you have enough for a day's supply
- Bottle and teat brush
- Detergent
- Plastic tongs
- Gloves
- Plastic grate or a plate to keep items submerged in the solution.

Process to use
- Check preparation instructions and immersion time of sterilisation solution (recommendations may vary from brand to brand).
- Wash hands.

- Rinse equipment with cold water.
- Wash equipment thoroughly using warm water, detergent and bottle brush, making sure there is no milk residue remaining on equipment.
- Rinse with cold water.
- Inspect equipment to ensure it is not damaged or that teats are not perished.
- Squeeze water through teat hole to clean and ensure there is no blockage.
- Place equipment in anti-bacterial solution ensuring equipment is fully immersed with no air bubbles. Leave for the minimum time advised in the instructions.

On completion
- Wash hands before handling sterilised bottle.
- Remove equipment using plastic tongs (to prevent skin irritation) and shake utensils, bottles and teats and store covered in refrigerator for up to 24 hours.
- Do not rinse sterilised equipment with tap water as this will re-contaminate equipment.
- If using plastic tongs, check that they are replaced in anti-bacterial solution.

Precautions
- Anti-bacterial solution must be changed every 24 hours. Wash out and rise the container and store out of direct sunlight to prevent chemical breakdown.
- Prepare anti-bacterial solution as per manufacturer's instructions to ensure correct solution concentration.
- Do not put metal equipment in anti-bacterial solution as it will rust.
- Ensure correct storage of sterilised equipment so it does not become contaminated.
- Make sure the prepared anti-bacterial solution tablets or concentrate are stored where they are out of the reach of children – sodium hypochlorite concentrate or tablets (an alkaline) can

cause burns if swallowed. Take great care to avoid steam burns when lifting the lid off the container.

ELECTRIC STEAM STERILISERS

Before using an electric steam steriliser you will need to carefully read the instructions. Steam sterilisers are automatic units that steam your equipment at a temperature high enough to kill bacteria.

- Put your clean equipment into the unit.
- Add water according to the manufacturer's instructions and switch on.
- The unit will switch itself off when it has completed the sterilising process.

There are also microwave steam sterilisers. These are like electric steam sterilisers, but you put them in the microwave oven. Read the instructions carefully before using.

BOILING WATER METHOD

Take extra care if using this method that you do not cause a burn or steam injury to yourself. As a safety precaution, make sure children are not in close proximity to you or the stove during this process to avoid splash burns or other accidents. Set a timer as a reminder and stay in the kitchen to avoid the pot boiling dry and equipment melting or burning.

In an emergency, when an anti-bacterial solution is not available, the boiling water method is an appropriate one to use.

Process to use
- Rinse all bottles and sterilising equipment with cold water.
- Wash equipment thoroughly using warm water, detergent and bottle brush, making sure there is no milk residue remaining on equipment.
- Rinse with cold water.

- Inspect equipment to ensure it is not damaged or teats are not perished.
- Squeeze water through teat hole to ensure there is no blockage.
- Put all the utensils in a large pot.
- Fill the pot with water until all the bottles and other equipment are totally submerged (remove any air bubbles) and cover with a lid.
- Put the pot on the stove, bring it to the boil and boil for five minutes.
- Let the water cool before removing equipment.
- Store equipment you are not going to use straight away in a clean sealed container in the fridge.
- Boil cleaning implements such as bottle brushes once every 24 hours.

On completion
- Wash hands before handling sterilised bottles.
- Remove equipment with metal or silicon tongs and store equipment in a covered container or assemble complete bottle, teats, collar and caps in the refrigerator for up to 24 hours.
- Do not rinse sterilised equipment with tap water as this will re-contaminate them.

Precautions
- It is safer to allow the water to cool before removing equipment.
- If the water is hot when removing equipment from the water, hold tongs to make sure hot water is not able to run down onto you hand or arm.
- Ensure correct storage of sterilised equipment so it does not become re-contaminated.

PREPARING INFANT FORMULA

There are several things you need to do before starting to prepare your baby's milk:

- Always wash your hands (see Chapter 15) before preparing food
- Ensure preparation area is clean
- Ensure bottles and teats are in good condition.

Set up the equipment you will need:

- Infant formula tin
- Sterilised feeding bottle with the cap and sealing disk
- Sterilised teat
- Cooled boiled water (if you are using bottled water this needs to be treated with the same precautions as tap water as it is not sterile)
- Sterilised plastic knife.

The preferred and safest way of making formula in the home is 'in the bottle' one at a time. If more than one feed is required, Tresillian recommends filling the required number of individual bottles using the following technique:

1. Carefully read and follow the instructions on the tin of infant formula.
2. Pour recommended amount of cooled boiled water into the bottle. Read at eye level to ensure an accurate measure.
3. Using scoop provided in the tin, measure and add the exact amount of formula into the bottle. Level the powder with a sterilised plastic knife. Do not pack the infant formula powder down as this will overpack the scoop and cause the infant formula to be too concentrated for your baby.
4. Place the disc, collar and cap on the bottle. Shake until the formula is thoroughly mixed.

On completion of infant formula preparation

- To ensure consistent and effective temperature control store formula bottles in the back of the refrigerator (not in the

refrigerator door) for up to 24 hours. If not used it is essential to discard after this time.
- Rinse and wash used equipment.

Precautions
- Check the expiry date of the infant formula powder before use.
- Discard any infant formula powder not used within a month after opening the tin regardless of the expiry date on the tin. Humid conditions can result in decreased shelf life of opened infant formula tins.
- Always store infant formula tins out of direct sunlight.
- Unused prepared formula to be discarded after 24 hours.
- Infant formula powder is considered clean not sterile.
- Make sure the required amount of water (as per instructions on the tin) is used. Too much water will result in a diluted infant formula and your baby will not gain adequate nutrition or weight and is likely to be very unsettled and difficult to soothe. If not enough water is used, the infant formula will be too concentrated and may cause constipation, put stress on the baby's internal organs such as their kidneys, and cause metabolic imbalances.

PRE-PREPARED INFANT FORMULA

This infant formula comes pre-prepared usually in 250 mL packs. As with all infant formula follow the instructions on the pack. Ensure you wash your hands before handling any infant feeding equipment or the pre-prepared infant formula pack.

TEATS

Finding the right teat for your baby can be a challenge. There are many styles of teats available for purchase, with lots of claims about how they can prevent different infant problems, e.g. colic or unsettled babies. There is no evidence to support many of these claims. It can be difficult finding the right teat – it is useful having a couple of teats that you regularly use. This will help avoid your baby having a favourite teat and makes it easier to introduce a new teat when the old one is no longer safe to use.

The flow of milk from the teat should drip steadily without pouring out in a stream. To test the milk flow through the teat:

- Hold the room temperature milk-filled bottle upside down over the sink – the milk should drip steadily but not pour out, i.e. one drop per second.
- If the bottle needs to be vigorously shaken and the flow is too slow, your baby might become frustrated and exhausted with the effort required to suck and go to sleep before drinking the necessary amount of milk.

Regularly check the teats, as silicone and rubber teats deteriorate over time and with use. When they start to deteriorate they can harbour bacteria and if pieces of the teat break off, they can become an inhalation or choking risk.

FEEDING YOUR BABY

Feeding your baby infant formula should be an enjoyable experience for you and your baby. A comfortable chair in a quiet place will help you relax and focus on your baby. Hold your baby so they can easily gain eye contact with you. Unwrap their arms so they can touch and explore while feeding. Gently talk and sing to your baby.

As you offer the bottle to your baby, be aware of the subtle and potent cues they are providing you (see Chapter 5). You may need to stop and change their position during the feed, provide a short break to burp or soothe if they become restless or upset.

If you have twins or triplets, whenever possible feed them one at a time. This provides some important individual time. Often when you are feeding them together, you are not always holding them but the bottles instead. This is especially so as they grow.

Equipment needed

- Bottle with expressed breastmilk or infant milk formula
- Teat held firmly in place by the collar of the bottle
- A container with warm water to heat bottle
- Bib or cloth to wipe your baby's mouth

Process

- Ensure your baby is comfortable prior to feed, e.g. nappy change. Unwrap your baby if possible so their hands are free to move.
- Wash your hands.
- Take feeding equipment to where you will feed your baby.
- Check temperature and flow of milk by dropping a little on the inner aspect of your wrist.
- Sit in a comfortable position holding your baby in the crook of your arm, placing the bib under their chin.
- Note the time when feeding begins – aim for between 20 to 30 minutes.
- If you put the teat to your baby's lips they will usually open their mouth.
- To prevent your baby sucking in air, hold the bottle at an angle, ensuring the teat and neck of bottle contain milk.
- Ensure the teat is above the tongue, and far enough back into mouth to enable the infant to suck in a coordinated manner.

- Some babies improve their suck if their lower jaw is supported by placing two fingers gently under their chin.
- Feeding time is an opportunity to enhance your relationship with your baby, so it is important that you encourage eye contact.
- Observe your baby's cues or approximately half way through the feed pause, sit your baby up, and help them to bring up wind by gently rubbing their back.
- Alternate the side you are holding your baby from right to left during the feed (as you would if breastfeeding) as this will help promote your baby's development and allow them to see you from both directions.
- Most babies like to be quietly spoken to during the feed.
- If your baby falls asleep during the feed and you do not think they have had enough milk, unwrap them and spend some time gently waking them by sitting them up (See Chapter 5 on 'quiet alert' stage).

THINGS 'NOT' TO DO DURING A FEED

- Using a microwave oven to heat your baby's bottles can be dangerous and is **not** recommended. The milk heats in an uneven way and presents the risk of severe burns to your baby's mouth or throat.
- **Do not** force your baby to feed by constantly jiggling their chin or squeezing their cheeks.
- **Do not** prolong feeds – preferably no longer than 40 minutes. If your baby becomes distressed or falls asleep after this time, cease the feed.
- **Do not** prop feed your baby by leaving unattended with their bottle propped on a rolled up towel or pillow. Milk can flow into your baby's ear canals and can cause an ear infection or the baby may inhale or choke on the milk.
- **Do not** leave your sleeping baby with a bottle in their mouth. The milk that is pooled in their mouth may cause tooth decay and recurrent ear infections.

FINISHING THE FEED

- Disassemble and wash the bottle and teat in cold water as soon as possible after finishing the feed.

TRANSPORTING PREPARED FEEDS

- The safest way to transport infant formula is to take the premeasured cooled, boiled water and the powdered formula in separate containers and mix them when needed. Warm the milk by placing the bottle in a container of warm water. Once the milk is warm, add the powder to the milk, replace the bottle top and collar before shaking the bottle until the infant formula powder is well mixed with the water.
- If you need to transport prepared formula or expressed breastmilk, it must be icy cold (5°C) when you leave the house. Carry it in a thermal cool bag with a cooling brick to keep it cold. You must use the feed within two hours if you're unable to refrigerate the bottle. If able to refrigerate the bottle within the two hours' travel time it can be stored for 24 hours from preparation time.

FEEDING CUPS

Feeding cups have come a long way in the last few years and these days there are many different brands available in all sorts of colours and styles. When you're choosing a feeding cup for your baby, look out for one that:

- Has a tight fitting lid not easily removed by your baby.
- Has two easy to grasp handles for small hands. Your baby will very quickly want to hold the cup.
- Is easy to clean without decorations that can trap milk – this makes cleaning difficult.

- Does not have any sharp edges.
- Is made from a safe form of plastic – it is now possible to buy bisphenol A (BPA) free plastic bottles and feeding cups.
- If your baby is learning to use a spout lid and cup, start with one that **is not** spill proof to encourage flow and an incentive to drink. Your baby can then move onto a spill proof one as they get to know how it works.

BOTTLE FEEDING PROBLEMS

Using a bottle to feed your baby is not always as easy as it may seem. It's not a matter of 'just put your baby on a bottle'. Some babies prefer to be breastfed and will actively refuse to take milk from a bottle, while other babies will fall asleep during feeds and then wake shortly after the feed wanting more food. Other babies will become agitated and upset, holding out for a familiar breastfeed.

Many bottle feeding problems start to occur when you are weaning the baby onto a bottle because you need to return to the paid workforce or for other reasons such as illness. For babies, sucking from a bottle is a very different type of suck to suckling milk from your breast.

The first thing to do is to try to identify the reason why your baby is refusing the bottle.

Check for these signs:
- Has your baby always had some difficulty taking a bottle and it has become more problematic?
- Is your baby unwell? Do they have a temperature; have they started to vomit or become unsettled more than unusual; is their urine becoming smelly and darker in colour or more concentrated; are their bowel motions different, e.g. very frequent, loose, mucousy, frothy or with spots of blood?
- Does you baby have a sore mouth? Sometimes oral thrush can result in the baby having a very sore mouth. There are also other infectious diseases such as human hand, foot and mouth disease that result in small blisters in the mouth (see Chapter 15).

If any of the above feeding issues are of concern, have your baby assessed by your child and family health nurse or doctor.

Once you have eliminated any health problems, there are several things to remember and strategies to try:

- Try not to become anxious. With time, patience and a gentle approach your baby will usually learn to take a bottle or in some instances a feeding cup.
- Find a quiet place to feed with minimal distractions and noise.
- If possible, ask your partner, family member or friend to try to do a feed. If breastfed, babies can smell breastmilk on their mothers and can become distressed when not offered the breast.
- Do not force your baby to feed by squeezing their cheeks or forcing their chin up and down. This type of forced sucking can create even more difficult problems to solve.
- If you do not have anyone in the house who can help for a few feeds, lay the baby in a comfortable elevated position in a rocker or pram to elevate so the head is raised higher than their shoulders. Feed your baby in this position, holding the bottle and gently touching and talking to them.
- Do not leave your baby with the bottle propped. This is very dangerous and can result in inhalation of milk into your baby's lungs or choking, or long term it may cause dental caries and ear infections.

WHEN BABY FALLS ASLEEP DURING A FEED

Some babies have a habit of falling asleep without finishing their bottle. This is not a problem unless they are waking and demanding a feed frequently or not gaining weight or are losing weight, or not passing adequate amounts of urine.

Check the following issues:

- Is your baby unwell?
- Are you offering too much milk at each feed?
- Is the infant formula correctly made up, i.e. is it too concentrated or too diluted?

- If on solid foods, try offering the bottle before solid foods
- Is the teat too slow or are the holes blocked?
- Does your baby have a rhythmical suck? If not, it may help to place your fingers under your baby's chin. This provides a slight resistance to suck against.

If bottle feeding your baby is becoming more and more difficult, it's important to talk things over with your child and family health nurse or doctor to ensure your baby has no physical reasons for this behaviour.

CHAPTER SUMMARY

- Infant formulas are usually made from cow's milk.
- Most infant formulas have a similar composition and nutritional value.
- Cow's milk should not be given to babies under 12 months of age.
- Infant formulas are modified to make them safer and more similar to breastmilk, however, they are not the same as breastmilk.
- Always make up infant formula as per the instructions on the tin or box.
- Never prop feed your baby as it is potentially very dangerous.
- Feeding time is a special time when parents and their babies can enhance their relationship.

Chapter Thirteen
WEANING

WEANING IS AN INEVITABLE EVENT for all babies. Nevertheless, mothers are strongly advised to fully breastfeed their babies until six months of age before commencing the weaning process with the introduction of solid foods. Many babies continue to breastfeed for several years because both baby and mothers find it an enjoyable experience.

It's often a mutual decision by mother and baby that the time has come to wean. However, if weaning has to occur suddenly, it can be difficult for both mother and baby.

The decision to wean must be made with care and you must be fully informed of the implication. Once you wean, it can be difficult to re-establish lactation. Although it is not impossible, as the hormones that support lactation remain elevated for several weeks and your breasts are capable of increasing your milk supply, it requires putting your baby back on the breast to feed at frequent intervals, in addition to regularly expressing breastmilk. This can be extremely tiring and stressful for you and your baby.

WEANING MYTHS AND MISINFORMATION

There are lots of myths and misinformation about breastfeeding that can result in mothers weaning unnecessarily.

Myth: *Your milk is too weak for your baby. This is why they are so unsettled!*

Fact: Breastmilk provides all the nutrients needed by your baby until they are around six months old. Mature milk looks much thinner and more watery than colostrum or transitional breastmilk in the first weeks of lactation.

Myth: *Babies are more settled and sleep through the night when given infant formula.*

Fact: There is no guarantee that if you wean, your baby will become more settled or sleep through the night. Often a baby's behaviour has nothing to do with what they are being fed. In most instances, their unsettled behaviour has more to do with their sleep patterns and their stage of emotional and physical development.

Myth: *When your baby starts to bite it means they no longer want to breastfeed.*

Fact: If babies bite the breast it is often just a mouthing action. If they get a surprise response from their mother, they are likely to try and get a repeat response performance. Babies may also bite if the breastmilk flow slows down while they are feeding. If this happens, you may need to manually start the flow by expressing and feed more frequently to increase your milk supply, but it does not need to be a reason to wean. Many mothers successfully feed, even when their babies have a mouth full of teeth. This is because to effectively breastfeed, your baby's tongue must sit over the lower gum, making biting impossible.

Myth: *It is not possible to return to the paid workforce and continue to breastfeed.*

Fact: Juggling work in the paid workforce and continuing to breastfeed can be challenging at first, but it is not impossible. It takes a bit of pre-planning, learning to express breastmilk and building a store of expressed breastmilk in the freezer. Many workplaces have policies to support their staff in continuing to breastfeed or express breastmilk for their babies during work hours.

WHEN TO WEAN

A purist view of weaning would be that it commences when you offer your baby anything other than breastmilk. However, most parents and health professionals consider weaning to occur when you make a decision to reduce breastfeeds or stop breastfeeding.

Weaning can be either baby-led or parent-led or mutual.

Baby-led is when the baby takes the initiative to cut back or stop breastfeeds. This can be distressing, especially if you and your baby have enjoyed the breastfeeding experience. Sometimes this may be a temporary weaning situation due to common hormonal or child development reasons. Seek skilled support and assistance if you want to continue to breastfeed your baby. Sometimes babies attempt to wean because of a low breastmilk supply. Often the problem can be resolved by increasing your breastmilk supply.

Parent-led weaning is when you decide it is time to stop breastfeeding. Weaning can be for many reasons including: returning to the paid workforce (it is often possible to continue to breastfeed), medical advice due to medication use or serious illness, or because your baby is unsettled (there is no guarantee that your baby will be more settled if given infant formula).

The older your baby is, usually the easier it is to wean. As your baby gets older, they have already started to reduce the number of feeds. For example, a nine-month-old baby may only demand three to four feeds a day and they will be enjoying two to three solid food meals per day.

GRADUAL WEANING

There are two ways to wean. One approach is to wean slowly or gradually over time; the other is to wean abruptly. The first is definitely the preferred method. It can take a little longer and is usually baby-led. It is easier if weaning is mutual, when both you and your baby decide that it is time to wean. Your breastmilk supply usually diminishes gradually and comfortably because of the decreased frequency and feeding pattern of your baby. The role of breastmilk transitions from being the primary source of your baby's nutrition to a lesser or secondary role.

A gradual approach allows your baby's digestive system to slowly get used to other food provided from another source. It also provides time for your breastmilk supply to gradually reduce. This lowers the risk of engorgement and mastitis (see Chapter 11). The amount of time it takes to wean will usually depend on how much time you have available. Gradual weaning can be either a relatively short period over several days, or progress slowly over several months.

Many women returning to paid work (see Chapter 17) partially wean, but continue breastfeeding for many months first thing in the morning, when they return home or overnight if necessary. Increasing the number of breastfeeds on the days you are at home will help sustain and support your breastmilk supply if there is no pressure to wean.

To gradually wean consider:
- The amount of time you will take to wean – a week, a month or three months.
- Which feeds are optimal for you and your baby to retain or which ones could be replaced. Wean at these feeds first. Keep the most enjoyable or essential feeds until last.

- Maintaining the first feed of the morning, as this is when you will have the most milk and your breasts need to be empty and comfortable before work, or the last feed of the day when you share quiet time together before settling into bed. The night feed will also keep your breasts feeling comfortable overnight.

HOW TO WEAN FROM BREAST TO BOTTLE

There is no right or wrong pattern to weaning. The following are examples of a gradual weaning pattern you can adapt to meet you and your baby's needs:

OVER A 4 WEEK PERIOD (5 FEEDS)					
		Feed 1	Feed 2	Feed 3	Feed 4	Feed 5
WEEKS	1	breast	bottle	breast	breast	breast
	2	breast	bottle	breast	bottle	breast
	3	breast	bottle	bottle	bottle	breast
	4	breast	bottle	bottle	bottle	bottle

OVER A 2 WEEK PERIOD (4 FEEDS)					
		Feed 1	Feed 2	Feed 3	Feed 4
DAYS	1	breast	bottle	breast	breast
	6	breast	bottle	bottle	breast
	10	breast	bottle	bottle	bottle
	14	bottle	bottle	bottle	bottle

ABRUPT WEANING

The abrupt weaning approach means making a decision to wean at a certain feed and then no longer offering the breast again. Your baby goes from being fully breastfed to being fully weaned. If possible this abrupt method should be avoided. There are very few reasons for abrupt weaning. The main one is if you or your baby require medical treatment that is not compatible with breastfeeding. In some situations with breast refusal, it is the baby who decides they will no longer go to the breast. However, you usually get some warning that they are no longer willing to breastfeed by their feeding behaviour and preferences.

If you are abruptly weaning, you will need to take special care of your breasts as they may become engorged, lumpy or uncomfortable. For the first five to 10 days you may need to intermittently massage and express your breasts, but only enough to make your breasts feel comfortable and drain lumpy areas. Removal of small amounts of milk for comfort only will not prolong lactation. If any lump remains persistent or painful, contact your child and family health nurse, lactation consultant or doctor for assistance. Any breastmilk you express can be stored in the refrigerator and offered to your baby.

CARING FOR YOUR BABY AND YOURSELF

Weaning can be an emotionally challenging time, so be kind to yourself and your baby. If at all possible, introduce the weaning process slowly. This is especially important if your baby has never taken either breastmilk or infant formula from a bottle or cup, as they will need time to adopt these new feeding skills.

If you know ahead that you will need to partially or fully wean due to returning to the paid workforce, or because you are going to be separated for a short period of time for a medical procedure, or other reasons, it may be useful to start offering regular feeds from a bottle or cup. Try to do this at least a few weeks prior to the first period of separation. This will allow enough time to help your baby to accept breastmilk or infant formula from a teat and bottle or via a cup.

When weaning keep in mind:
- How your baby might be experiencing this new way of feeding.
- What feelings your baby may be having.
- How you can minimise any distress that you or your baby might be experiencing with this changed feeding experience.

Sometimes babies will be confused or upset because of this necessary change and will totally refuse the offered bottle, even if it contains breastmilk (see Chapter 12 for strategies to assist).

Having a support person available during the weaning period can provide you with the emotional and practical support that may be required. Your baby may cry more than usual, requiring you to be even more attentive than usual. If your baby is refusing the bottle, it may be helpful to get your partner or support person to feed your baby for a few feeds. Monitor the number of wet nappies your baby is having as this is a good measure of hydration. If you become concerned about your baby's refusal to feed via a bottle or cup, contact your child and family health nurse or doctor.

TRANSITION FROM BREASTMILK TO INFANT FORMULA

The decision about what type of milk you will provide for your baby will be dependent on their age. Babies under the age of 12 months cannot tolerate full strength cow's milk to drink as it places too much stress on their kidneys. Small amounts of cow's milk are tolerated in the preparation of their solid food after six months of age (see Chapter 14). So if your baby is under 12 months of age they should be offered an infant formula (Chapter 12).

USING A CUP

Whether you bypass the bottle and wean your baby onto a cup will depend on your baby's age, developmental ability and your preference. For example, if your baby is at least 6–7 months or older, weaning onto a cup may be a practical option and can save on the purchase of teats and bottles. Ideally you will offer three to four cups of 100–150 mL of milk each day to meet the energy, nutrition and fluid needs of your baby.

Milk intake becomes less important after solid foods have commenced as the energy and nutrition in milk can be supplemented through feeding your baby with rice cereal made with milk, yoghurt, cheese and other high calcium products. After six months of age small amounts of cooled boiled water can also be offered via a cup.

If going straight onto a cup, do not forget to give extra cuddles that may be missed if you had been breastfeeding or bottlefeeding. Do this by having a special time, before or after the feed, to cuddle and gently talk to your baby.

In an emergency, if you don't have a bottle that has been effectively cleaned and sterilised or feeding cup, you can use an egg cup, especially one with a thicker rim, as it is easier for your baby to grasp with their lips than a regular cup or plastic mug. An egg cup also contains a smaller amount of milk and can be easier for your baby to manage while getting used to this new way of drinking. Expect some spills to start with, so be prepared with a protective bib or hand towel.

WEANING AND CONTRACEPTION

Some mothers very quickly start to ovulate (produce an ovum) when they reduce the number of breastfeeds given. With an increase in fertility the progesterone-only (mini pill) may no longer be an adequate form of contraception. You may need to change to a combined pill (contains both oestrogen and progesterone), or explore with your doctor or family planning service other contraceptive options prior to starting the weaning process.

CHAPTER SUMMARY

- Weaning is an inevitable event for all mothers and babies.
- Weaning can be either baby-led or mother-led or mutual.
- Weaning can occur either abruptly or gradually. Gradual is usually the preferred choice for baby and mother.
- Weaning is rarely the answer to managing an unsettled baby.
- If possible give yourself and your baby lots of time to wean.

AT AROUND SIX MONTHS OF AGE, your baby will become increasingly curious about food and will be ready to experience a variety of different foods to complement their milk intake. By seven months of age, your baby should definitely have started to take food other than breastmilk or infant formula.

How will you know your baby is ready for solid food? By six months you may notice some of the following behaviours:

- Your baby has the ability to sit up straight – this requires good head, neck and shoulder control.

- Shows interest in food – this includes the food on your plate.
- There is an increase in appetite; your baby is demanding more frequent breastfeeds or bottle feeds.
- There is an increase in hand-to-mouth behavior – this includes putting toys in their mouth.
- Your baby opens their mouth in anticipation when you offer food on a spoon.

Don't be surprised if your baby changes their behaviour once they start to eat solid foods. You might find they sleep for longer at certain times of the day or night. They might become less interested in drinking breast or formula milk. Their bowel motions will change in frequency, texture, colour and smell. Some days your baby will be interested in eating and other days they may refuse. Going slowly and following your baby's lead is the best way to progress. Never force them to eat.

WHEN TO START INTRODUCING SOLID FOODS

The starting time of around six months of age to introduce solids has been identified because:
- A baby's appetite and nutritional needs are not fully satisfied by breastmilk or infant formula and they need additional types of food.
- In exclusively breastfed babies, their zinc and iron stores are starting to deplete and this becomes a health concern after six months.
- Your baby's tongue thrust reflex (when anything is placed on their tongue it pushes out) has disappeared (this may go from around four months), and their ability to sit without support has improved. They can now manage food that is a much thicker texture than milk.
- By seven to eight months they are able to chew.
- Due to their maturing digestive system, your baby can now digest starches.
- Your baby is interested in their environment and they are much more willing to accept new textures and flavours.

NHMRC 2012, *Infant feeding guidelines: information for health workers*, Australian Government, Canberra.

Introducing foods other than breastmilk or infant formula too early (before six months) increases the risk of allergies and diarrhoeal disease, as their digestive tract and immune system are still immature.

There are a number of good reasons why your baby should be offered a variety of solid foods from around six months of age:

- Babies need a variety of nutrients from a range of foods for the growth spurts that will occur in their first 12 months.
- Healthy foods support immunity against infection.
- To increase their zinc and iron levels, which are so important for heart and brain health.
- To encourage baby to learn how to chew food properly – this is another important step in their development, and the muscles used to chew are also important for the development of speech.

HOW TO INTRODUCE YOUR BABY TO SOLIDS

Introducing your baby to solid food can be great fun as you watch their reaction to this new experience, especially the strange faces they pull when they try a new texture or unfamiliar flavour. It is a great time for interaction as you help your baby learn new skills. By six months of age, the tongue thrust reflex babies have to protect themselves has disappeared (this goes at around four months of age). At first, some babies might spit out the food you place in their mouth. Remember this is a totally new experience for them, which will require very different movements of their tongue and jaw.

When you first start to offer solid food to your baby, their milk (either breast or infant formula) remains the most important part of their diet. Use a clean small unbreakable bowl and a small plastic or silicon baby spoon when offering the food to your baby, and allow them to suck the food off the spoon.

- Start with small amounts (one tablespoon) of one food (four teaspoons = one tablespoon).
- Increase each day until your baby is taking two tablespoons.
- When taking two tablespoons, you can start offering your baby two meals twice a day.

FOOD TEXTURE

Start by offering a smooth puree consistency, introducing one food at a time, until they are eating a variety of foods from all the food groups. As your baby masters the pureed foods, gradually increase the texture and consistency from fine to coarse, mashed, then minced, and then chopped by 12 months. This increase in texture and consistency may take many months to move through the stages.

By eight months, eye-hand coordination is well developed and most babies can manage and enjoy finger foods. At this stage, they will enjoy having food from your plate.

Puree	Mashed and minced	Chopped
6 months	8 months	12 months

> **NOTE:** Never force your baby to take food. Offering solid food is about educating your baby and helping them develop the necessary chewing and swallowing skills.

FOODS TO OFFER

Even though you may think your baby's diet tastes bland and boring, avoid adding sugar, salt or strong seasoning agents. Babies have delicate palates, but can quickly learn to enjoy the family's normal cultural diet and a healthy mix of family foods without the need for extra sugar or salt.

When deciding on the food to feed your baby, you are sure to be offered lots of advice from family and friends. Often the food you offer your baby will be dependent on your cultural background. Babies in China are often started on congee. Congee is plain rice that is cooked for a long time until it becomes porridge like. It is a popular food for many in China where they add vegetables, tofu, chicken or pork. In South America, maize-based porridge is a common first food.

In Australia, it is now recommended to start offering iron-rich family foods from six months including meat, fish and chicken. By using breastmilk or infant formula on your baby's first food, the taste difference will be reduced and this may help your baby to accept the solid food being introduced.

SOURCES OF IRON-RICH FOODS

Babies need iron rich and nutrient dense foods – in other words, a balanced diet. This is a wonderful opportunity to check your own diet to ensure the whole family is eating a very healthy diet. Very quickly your baby will be demanding and eating the same food you are eating.

Good	Medium	Low	Very little
Chicken Fish (fresh & canned) Lamb Beef Pork Liver/kidneys	Beans (e.g. kidney & soy) Legumes (e.g. lentils) Cereals with added iron Tofu	Rice Pasta Dried fruits Green vegetables Bread	Milk/dairy foods Eggs Other vegetables Other fruits

Over the past decade the sequence, variety and type of foods to introduce babies to solid food have significantly changed, becoming far more flexible. This reflects a greater understanding of cultural variations when introducing infants to solid foods and the later age at which infants are now introduced to them.

AT SIX MONTHS

Foods can be introduced in any order provided they have an appropriate consistency for your baby's developmental age and some foods need to be iron-rich (e.g. rice cereal that has been iron fortified). Solids may include rice cereal, pureed meat, poultry, fish and liver, or cooked tofu and legumes. Vegetables, fruits, and dairy products such as full-fat yoghurt, cheese and custard can then be added. The following table is only an example of the sequence and amounts to give. You can introduce other food, increase the rate of new food introduction and vary the amount depending on your baby's hunger level and ability to tolerate the new foods. Offer your baby their breastfeed or infant formula before solids so that they continue to receive adequate milk until their intake of solid foods is well established.

You will get to a stage when you stop measuring and provide your baby with a varied and changing diet that reflects the family diet. This will reduce the time you spend in the kitchen.

If your baby is in childcare talk to the centre staff to ensure your baby is offered appropriate and safe foods as they learn to tolerate solid foods.

FROM EIGHT MONTHS

From about eight months of age your baby will start to chew on their gums. When this starts to occur it is a sign that they are ready to try more coarsely mashed or minced foods. By eight months they will want to help feed themselves; so giving your baby a spoon can encourage eating skills and independence at feedtimes. The amount of food you offer your baby will depend on their appetite.

Increase the variety of cooked or raw vegetables (e.g. carrot, potato, tomato), fruit (e.g. apple, banana, melon), whole egg, cereals (e.g. wheat, oats), bread, pasta, dairy foods such as full-fat cheese, custards and yoghurt.

This is a good time to introduce finger foods such as toast fingers, sugarless rusks, cooked vegetables (e.g. beans and carrot) sticks or tomato slices.

If your baby is in childcare make sure they are receiving an adequate diet that contains iron-rich foods.

AT 12 MONTHS

Around 12 months of age, your baby will be ready to eat most things the family is eating. They will actively reach for food. Foods can now be chopped up. Full-fat cow's milk and water can become the main drinks. Milk should be limited to no more than 600 mL per day. If your baby is still breastfeeding or taking lots of milk-based foods then offer less cow's milk. Some babies will reduce their milk intake well below 600 mL per day. Remember, they will gain additional fluid from the food you offer (e.g. fruit and vegetables often have a high water content) and calcium from dairy products such as yoghurt and cheese.

If they are attending childcare they will now be eating the food the centre offers to toddlers.

Age	Suggested progression
6 months	• Start with one meal per day. • Gradually increase the amount and variety of foods. Start with one teaspoon of pureed food and each day gradually increase. At first the puree will be reasonably fluid, as they learn to eat increase the thickness of the puree. Introduce only one type of new food at a time. • Some babies are happy on one meal a day while others will show obvious hunger and quickly demand two meals per day. • Remember to offer a breastfeed or infant formula before solid food.
7 months	• By this time your baby will be on at least two meals a day while some may be demanding three meals. • Continue to increase the amount and variety of foods. Allow your baby's behaviour during meal times to guide how much you offer them to eat. • The texture of the pureed food offered can now be thicker. • Continue to offer a breastfeed or infant formula before solid foods.

8 months	• Three meals a day will be eaten by your baby. • Continue to increase the amount and variety of foods guided by your baby's behaviours and feeding cues. • Mashed and minced food will now be enjoyed. • Continue to offer a breastfeed or infant formula before solid foods. • Your baby will enjoy having their own spoon to help at meal times.
9 months	• Three meals will be enjoyed by your baby especially if they eat with the rest of the family. • Now is the time to introduce a healthy snack either in the morning or afternoon. • Continue to increase the amount and variety of foods. • Your baby will have started to develop their pincer grasp (thumb and finger used to pick up objects) and enjoy finger foods and helping to feed themselves. • Remember to always closely supervise while eating. • Allow your baby's behaviour to guide whether you offer a breastfeed or infant formula before or after their solid food.
12 months	• Three meals that are the same as the rest of the family meal. • Food is cut up in baby bite size or mashed with a fork, with lots of finger food. • Two healthy snacks per day will be enjoyed especially if they can feed themselves. • Remember to always closely supervise while eating and have your baby sitting securely in their high chair or on your lap. • Allow your baby's behaviour to guide whether you offer a breastfeed or infant formula before or after their solid food.

KEEPING BABY SAFE

Choking is always a concern for parents when their baby starts eating chopped or finger foods. Great care needs to be taken when offering some foods, especially those with bones or raw crunchy fruits and vegetables. When buying fish, choose fillets that do not have bones. Even if they are advertised as not having bones, it is important that you check the fish for bones. Babies love to suck on chop bones. Make sure there are no sharp edges that might cut your baby's mouth, or pieces of bone that will fall off and cause a choking hazard.

It is impossible to completely remove the danger of choking simply by excluding certain foods, however some simple safety tips can lower the risk:

- Your baby should always be seated when eating, e.g. high chair or a baby chair. Make sure you use the safety harness.
- Don't give finger food if your baby is laughing, crying or otherwise upset.
- Never force your baby to eat.
- Act as a role model – encourage your baby to chew well and not to overfill their mouth.

MOST IMPORTANTLY you or another adult should always be present and actively supervising when your baby is eating.

FOOD SAFETY

When preparing foods, care must be taken to ensure your baby and family are protected from infections such as gastroenteritis.

- Wash your hands before you begin to prepare food.
- Wash your hands after you have prepared the food.
- Wash cutting boards, utensils and dishes between different foods
- Use different boards for produce such as raw meats, poultry, fruits and vegetables.
- Different coloured boards are ideal for this purpose.
- When tasting your cooking, do not reuse the spoon.
- When preparing or testing your baby's food use a different spoon from the one you use for your baby.
- Keep food equipment and preparation areas clean.
- Cooking and dining equipment (except bottles) do not need to be sterilised. It is fine if they are washed in hot soapy water and scalded with boiling water prior to use or washed in the dishwasher.
- Wash all fruit and vegetables thoroughly; this will remove pesticides and dirt.
- Do not keep food warm for extended periods. It should be cooked, served and eaten without a delay.
- Discard food your baby has left on their plate. A small amount of their saliva can result in left over food becoming contaminated.
- Fish needs to be double checked for bones – use clean fingers.
- Fruit must have any seeds removed before offering to your baby
- Always check the temperature of your baby's food before offering to ensure it will not burn their mouth or lips.
- If using a microwave oven to cook food, check the middle as well as the outside edges of the food. The outside may be cool but the middle may be extremely hot.
- Avoid using flysprays or other pesticides in or near the food preparation area. Cover food if you do need to use a pesticide in your kitchen.

Some foods do not freeze well, e.g. potato. To overcome this problem, mix foods such as potato with other vegetables. When they are thawed the food may be watery. Mix with a little rice cereal or cottage cheese to thicken. Consider using ice-cube trays to freeze baby food especially in the early months when baby is only eating small portions.

When freezing foods they should:
- Be stored at a temperature of minus 15°C (0°F). Check your freezer to ensure it is able to maintain this temperature.
- Always label food to be frozen with contents and date
- Do not store longer than 2–3 months.
- Once the food has been thawed never refreeze it.

When thawing foods, place:
- In the fridge if you are not in a hurry.
- On a plate over a bowl of hot water for a short period of time only. Make sure it is covered.
- In a microwave on the defrost setting.

Heat foods just before you are serving. Keeping food warm for extended periods is a potential risk of bacterial contamination.

If you need to transport your baby's food, leave frozen or unheated in an insulated freezer bag with a cooler brick.

Learning about food product labelling can help you avoid giving your baby foods high in artificial colours and flavour enhancers, trans fatty acids, saturated fat, sodium (salt) or sugar.

It is also important to store foods as recommended on the packaging. Check use by dates on the packaging.

VEGETABLES

To get the most nutritional value from vegetables:
- Peel just before you cook.
- Don't leave vegetables to soak – water-soluble vitamins can leach out into the water.
- Microwave or steam vegetables – cook till soft enough to mash, chop or puree.
- Avoid overcooking.

- Cook extra vegetables when preparing the family meal. Store immediately in the fridge for the next day or freeze in small portions for later use.

Foods to be cautious with until your baby is older:
- Never give raw eggs and poultry that have not been cooked properly, as these may contain salmonella bacteria.
- Honey, as it can be contaminated with botulism spores, and cause your infant to become very unwell. Tresillian advises not to offer honey until your baby is over 12 months of age.
- Nuts, as they pose a choking hazard. If whole or in small pieces they can be inhaled. Whole nuts are not recommended for children under five years of age. Nut pastes may be offered but observe for possible food reactions.
- Fatty foods, such as the skin of chicken, fried meats, battered fish and chips, and many take-away foods. These foods frequently have a high saturated fat and salt content.
- Fruit juice is not necessary or recommended for children under 12 months as it can contain excessive kilojoules (calories) and displaces food intake.
- Do not offer your baby tea, herbal teas, coffee or sugar-sweetened drinks (soft drinks, cordials).

WATER AND OTHER DRINKS

After six months of age your baby can be offered drinks other than breastmilk or infant formula. Of course, cooled boiled water is the additional drink of preference. Boiled tap water contains fluoride that is essential for your baby's future dental health. Your baby's teeth can gain benefit from the fluoride in the extra water you provide your baby. The best way to encourage a baby to drink water is to see their parents drinking water.

Fruit juice, either commercial or freshly squeezed, is not recommended until your baby is over 12 months of age. The juice can cause loose bowel motions and reddening and burning of their bottom due to the acid and high vitamin C content.

OFFERING ADDITIONAL DRINKS USING A CUP

Using a cup for fluids works well for most babies. There are real risks using a bottle for long periods of time. The use of a bottle, especially if offering juice, milk or fluids other than water is risky as they contain natural sugars or in some cases added sweeteners. Over the longer term these can cause tooth decay. This is much less likely if a cup is used. Bottles can also be an issue if your baby is going to go to a childcare centre where they discourage children from having a bottle.

COMMERCIAL BABY FOODS

While fresh home-prepared baby food is by far the best for your baby, it is not always convenient to prepare or available. Commercial baby food can be a useful stop-gap for busy parents when out visiting or travelling.

Commercial baby foods have the advantage of being consistent in taste and texture and there are now many varieties available in all kinds of packaging. When buying any baby food, always check the expiry date on the packaging and the condition of the package, pouch or jar to make sure they are in good condition. If frozen, return to the freezer as quickly as possible so they don't start to thaw.

If you're really time poor, consider investigating the many online providers of freshly-prepared baby food.

While commercial foods do have a lot of advantages, they also have some disadvantages. Their flavours are often blended together, giving them a different taste and look (bland) to their fresh equivalents. They can also be quite expensive.

Between six and 12 months, your baby should progress from eating plain foods to eating a mashed up version of the meal that the rest of the family is eating.

VEGETARIAN BABY DIETS

Vegetarian diets are a healthy alternative and babies quite enjoy vegetables. However, it's important that your baby is provided with sufficient iron, protein, vitamin B12 and calcium. At Tresillian, we suggest parents who want their baby to have a vegetarian diet consult a dietician. This will ensure the food offered to your baby will meet their nutritional requirements.

Lacto-ovo vegetarians – Obtain protein from dairy products, eggs, beans, legumes, pulses and nuts. They exclude red meat, offal, fish and poultry from their diet

Lacto-vegetarians – Obtain protein from dairy products, beans, legumes, pulses and nuts. They exclude red meat, offal, fish, poultry and eggs

Vegans – Obtain protein from beans, legumes, pulses, nuts and soy products like tofu. They exclude red meat, offal, poultry, fish, eggs and dairy products. Babies on a vegan diet must have vitamin B12 added to their diet as they are not having any animal products or B12 via infant formula.

MANAGING THE MESS

Learning to eat can be a messy process, especially if you have a baby who loves to learn through exploring. Very quickly your baby will want to help put the food into their mouth. They will often grab onto the spoon. The easy way to manage this is to give your baby a spoon to help, even though they will not be competent using the spoon until they are about 18 months old.

Other things to support your baby's attempts to learn to feed independently include:

- When your baby is able to sit up, place them in a well supported and stable feeding chair with an attached tray – make sure you use the five-point safety harness (see chapter 3).
- A large sheet of plastic, shower curtain or newspaper under the chair that will catch the dropped food.
- A bib to protect clothing from the food.
- A damp washer to clean hands and face.
- Wearing an apron can also help you remain splatter free.

MY BABY IS REFUSING SOLID FOODS

Not all babies are ready to start eating solid foods when books (such as ours) advise! Remember, the food offered during the first couple of months is about helping your baby learn about new tastes, textures and smells. The important thing is not to force your baby to eat. Feeding times should be relaxed and enjoyable for both you and your baby.

Things to try to encourage eating:

- Reduce distractions, e.g. turn off the television, mobile phone and laptop, and ask others in the room to try and be quiet.
- Try offering the food before giving a milk feed.
- Use a shallow spoon so your baby can easily suck the food off the spoon to start with.
- Position your baby so they can see your face; make sure your smile is encouraging. Avoid pulling a face if you don't enjoy or like a specific food.
- Offer food when your baby is calm and alert and showing obvious signs of hunger.
- Give your baby a spoon to help them feel part of the experience.
- Give small breaks when your baby is showing disengagement cues (see Chapter 5).
- Talk to your baby in a calm and descriptive way with lots of encouraging words and praise.

If possible, try and feed your baby with the rest of the family from as early as possible. They will soon learn that meal times are not just about food, but also about social interaction. Importantly your baby will learn by observation and while there might be some messy moments, try and remain patient and calm.

ALLERGIES AND INTOLERANCES

Some babies may have an **allergy** to certain foods. An allergy to a food is defined as your immune system reacting to a food substance, as if that substance is toxic. Research has shown there is minimal evidence to support the delayed introduction of solid food beyond six months of age. If foods are restricted because you are concerned about the risk of your baby developing an allergy, discuss this with your baby's doctor and a dietician. Restricting the type of food offered to your baby can result in a dietary deficiency.

The common food allergies for babies tend to be:

- Cow's milk (a good reason to avoid early introduction to cow's milk as their main source of nutrition)
- Eggs
- Soybeans
- Peanuts
- Tree nuts (cashews, almonds, brazil nuts)
- Wheat
- Fish and shellfish.

To try and protect your body, the immune system releases chemicals (such as histamines) into the body's tissues. The effect on the body can be quite major, even with tiny amounts of food. A reaction can be unsettled behaviour or a mild skin rash or respiratory distress. The onset of a reaction can be immediate to a few hours later. In some circumstances it can be delayed for up to two days after exposure to the allergen. If your baby has a moderate to severe reaction ring 000 for an ambulance immediately as some allergic reactions can be life-threatening. These reactions may include:

- Breathing problems, wheezing
- Swelling of lips or throat
- Diarrhoea or vomiting
- Severe red rash
- Pain.

Most children grow out of their food allergies (especially egg and cow's milk) and very few babies, in fact, experience food allergies.

Some babies have a **food intolerance**. A food intolerance is different to a food allergy, as it is generally a less severe reaction and is not caused by the immune system reacting to the food. Common food intolerances include:

- Dairy products
- Lactose

- Strawberries
- Citrus fruits
- Tomatoes.

Intolerances can still cause a lot of discomfort, however, there are generally fewer symptoms with intolerances than with allergies. Most common symptoms are:
- Constipation
- Diarrhoea
- Skin redness
- Dermatitis.

USE OF COW'S MILK (FULL CREAM COW'S MILK)

Cow's milk is not suitable for babies under the age of 12 months due to its high electrolyte and protein concentration. Babies' immature kidneys can have significant problems and risk damage when cow's milk is a regular source of their fluid intake. It is strongly recommended that babies under 12 months of age are either breastfed or fed infant formula.

Although cow's milk is not advised as a main drink for babies, small quantities in the preparation of their solid foods is safe. For example, use in custards and mashed potato, and on cereal. Do not use low fat milk with children under two years of age or skim milk under the age of five years.

KITCHEN SAFETY

Kitchens are dangerous places for babies especially if you are busy cooking.
- Keep your baby outside the kitchen when cooking. There are many dangers when you are busy and distracted.
- Place a safety gate near the entrance to your kitchen. It will allow your growing baby to see you while you work.

- Get into the habit of turning saucepan handles inwards. If you get into this habit now, it will be well entrenched by the time your baby is walking.
- Curly or shortened cords will help keep them out of reach.
- If you get called away from the kitchen, turn off pots that are boiling or have oil in them and take your baby with you.
- Baby's feeding equipment should be unbreakable, smooth and easy to clean.
- Avoid using tablecloths as they make it very easy for your baby to reach out and pull the table contents down onto them. It also saves a very big mess.
- To avoid slipping or falling, wipe up spills as they happen.
- Do not carry your baby in a pouch when cooking as it places them at significant danger of splash injuries from hot oil or other fluids.

CHAPTER SUMMARY

- The recommended time to introduce your baby to solid foods is six months. Start with iron rich foods.
- Breastfeed or offer their infant formula *before* their solid foods.
- During the first few weeks introduce new foods slowly but once your baby is used to the new tastes and textures you can be more adventurous.
- Be prepared for a mess; babies like to feel and experiment with their food. This is all part of providing an important learning experience.
- By 12 months of age your baby should be eating most foods that you or your family are eating.
- Babies very quickly like to help feed themselves, so give them a spoon.
- Remember, meal times are a social time and it should be enjoyable.

Part Four

BABY'S HEALTH AND SAFETY

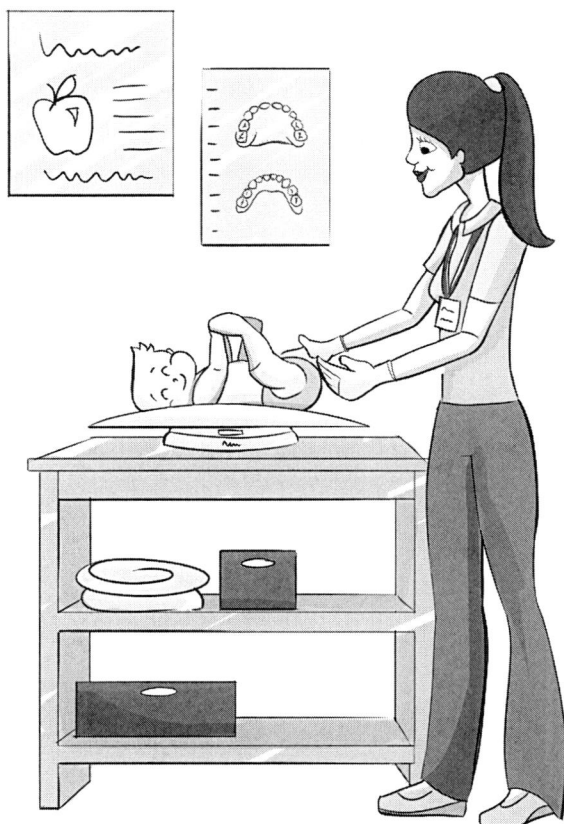

Chapter Fifteen
CHILD HEALTH

KEEPING YOUR BABY HEALTHY is one of the most important parenting tasks. Your baby's immune system is still immature at birth, placing them at risk of developing lots of minor illnesses. They are also very vulnerable to more serious infections.

Parents can do many positive things to reduce the risk to their baby's health and development. You can:

- Provide age appropriate nutritious foods, and if possible, breastfeed until your baby is six months old or longer.

- Give your baby lots of activities that encourage their physical, social and emotional development.
- Check that your home environment is clean, but not so clean that it reduces the baby's exposure to normal household bacteria. This is necessary to stimulate their immune system.
- Ensure your baby has regular health checks that include a developmental check.
- Make sure that your baby's, your own and other family members' immunisations are up-to-date.
- Maintain safe and hygienic food handling and storage practices and precautions.
- Practise regular hand washing. It is one of the most effective illness prevention strategies you can use.

Parents are usually the best judges of their baby's health. If you are concerned that your baby is unwell or there is a problem with their development keep asking questions. As you have 24-hour contact with your baby, you can often detect subtle changes that health professionals find hard to detect.

Regular visits to your child and family health nurse and doctor are essential. If they are familiar with you and your baby, it becomes much easier to pick up any health and developmental problems your baby may have. There are many common childhood problems that your baby may experience. If identified early and treated, they are usually easily resolved.

AUSTRALIAN CHILD AND FAMILY HEALTH SERVICE

Australia has a unique, free universal child and family health service. There are slight differences in each state, but the focus of every state service is to ensure your baby remains healthy and developing at a normal or better than normal rate. The service is also interested in the mental health of parents as we know your physical and mental health can have a significant impact on your baby's health and development (see Chapter 2).

The child and family health nurses are registered nurses with, as a minimum, an additional qualification in child and family health nursing. Many of these nurses also have qualifications in midwifery, infant mental health, adult mental health or paediatric nursing. In some states they are called maternal child health nurses or child health nurses.

In most states, the child and family health nurse provides a home visit as their first contact with you. If needed, they may be able to continue visiting at home at times when you are unable to come to the health centre or require additional support. This is an excellent free service for families particularly in the early months.

The child and family health nurse can:

- Provide you with support and guidance to help you develop a strong and enduring relationship with your infant.
- Give baby regular developmental checks, including monitoring your baby's growth, checking eyesight and hearing (up to 6 years of age).
- Advise you on breastfeeding, including when breastfeeding problems occur.
- Support you to learn about bottle feeding your baby (if necessary).
- Guide and inform you when you are ready to wean your baby.
- Advise on the transition of your baby to solid foods.
- Help you learn about the physical care your baby requires, especially if you are feeling unsure about what your baby needs and what parenting skills you should adopt.
- Help you understand your baby's sleep patterns and the best and safest ways to settle baby.
- Assist you in identifying and managing common health problems that are causing you concern, but don't need to be seen by a doctor – e.g. cradle cap, nappy rash, oral thrush.
- Discuss concerns you may have about your own emotional health – e.g. postnatal depression and anxiety.
- Provide referrals to other health professionals or organisations such as Tresillian Family Care Centres (if necessary).
- Facilitate parent education groups such as 'New Parents' groups.

The child and family nurse will encourage you to participate in a *psychosocial* assessment to see if you need additional support. This will include a series of questions about your social and emotional state. You will also be asked to complete the Edinburgh Depression Scale questionnaire. Once the nurse has finished gathering this information, she will discuss it with you and, if necessary, will work out a course of action with you.

The personal health record book you were given at the birth of your baby is used to record your baby's health and developmental progress. The colour of the book cover will vary from state to state. For example, in NSW and Tasmania it has a blue cover and is often referred to as the 'blue book'. It is important to have this book with you when you take your baby to see your child and family health nurse or doctor. They will record information about your baby that includes: weight, head circumference and length, outcome of developmental checks, and information about their health status. The book also contains lots of useful information that will help you care for your baby.

Having a doctor who knows your family and your baby is also extremely important. If possible, see the same doctor at each visit. If your baby becomes unwell, it is much easier for the doctor to make a diagnosis if they have examined your baby previously and know your family's health history.

Regardless of the health professional you choose to help guide you through the early years of your baby's life, they must have a good working knowledge of child development and be used to seeing lots of babies and young children on a daily basis. You are relying on them to provide a safety net for you and your baby. Ideally, they should have specialist qualifications in child and family health or paediatrics.

SCREENING

Regular developmental screening is a good way to check that your baby is developing within or above the expected developmental norm. Should there be a problem, it's much better if it's picked up early and the appropriate treatment begun. This is known as early intervention. Some screening tests will commence at birth, while others will be conducted on a regular basis through your baby's first year of life and periodically each year as they grow and develop.

Mistakes can be made or problems missed as the problem may not have been obvious or present at the time of the testing. If your baby is upset, hungry or very tired during a screening test, this may influence the result. If a screening test is postponed because your baby is upset, make sure you reschedule the test. Ask your doctor or child and family nurse for advice if you have any concerns about your baby's developmental health.

APGAR

The *Apgar* is a scoring system developed to assess the health of a newborn baby, and is the very first screening your baby will undergo from birth. It helps the midwives and doctors assess vital signs and to make a decision about when medical intervention or help is needed. The Apgar score is based on five simple criteria; Appearance, Pulse, Grimace, Activity and Respiration and ranges from zero to 10. It is completed three times: at birth, then one minute, and at five minutes after birth. Heart rate, breathing, muscle tone, reflex irritability, and skin colour are assessed each time. Each category is given a score from 0 to 2, with a total possible score of 10.

If your baby is given a score of 0 to 3, resuscitation is commenced immediately. If your baby has needed resuscitation and their five-minute Apgar score is less than 7, the score is repeated at five-minute intervals until your baby is 20 minutes old.

Score	0	1	2
Heart rate	Absent (no pulse)	Below 100 beats per minute	Normal (above 100 beats per minute)
Breathing	Absent (no breathing)	Slow or irregular breathing, weak cry	Normal rate and effort, good cry
Muscle tone	No movement, floppy tone (limp)	Arms and legs flexed with little movement	Active spontaneous movement
Reflex irritability	Absent (no response to stimulation)	Facial movement only (grimace) with stimulation	Pulls away, sneezes, coughs or cries with stimulation
Skin colour	Bluish-grey or pale all over	Normal colour (but hands and feet are bluish)	Normal colour all over (hands and feet are pink)

Many healthy newborns do not get a score of 10 because their body is not completely pink. How immature your baby is will impact on the score, e.g. premature babies are likely to have a lower score.

GUTHRIE (HEEL PRICK) TEST

The Guthrie is a voluntary test done 48 to 72 hours after birth. A few drops of blood are collected on a piece of special filter paper from a prick to your baby's heel. You might like to breastfeed your baby while they have their heel pricked. Research shows that they will experience less pain if they have a slightly sweet solution just before a medical intervention that may cause them some pain or discomfort.

The Guthrie test is used to detect some rare genetic disorders. These include:
- Cystic fibrosis
- Phenylketonuria (PKU)
- Primary congenital hypothyroidism.

You will be contacted if there are concerns about the test results. Commencing early treatment for these conditions and others is very important as it can make a huge difference to the health and development outcomes for your baby. If you are discharged from hospital before your baby has this test, talk to your doctor about having it done. Not all genetic disorders are tested for on the Guthrie. If you have a family history of a genetic illness, please tell your doctor as they may be able to have it included in the range of disorders tested.

HEARING TEST

The ability to hear is key to ensuring language development occurs within or above the norm. In most states hearing is tested at birth. If this does not occur arrange a hearing test for your baby. Hearing will also be tested at other times during your baby's early years of life, as hearing ability can deteriorate over time.

Your child and family health nurse or doctor will regularly ask you about your baby's ability to hear. The questions asked will depend on their age and are from the personal health record book. These will include:

- Do you have any concerns about your baby's hearing?
- Does your baby turn their eyes/head toward sounds or voices?
- Does your baby hear you and listen to your voice?
- Has your baby started to make noises to indicate pleasure or displeasure?
- Does your baby babble, e.g. 'mama, dada, baba'?
- Does your baby vocalise and change the pitch of their voice to get your attention?
- Does your baby respond to their own name and 'no'?
- Does your baby respond to music and singing?
- Does your baby have a constant cold or green runny nose?
- Has your baby had an ear infection or discharge from their ear?

As with all health problems, the earlier recognition and intervention occurs, the greater the likelihood of a positive or improved outcome for your baby.

VISION

Vision is another important sensory skill and is regularly tested during the first year. Your baby's vision will naturally change over time (see Chapter 7 for vision development). You can expect your child and family health nurse or doctor to ask you these questions from the personal health record book about your baby's vision:
- Do you have any concerns about your baby's vision?
- Does your baby move both eyes together?
- Does your baby look at you and follow you with their eyes?
- Does your baby have a lazy or turned eye (strabismus or squint)?
- Does your baby look at their hands and other objects?
- Have you noticed one or both of your baby's pupils are white?
- Do any members of your family have vision problems?

HEART

Your doctor will check the condition of your baby's heart. They will check their colour and breathing, feel their pulse and finally listen to their heart. Sometimes heart conditions are not picked up at birth, so it is important to check when visiting your doctor.

HIPS

Some babies are born with developmental dysplasia (dislocated hips). If this condition is not treated they will have difficulty standing and walking. There are two types of hip dysplasia: the first is congenital hip dysplasia which is a genetic condition and often passed down in families; the second and more common reason for hip dysplasia can be the result of such occurrences as a breech birth or multiple pregnancy. In both cases the structures that support the hips might be loose and the hip joint socket shallow. Your child and family health nurse will do a simple test to check if the hips dislocate on movement. Early detection and treatment is important as it can reduce the interventions needed to correct the condition.

When swaddling your baby, avoid wrapping them in a manner that restricts the movement of their hips and legs. Make sure when you wrap, their legs are not held in a straight position (see Chapter 5).

WEIGHT, LENGTH AND HEAD CIRCUMFERENCE

Regular monitoring of your baby's physical growth will provide a record of the amazing level of physical growth that occurs during the first year of life. Weight is the most commonly used measure of growth and health. However, avoid being too focused on the weight of your baby. Weight is only one measure of health.

Weight, length and head circumference are three important areas of physical growth. Growth refers to an increase in size. At birth, the head is approximately one-quarter of the baby's total body length, while the legs only take-up one-third of the total body length. By approximately five months most babies have doubled their birth weight. By 12 months their length is more than 50% greater than at birth. By two years, a baby's head accounts for one-fifth and their legs for nearly half of the total body length.

During the first two years a baby's head circumference will increase rapidly. This is due to the rapid growth in brain size during this period. A baby's skull is structured to allow this growth. At birth, the bones of the skull are separated by six sutures or gaps, and form two *fontanelles* or 'soft spots'. The anterior fontanelle is on the top of the baby's head and easily felt. It closes over by a baby's second year of life. The second smaller posterior fontanelle is at the back of the head and it closes more quickly. The sutures and fontanelles enable the bones of the skull to overlap during the birth process. At first your baby's head might appear misshapen; this usually improves within a few weeks.

Your child and family health nurse or doctor will monitor weight, length and head circumference changes on a regular basis, and record these in your baby's personal health record on the supplied growth chart. Weight, length and head circumference are plotted on a graph in order to determine your baby's growth curve from one visit to the next. The growth chart has curved lines drawn on them that indicate a normal growth range – these are called *percentiles bands*.

These percentile bands range from the 3rd to 97th percentile. This means that a baby whose weight is on the 50th percentile is heavier than a baby on the 3rd percentile. Or a baby whose length is on the 97th percentile is longer than a baby on the 3rd percentile.

Be aware that growth charts are only a guide for parents and health professionals.

The preferred charts used for Australian babies have been developed by the World Health Organization (WHO). These charts are based on the growth of children ages 0 to 59 months living in environments believed to support optimal growth of children. The charts show how infants and young children grow under these optimal conditions, rather than how they grow in environments that may not support optimal growth.

Measurements are done on a regular basis – more frequently in the early weeks of your baby's life. The child and family health nurse will take your baby's measurements at the first visit, and then at subsequent visits. It is recommended that measurements are checked as per your baby's personal health record, at least monthly until eight weeks, then at six months and 12 months (these times may vary slightly in different states). At these times, the child and family health nurse or your doctor will usually complete routine screening activities to check on your baby's development.

A baby's weight is usually done without clothing to ensure a consistent measurement, and using digital baby scales. Length is measured using a board. Head circumference is done with a paper tape measure (as a cloth measure can stretch with use). The nurse or doctor will place it around your baby's head slightly above their eyebrows.

Many things including culture and genetics will govern the percentile your baby is on. Use these charts as guides only, as children grow at different rates. You will notice over your baby's first year that sometimes their weight does not increase, or may even decrease. Weight is influenced by so many things that are happening in your baby's life. There are many short-term reasons why babies have periods where they slow down or don't gain weight. For example, having a cold, weaning or starting a new childcare arrangement can all impact your baby's ability to gain weight.

WHEN FURTHER INVESTIGATION IS NEEDED

Weight is an important measure for the status of your baby's health. When your baby is assessed by your doctor or child and family health nurse, they will investigate further if your baby:

- Continues to lose weight after the first 10 days of life
- Does not regain their birth weight by the time they are three weeks old
- Consistently does not gain weight of at least 100 grams a week during the first three months
- Their weight, when plotted on a growth chart, is less than the 3rd percentile or significantly drops below the previous percentile.

IMMUNISATION

Immunisation has had a major impact on reducing child deaths from infectious diseases. Unfortunately, some parents have chosen not to immunise their young children. This has resulted in a lowering in the 'herd' immunity of our community. Most babies are born with some level of immune protection from their mother, especially if breastfed. Nevertheless, there can be significant risk of infection for young babies until they are old enough to be immunised. Babies and children who are unable to be immunised due to illness or their fragile health status are placed at even greater risk of contracting devastating illnesses.

Immunisations are a simple, safe and effective way to protect your baby. If your baby is immunised they will not be a danger to other younger babies. Importantly, immunisations are not only for young children, but adults need to ensure they are fully immunised. Do you know if your immunisations are up-to-date? It's also important to ask other family members and friends to have a booster injection if they are not up-to-date. Immunisations can be done by your doctor, some child and family health nurse and some local councils.

If you live in New South Wales, immunising your baby is necessary if you intend enrolling them in childcare. Laws were introduced in 2012 that childcare operators have the right to exclude unvaccinated children from state-run childcare facilities. This ruling is expected to extend Australia-wide.

Of course there are always exemptions. If your baby has a medical condition or you have an objection to your child being immunised on religious grounds, you can apply for an exemption to your GP, but only after receiving counselling.

Child Programs 0–4 years	
Birth	• Hepatitis B (hepB)
2 months	• Hepatitis B, diphtheria, tetanus, acellular pertussis (whooping cough), *Haemophilus Influenzae* type b, inactivated poliomyelitis (polio) (hepB-DTPa-Hib-IVP) • Pneumococcal conjugate (13vPCV) • Rotavirus
4 months	• Hepatitis B, diphtheria, tetanus, acellular pertussis (whooping cough), *Haemophilus Influenzae* type b, inactivated poliomyelitis (polio) (hepB-DTPa-Hib-IVP) • Pneumococcal conjugate (13vPCV) • Rotavirus
6 months	• Hepatitis B, diphtheria, tetanus, acellular pertussis (whooping cough), *Haemophilus Influenzae* type b, inactivated poliomyelitis (polio) (hepB-DTPa-Hib-IVP) • Pneumococcal conjugate (13vPCV) • Rotavirus
12 months	• *Haemophilus influenza* type b and *Meningococcal C* (Hib-MenC) • Measles, mumps and rubella (MMR)
18 months	• Measles, mumps, rubella and varicella (Chickenpox) (MMRV)
4 years	• Diphtheria, tetanus, acellular pertussis (whooping cough) and inactivated poliomyelitis (polio) (DTPa-IVP) • Measles, mumps, rubella (MMR) (to be given only if MMRV vaccine was not given at 18 months)

Australian Government, Department of Health 2013

Your baby's immunisations will be recorded on the National Childhood Immunisation Register. You will receive a card for the health professional to record your baby's immunisation history. This is used as a proof of immunisation for entry to childcare and school.

Some babies need to have the timing of their immunisations delayed if they are unwell with a high temperature or their health is otherwise significantly compromised. However, if your baby has a runny nose or on antibiotics but is otherwise well, they can be immunised.

REACTIONS TO IMMUNISATIONS

It is possible that your baby will have a minor side-effect following their immunisation. It is very rare for major side effects to occur. If you are concerned you need to take your baby to the doctor straight away.

Minor side-effects may include: being unsettled or grizzly, minor fever or redness and swelling at the site of the injection. Giving your baby extra fluids to drink and dressing in loose comfortable clothing will help. Paracetamol is no longer advised for infants. A small hard lump at the injection site may persist for weeks or months, but will eventually disappear and does not require treatment.

DENTAL HEALTH

Your baby is born with all of their baby or primary teeth, but they remain hidden for many months. Baby teeth start to form at about eight weeks after conception. The first tooth will usually start to appear between six to 10 months on the lower jaw. Your baby should have their 20 first teeth by the time they are three years of age.

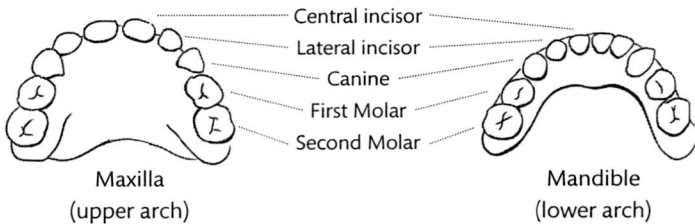

Central incisor
Lateral incisor
Canine
First Molar
Second Molar

Maxilla (upper arch)   Mandible (lower arch)

Healthy teeth are important to:
- The development of speech.
- Be able to eat a varied and nutritious diet.
- Reserve the space for permanent teeth. Early loss can cause misalignment or crowding of the permanent teeth – this will effect your baby's facial features.

Babies are born without the bacteria in their mouths that cause decay. Bacteria is easily and rapidly passed from others. Don't use your mouth to clean spoons, bottle teat or dummies before giving to the baby, or kiss the baby on the mouth. Parents need to regularly brush their teeth to avoid passing bacteria to their baby.

As your baby reaches six months of age your child and family health nurse or doctor will start to ask you about your baby's teeth and gums. These questions may include:

- Does your baby have any teeth?
- Has your baby had any problems with teething or with their teeth?
- Does your baby go to bed with a bottle to get to sleep?
- Does your baby, when drinking, ever walk around with a bottle or feeder?
- Have you started to brush your baby's teeth?

TEETHING

Teething affects all babies slightly differently. Some babies don't react at all while others develop swollen gums, red cheeks and may dribble excessively.

Parents blame a range of symptoms on teething including fever. However, several studies have shown there is no measurable change in a baby's temperature in the three days leading up to or on the day the tooth erupts through the gum. As babies contract a lot of minor infections and high fevers in their first year of life, many parents are convinced that teething is the cause but it is purely coincidental.

If you think your baby is experiencing pain from their erupting teeth, a very thin film of teething gel can be applied to their gums. Ask your pharmacist about the best teething gel for your baby and follow the teething gel instructions.

If your baby has a dummy don't use anything on the dummy to soothe them, e.g. honey or jam. We also suggest that when your baby is around 12 months of age you try and wean your baby off the dummy altogether. The best way to do this is by restricting the dummy to bedtime only. At other times, replace the dummy with a toy or blanket for comfort. If you do this over a period of weeks it won't be nearly as distressing for you or your baby.

CLEANING GUMS AND TEETH

Clean your baby's gums well before the teeth start to appear by wiping them with a clean, thin, damp washer.

As soon as your baby's teeth start to appear:
- Clean them twice a day; in the morning and before their night time sleep.
- Use a clean, damp, thin washer to wipe the teeth first.
- A very soft toothbrush with a small head can be used if your baby does not object.
- The best time to start using toothpaste is when your baby is 18 months old, and then only a very small smear of a toddler-safe toothpaste, unless directed by your dentist to use earlier.
- Don't let your baby suck on the toothpaste tube.

If using a toothbrush:
- Hold your baby in a position where you can see their mouth and they feel secure.
- Cup your baby's chin in your hands and allow their head to rest against your body.
- Clean your baby's teeth by using soft, circular motions.
- Lift their lips to brush the front and back of the teeth and at the gum line.

Cleaning the toothbrush:
- Rinse well with tap water.
- Store the toothbrush in an open container to air-dry.
- Do not allow contact with other toothbrushes, as this will reduce the risk of decay causing bacteria transferring onto your baby's toothbrush.
- Toothbrushes should be replaced every three to four months or when the bristles get worn or frayed.

Importantly, cleaning teeth helps prevent tooth decay, but diet and the way you feed your baby will also significantly contribute to the health of their teeth and gums. If you are unsure or tentative about cleaning your baby's gums or teeth the child and family health nurse will demonstrate how to do it.

TONGUE TIE

Tongue tie is a condition that is caused by a short string of tissue underneath the tongue (*frenum*) that restricts the tongue's movement. The frenum usually loosens by itself during the early childhood years, allowing the tongue to move freely. It is very rare for treatment to be necessary. If you are concerned about your baby's ability to feed adequately, it is important to check with your doctor or child and family health nurse.

OBESITY

Obesity has become a significant problem in Australia. Preventing a baby from becoming obese is important for future health as the extra fat cells formed in early childhood are likely to remain throughout childhood and into adulthood. The onset of many adult illnesses start in early childhood and many are related to obesity, for example, heart disease and diabetes.

Obesity is most often a problem of infant formula fed babies, when parents urge their baby to finish the bottle, even when they are showing obvious signs of being full and satisfied. The introduction of solid foods is another transition point where parents can overestimate the amount of food their children need. The most powerful obesity prevention strategy is for parents to model a healthy lifestyle – eating a varied and nutritious diet, using water as their drink of choice, and participating in regular daily exercise.

HEAT RASH

Prickly heat or *millaria* are the other names for a heat rash. When your baby gets hot, their underdeveloped sweat glands can become blocked. Perspiration then becomes trapped under the skin and forms blisters. It can occur when a baby has a fever or they are overdressed, especially in summer. Take your baby to a doctor if:

- The blisters fill up with pus or turn red (this means they have become infected).
- The rash is present for more than two to three days.
- As well as having the rash, your baby is unwell, is not feeding well or has a fever.

The rash should disappear in two to three days. Make your baby feel comfortable by giving them a bath in lukewarm water, dress in light cotton clothing and try to keep them cool, but not chilled.

Not all rashes are heat rashes, so if you are concerned about the rash take your baby to your doctor or child and family health nurse.

BIRTHMARKS

Some babies are born with a red or purple mark that is commonly called a birthmark, while other babies develop a red mark several months after birth. Most do not require any treatment and can fade as the baby grows. Some birthmarks can benefit from treatment, resulting in a reduction in size and appearance. It is important to have any marks reviewed by your doctor.

SALMON PATCHES AND STORK MARKS

Salmon patches and stork marks are common on newborn babies. They appear as a faint, dull pink capillary marking on the forehead (salmon patch) or on the nape of the neck (stork mark). They fade with time and without treatment.

PORT WINE STAINS

A port wine stain is a result of an abnormality in the formation of the blood vessels under the skin surface. It is present at birth and persists throughout life. These birthmarks affect approximately one person in every 3000. It can occur on any part of the body as a red or purple flat area of skin.

If your baby has this type of birthmark, they will be referred to a specialist for treatment. In most instances, treatment is successful in removing or significantly reducing the birthmark.

BLUE SPOTS

Blue spots (sometimes called Mongolian blue spots) are irregular shaped flat blue or blue/grey spots that feel like normal skin. They commonly appear at birth or shortly after birth. They are most commonly located at the base of the spine, on the back or buttocks. These blue spots can also occur on other parts of the body. They are common amongst people with darker skins. Blue spots are not associated with an illness or condition, although they are sometimes wrongly mistaken for a bruise. No treatment is needed or recommended. They usually fade over time.

JAUNDICE

Jaundice (*hyperbilirubinaemia*) occurs in up to 50% of full-term babies, and even more frequently with pre-term babies within the first few days of life. Jaundice is the result of the normal breakdown of red blood cells. However, your baby's liver may not be mature enough to get rid of the end product of *bilirubin* and the baby will develop a yellowish tinge to their skin.

Jaundice usually resolves without treatment, during the first two weeks of life for full-term babies and three weeks for pre-term babies. Some jaundice is linked to breastmilk. This is due to a chemical in breastmilk that interferes with baby's ability to break down the bilirubin and usually resolves within a couple of weeks. It is highly recommended you continue to breastfeed your baby unless advised by your doctor. A blood test might be done if the jaundice level is thought to be too high.

You will be encouraged to continue to breastfeed at regular intervals to ensure your baby remains adequately hydrated. Some babies will be very sleepy and not wake for feeds at frequent enough intervals. You may be advised to wake your baby every three to four hours for a feed while they are jaundiced.

You will need to return to your doctor with your baby if:

- The jaundice is still present after two weeks or three weeks for pre-term babies.
- Your baby is unwell or feeding poorly.
- Bowel motions are pale or urine is a dark colour.
- They are not weeing adequate amounts each day.

CRADLE CAP

Cradle cap or *seborrheic dermatitis* is a build up of a thick pale yellowish, oily scale on the scalp, due to excess serum production. It can also cause inflammation or redness of the scalp. Similar patches of crusty roughened skin may also appear in other areas on your baby's eyebrows, behind the ears, upper chest, under arms and shoulders. Some babies seem to be more prone to developing cradle cap than others.

The exact cause is unknown, although it has been suggested it is related to the mother's hormones still circulating in the baby's bloodstream after birth. It is very common and usually easily treated.

To treat:

- Wash and massage your baby's head regularly.
- Use a mild soap and water or your usual bathing solution. Massage the affected area.
- After bathing, use the flats of your fingertips to apply and massage in oil (suitable for baby massage) or other moisturising agent (e.g. sorbolene) to affected areas. If possible leave on overnight.
- Repeat this over several nights until the scale has been removed.

Avoid picking at the scale as this may cause your baby's scalp to bleed. Regularly massaging your baby's head using the pads of your fingers can be helpful in limiting the onset of cradle cap. Don't forget to massage the fontanelle areas.

There are commercial cradle cap treatment products available from your pharmacist.

MISSHAPEN HEAD (*positional plagiocephaly*)

Some babies have a misshapen head. In most instances, this does not affect the development of their brain. A misshapen head can be an outcome of their birth. By the time the baby is six weeks old, the baby's head should have been remoulded. Your child and family health nurse or doctor will check your baby's head to monitor its growth. They will also check the sutures and fontanelles in your baby's skull do not close prematurely.

A very common cause of a misshapen head is due to the baby being placed in the same position to sleep and play. It's important to place your baby on their abdomen to play for increasingly longer periods each day (see Chapter 8). If your baby is laying on their back, changing their position or that of the bassinet or cot in the room, or varying the placement of a toy will encourage them to move and vary the position of their head. Remember to always put your baby to sleep on their back.

NAPPY RASH

Nappy rash is a dermatitis occurring in the area covered by the nappy. There are several things that can contribute to your baby developing a nappy rash:
- Ammonia produced in your baby's urine.
- Faeces, especially if your baby has diarrhoea.
- Soaps, powders and creams can be an irritant.
- Friction between the nappy and your baby's skin.
- Not changing the nappy frequently enough.
- *Candida Albicans* or thrush that is present in faeces. Thrush infections thrive on moist and warm skin areas.

To assist in clearing up your baby's nappy rash it is helpful to:
- Use disposable nappies until the rash disappears.

- Wash and rinse cloth nappies thoroughly.
- Increase the frequency of nappy changes. Avoid leaving your baby in a wet or dirty nappy for extended periods.
- Clean your baby's nappy area using a wet washer or olive oil on cotton wool or non-perfumed wipes.
- Avoid using plastic pants.
- Use a cream to form a barrier at each nappy change to keep moisture from your baby's bottom, e.g. zinc cream works well. Your pharmacist will also be able to provide advice as to the best barrier cream to use.
- Leave your baby without a nappy for as long as possible during the day.

If the rash persists for more than a couple of days there is likely to be an underlying infection such as thrush or a bacterial infection. Thrush is a fungal infection that thrives in moist warm areas. It will need to be treated with an antifungal cream. Your local pharmacist will provide you with advice.

If your baby is distressed or in pain as a result of the rash or the rash is not responding to treatment, check with your child and family health nurse or doctor.

BOWEL MOTIONS

It is amazing how the bowel functions of a baby can become an endless source of fascination and worry for some parents. They are either too frequent or not frequent enough, or too loose or too firm.

As a parent the things to take notice of are:
- How often your baby poos
- Its colour
- Its consistency – firm, runny and everything between
- And the smell of the poo.

Things that impact on the poo's appearance, frequency and smell:
- Your baby's age
- Whether they are breast or bottle fed

- If they have commenced solid food
- What type of food they are taking. Poos get more smelly if they are drinking infant formula, or as baby begins eating solid foods.

Newborn babies	• Sticky thick dark black/green (tar-like) substance called *meconium*. It is a collection of waste products that the fetus forms. These include bile, fats and proteins • Some babies pass meconium during labour if they become distressed and others wait till after birth. Meconium is usually passed within the first 24 hours after birth • Around the 2nd or 3rd day the poo will start to change consistency and colour and becomes loose and green. It can look like diarrhoea – this is a transition stool • By the 4th day breastfed babies pass 3 to 4 light yellow poos • If your baby is jaundiced its poos are likely to be bright green, due to their increased excretion of *bilirubin* (see section on Jaundice for further information)
Breastfed babies	• Can be quite runny • Often yellow-orange in colour, but can be green sometimes • At first your baby may have very frequent poos, several each day • As the weeks and months go by, they can become less frequent, every couple of days and some babies go for even longer • Usually minimal odour, but can have a sweet smell because breastmilk has a high level of lactic acid
Infant formula fed babies	• Firmer poo, lots of colour variations depending on the infant formula • A newborn receiving an infant formula will pass 2 to 3 bright yellow poos each day • Infant formula fed baby's poos will have a slightly more noticeable odour than a breastfeeding baby's poo
Solid foods	• Consistency and colour will be influenced by the variety and amount of food your baby eats. It is often a shade of brown • At times, their poos will be quite smelly • As the food they take becomes more solid, you might find lumps of carrot or whole peas until they get use to chewing their food

CONSTIPATION

Parents and other family members often think their baby is constipated because they grunt, grimace, their face turns red and they look like they are straining when doing a poo. This is normal baby behaviour.

Breastfed babies rarely become constipated. But infant formula fed babies can become constipated, especially if the formula is incorrectly prepared with not enough water added to the formula powder (always follow the instructions on the infant formula tin).

Sometimes your baby's poo can look like little pebbles. If it flattens easily when squeezed between two layers of nappy, it is fine. If it is hard to flatten, then your baby may be constipated.

There are some disorders that can cause babies to be unable to have a normal bowel motion. If constipation is a problem, there is blood in the poo or it persists for over a week, your baby needs to be checked by a doctor. If you are concerned but unsure about going to the doctor, visit your child and family health nurse.

If your baby is being fed an infant formula, or over six months of age and breastfed you can offer:

- Additional cooled boiled water between breastfeeds or bottle feeds (approximately 30 to 50 mL). Be careful not to offer too close to a normal feedtime.
- Increase the fibre in your baby's diet (if over six months of age), e.g. more apples, pears or rice.

ORAL THRUSH

Oral thrush occurs in and around the mouth. It is very common during the first 12 months of life. Oral thrush is caused by a fungus called *Candida Albicans*, an organism that exists in everyone's body. When there is an imbalance in the body's organisms within a baby's gut, an infection can occur, as thrush can easily multiply. This can occur after a course of antibiotics.

Thrush can be picked up by your baby during their passage through the vagina during childbirth, or from objects already infected by thrush (your nipples, a dummy or teats). A very common way of your baby developing thrush is if you place their dummy or a spoon in your mouth and then put it into your baby's mouth.

If your baby has thrush, you will see white patches in your baby's mouth and on their tongue. It doesn't usually cause discomfort, unless your baby's mouth and tongue look red and inflamed. Sometimes a baby with oral thrush may be reluctant to feed or eat.

Your child and family health nurse or pharmacist can provide advice about the treatment of thrush. Go to your doctor if your baby:

- Has a fever.
- The thrush infection keeps coming back, even though you have been using treatment recommended by a health professional.

It is very easy to re-infect your baby with thrush. Ensure that you wash your hands before and after handling your baby, and before preparing food. If you are breastfeeding, your child and family health nurse, doctor or pharmacist will usually advise treating both your baby's mouth and your nipples with an antifungal treatment to decrease the risk of re-infecting each other. If bottle feeding your baby, make sure you disinfect their bottle and carefully wash the teat and dummies.

If your baby has oral thrush they are also likely to develop anal thrush (see nappy rash).

HAND WASHING

Every time you attend to your baby you should either wash your hands or use a hand sanitising gel. This is especially important to do after changing your baby's nappy or before and after handling food if it poses a risk to your baby, e.g. raw chicken and meats. It is also good practice to wash your hands after returning home from excursions outside the home or after handling pets.

This very simple precaution can help keep your baby safe from infections that can be uncomfortable for an adult, but dangerous for an infant or young child.

The trick with handwashing is to make sure you do it well. Use soap, rinse your hands and dry them well with a hand towel. Of course it goes without saying that your fingernails should also be clean.

- Your baby's immune system is immature at birth, so extra care is needed.
- Practise regular handwashing – it's one of the best protections against infection for your baby.
- The child and family health nurse is a free service that will provide you with parenting and child health advice and support.
- If you have any concerns about your baby's growth or development make sure you speak to your doctor or child and family health nurse.
- Try to visit the same doctor so they can become familiar with your baby. It becomes much easier for them to pick up health and developmental problems if they know you and your baby.
- Baby's weight is only one measure of health so don't be too focused on it.
- Make sure your baby's, your own and other family members' immunisations are up-to-date.
- A very common cause of a misshapen head is that the baby is being placed in the same position to sleep and play. Remember to always sleep them on their back.

Chapter Sixteen
WHEN BABY IS UNWELL

IT IS COMMON FOR BABIES to have times when they are unwell during the first year of their life. Mostly these illnesses are minor and require minimal contact with health professionals, however there are times when you need to take your baby to the doctor for assessment without delay. For example, if baby:

- Has difficulty breathing or their breathing is rapid.
- Has a fever.
- Is vomiting (if unusual for them or more frequent than normal).

- Has a reduced appetite or is refusing their milk and, if over six months, other foods you offer.
- Is drowsy, unresponsive or floppy. You may notice they are making less eye contact with you and are less interested in their surroundings.
- Has a stiff neck.
- Is affected by (sensitive to) bright lights.
- Has continuing diarrhoea.
- Has cramps or a tense abdomen.
- Poor circulation; your baby looks very pale, with cold hands and feet. They can also have a blue tinge around their lips.
- Has a rash – this is often common and is usually due to a viral infection. If the rash is red or purple, your baby requires urgent investigation by a doctor, as it could be meningococcal disease.
- Has poor urine output or less wet nappies then usual.

When baby is unwell try to reduce contact between your baby and other children. A sick baby can get worse very quickly, so it's important that you don't hesitate in getting medical help.

This chapter provides information about several common illnesses and infections that your baby may experience in the first year of their life.

IN AN EMERGENCY

There are several things parents can do to prepare for both minor and major emergencies:
- Invest in a basic first-aid kit. Having a first-aid kit will assist you in managing minor accidents that will inevitably occur at some time during your baby's early years.
- Learning first-aid skills by attending an accredited course will ensure you are prepared for both minor and major emergencies if they should occur.

- As part of your first-aid course you will learn infant resuscitation – a crucial skill for all parents. This is even more essential if you live near water or have a swimming pool.
- Develop a list of emergency contacts and details that includes:
  - emergency numbers
  - name any cross streets, that is, the nearest intersection to your home
  - your doctor's name and contact details
  - poison information service
  - partner's mobile and work contact details.
- Keep your emergency list on your fridge or somewhere easy to find.

SPITTING UP OR VOMITING

It is not uncommon for babies to spit up milk (sometimes called *posseting*) or to vomit milk. In the early days it is often related to the amount and flow of the milk. The milk will usually just flow out of your baby's mouth without any force during or after a feed. If you are using an infant formula to feed your baby, there is usually no value or advantage in changing the brand of infant formula.

Posseting and vomiting in otherwise healthy babies is usually related to an overflow of milk due to an immature valve between the oesophagus and stomach (sometimes called *oesophageal reflux*). In most instances, the vomiting and posseting resolve without treatment as your baby learns to sit up and is physically more active. However, if your baby is not consistently gaining weight or is losing weight, is drowsy most of the time or distressed, further investigations are urgently needed.

For lots of parents, a large bib helps protect their baby's clothing – and their own. A towel placed over a parent's shoulder saves a lot of curdled milk smelling clothes.

At bath time, pay special attention to your baby's neck area, making sure it is clean and dry. Several times a day, use a cream that will protect the skin while repelling moisture to ensure that baby is comfortable. This cream will help reduce the risk of the neck folds becoming reddened and sore.

Any medication for vomiting should only be recommended by a doctor, after excluding any underlying cause for the vomiting.

Treatment:
- Avoid large feeds when your baby is very hungry. Increase the number of feeds (feeding more frequently) and reduce the amount you offer your baby each time.
- If breastfeeding, try expressing for a minute or two before putting your baby on the breast. This may help to take away the initial gush of milk.
- If bottle feeding try using a slower teat.
- Check the formula preparation method and strength of formula to make sure you are accurately following the instructions on the formula tin.
- Play more vigorously with your baby *before* a feed. Use quieter, gentler handling and play *after* feeds.

WHEN TO GO TO THE DOCTOR WITH A VOMITING BABY

See your doctor if your baby:
- Has started vomiting, but does not usually vomit
- Has diarrhoea
- Is forcefully vomiting
- Has a high temperature
- Has become unsettled or difficult to soothe
- Is drowsy or lethargic
- Is not having their normal number of wet nappies, or their urine appears concentrated and/or smelly
- Has smelly and unpleasant vomits; contain blood or bile (yellow or green colour)
- Is refusing the breast, bottle and/or solid foods.

DIARRHOEA AND ASSOCIATED VOMITING

Diarrhoea is a common occasional problem for most people. It can also be associated with vomiting. This is often referred to as *gastroenteritis* or gastro. It usually resolves with rest, additional fluids and a modified diet. However, for babies, diarrhoea on its own or with vomiting can be extremely dangerous. They can dehydrate and their condition can rapidly deteriorate.

If your baby has diarrhoea, their poos will usually be large, smelly, runny, watery and frequent. This may lead to dehydration. They may be unsettled and in pain. It is important that your baby is checked by a doctor. Do not give your baby anti-diarrhoeal agents as they can mask the condition of your baby.

The most common cause of diarrhoea and vomiting is a viral infection, such as *rotavirus, adenoviruses* and *norovirus*. There is now a rotavirus vaccination given as part of the immunisation schedule and it is now no longer a major cause of chronic diarrhoea. Some diarrhoea can be caused by a parasitic infection (*giardia*). Bacterial infections such as *salmonella, shigella* and *campylobacter* can also be a common cause.

There can be other reasons for diarrhoea, including a reaction to some food (intolerance or an allergy), or medications (antibiotics). Too much fruit juice can also cause your baby to have diarrhoea, or coeliac disease (occurs after solid foods have commenced and is an intolerance to gluten in wheat, oats and rye-based products).

Gastrointestinal diseases occur when germs enter the body via the mouth. This can happen if your baby eats contaminated foods or drinks fluid that is contaminated. This usually occurs because the person handling the baby's food has not washed their hands after going to the toilet or changing their baby's nappy. Inadequate food preparation and storage can also result in the growth of gastroenteritis causing bacteria. For example, using the same chopping board to prepare chicken as you would to prepare other foods, such as raw vegetables that will not be cooked.

To reduce the risk of gastroenteritis:
- Wash your hands after using the toilet or handling nappies.
- Wash your hands, before handling food.
- Make sure infant formula and baby foods are stored and transported safely.
- Continue to sterilise your baby's bottles and teats until your baby is 12 months old.
- Store food correctly in the refrigerator.
- Make sure there is no contamination between raw meats (especially chicken) and other foods.
- Discard leftover food from your baby's bowl at the end of a feed and do not reuse.

Treatment:
To reduce the risk of infecting others, wash your hands after changing your baby and before preparing or handling food (see Chapter 14).

Your baby needs to be adequately hydrated at this time. If you are breastfeeding, keep offering your baby the breast. Your baby might need more frequent feeds. If your baby is fed with infant formula, continue to offer full strength feeds. Additional rehydration fluids may be recommended. Your doctor or pharmacist will be able to assist you in deciding on the appropriate rehydration fluid and amount to give your baby. Giving your baby sugary or salty drinks is likely to cause more diarrhoea and dehydration.

NOTE: You will be asked to keep your baby home from childcare for at least 24 hours after the diarrhoea has stopped.

Take your baby to the doctor if they:
- Have 8–10 watery poos or 2–3 very large poos a day.
- Are vomiting often and can't seem to keep any fluids down.
- Seem to be dehydrated – not passing urine, are pale and thin, have sunken eyes, cold hands and feet, drowsiness or significant irritability.
- Develop severe abdominal pain or are very unsettled.
- Have blood in their poo.
- Vomit and it is a green colour or very watery.

FEVER

A fever is when the body temperature is significantly higher than normal. Your baby's normal temperature should be between 36.5 and 37.5°C. So if your baby's temperature reaches and remains at 38°C or above, it is considered a fever. Rather than being a negative event, a fever is one of the body's natural defences. During a fever, white blood cell production and interferon, the body's natural virus-fighting substance, are stimulated. Fever is a symptom not a diagnosis and is rarely harmful. An underlying infection is usually the main cause of a fever.

As a fever is the body's way of dealing with a high temperature it is now strongly advised not to give infants or young children medication to reduce the temperature (e.g. paracetamol or ibuprofen) without medical advice. These medications may slow down the body's process of fighting the infection. There is also a risk of toxicity occurring if your baby starts to become dehydrated. Your doctor may recommend the use of medication to reduce your baby's fever. Follow the instructions carefully. As a safety measure it is important to record when you give the medication so that you or others do not overdose your baby. Never use aspirin as it can cause Reye's syndrome – a rare but serious illness.

Babies under the age of three months with a fever should be checked by a doctor as soon as there is evidence of a high fever as their condition can deteriorate very quickly. If your doctor is unavailable take your baby to a late-night medical service or your local hospital emergency department.

Take your baby to a doctor immediately if they have fever and any of the following symptoms:
- difficulty breathing or their breathing is rapid
- vomiting (if unusual for them)
- drowsy, unresponsive or floppy
- a stiff neck
- continuing diarrhoea
- affected by (or seems sensitive to) bright lights
- cramps or a tense abdomen
- a rash.

Taking your baby's temperature can be helpful if you feel your baby has a raised temperature. However, temperatures often fluctuate throughout the day. Body temperature is usually lower in the morning and higher at night.

In the past many families used a mercury glass thermometer to take their child's temperature, however these are no longer recommended for babies as there is a risk of breaking the glass and releasing the highly toxic mercury. Instead, consider using a digital thermometer. Digital thermometers allow the measurement of the temperature via the ear. These are quick, easy, accurate and safe to use with infants.

Having a fever will cause your baby to feel uncomfortable and unwell. They are likely to be unsettled and grizzly; wanting you to hold them and provide comfort. The treatment that is usually advised is to help your baby feel more comfortable:

- Dress them in enough clothes so they are comfortable and they are not shivering or sweating. Use light, loose fitting clothing. Leaving some clothing on them, even if very hot, will help absorb any moisture and keep them from shivering.
- Offer them frequent regular fluids and continue to breastfeed. If bottle feeding you might offer, between feeds, a small amount of cooled boiled water.
- Avoid having a fan directly blowing on your baby and don't sponge them with cool water. These actions can make your baby feel even more uncomfortable.
- Follow any additional treatment your doctor advises.

COMMON COLD

A common cold is just that, a common illness for most families. When there are infants and young children in the family, colds can occur up to 10 times per year, especially if they are attending a childcare centre. All babies are prone to catching colds due to their immature immune system, especially once the immunity gained from their mother begins to wane. Breastfeeding your baby will provide some added protection from developing infections such as the common cold. Unfortunately, it is nearly impossible protecting your baby from developing a cold, as the cold causing virus is airborne. So just being out and about in your community can result in contact with someone with a cold.

Your baby will usually have symptoms such as: a runny or stuffy nose, sneezing, a raised temperature (above 37.5°C), be grumpy and unsettled, be lethargic and have lost interest in food. Your doctor will usually advise against the use of antibiotics as they are not an effective treatment for illnesses caused by a virus.

Treatment
- Provide extra fluids – frequent and small amounts, especially if your baby is vomiting.
- Dress them in comfortable loose clothing.

- Saline nasal drops may reduce your baby's snuffly or blocked nose (talk to your pharmacist about the most appropriate product).
- Your baby may need lots of cuddles and attention.
- Avoid using cough medicines and decongestants as they can cause an increase in heart rate and jittery behaviour.

The difficult thing about your baby having a cold, is that often it's passed on to everyone else in the family. Keep in mind that it's very easy for parents to become run-down with the added demands of an unwell baby, so try and look after yourself at this time and accept offers of help from friends and family. Remember to regularly wash your hands, practise cough and sneeze etiquette and discard used tissues.

COUGH AND SNEEZE ETIQUETTE

- Cough or sneeze into your inner elbow rather than on your hand.
- If you use a tissue to cover your nose or mouth when sneezing or coughing, put the tissue in the bin straight away.
- Wash your hands with soap and water or sanitising gel.

SORE THROATS

Babies can get sore throats though it is often hard to identify. Sore throats can be caused by a virus or bacteria. Viral sore throats usually disappear within a few days and are not usually serious. Bacterial sore throats are caused by *streptococcus* and complications can occur. These infections are spread by airborne droplets from sneezing and coughing. It can also be spread from contact with contaminated surfaces, e.g. hands, toys, tissues and eating equipment.

Treatment is dependent on whether the sore throat is caused by a bacterial or viral infection. A bacterial infection can be treated with antibiotics prescribed by your doctor. Your baby will be fussy and upset so:

- Provide extra fluids – frequent and small amounts, especially if your baby is vomiting.
- Dress your baby in comfortable loose clothing.

- Your baby may need lots of cuddles and attention.
- Avoid using cough medicines and decongestants as they can cause an increase in heart rate and jittery behaviour.

EAR INFECTIONS

Infections of the middle ear (*otitis media*) or outer ear infections (*otitis externa*) are reasonably common infections during infancy and early childhood. Otitis media frequently occurs after having a cold with a runny nose and sore throat. It can cause significant discomfort and pain, with associated fever and vomiting. Your baby may be very irritable and difficult to settle. They may also be pulling or rubbing their ear.

The structure of the ear in infancy is a major contributing factor to middle ear infections. A baby's Eustachian tubes that connect the throat to the middle ear are much shorter and straighter than an adults. This makes it very easy for germs to enter into the middle ear from the nose and throat. It can happen when your baby has a cold, or if your baby is prop fed and the milk flows into the middle ear. As your baby's head grows and changes, the Eustachian tubes extend and curve.

An outer ear infection is usually due to excessive moisture in the ear (e.g. from swimming) or from damage to the ear canal after the use of a cotton bud or from scratching. Do not poke anything into the ear to try and clean as damage can be easily caused to the structures of the ear.

Treatment
It is important to see your doctor, as there is a risk of hearing and other problems if your baby has reoccurring infections.

BLOCKED TEAR DUCT

A blocked tear duct will cause your baby to have watery eyes or a discharge from their eye, especially when they wake up. It is often called a sticky eye. Your doctor needs to check your baby's eyes if:
- Their eye or eyes look red.
- There is a greenish discharge – this means it is infected.

- The tear duct is still blocked after your baby has reached 12 months.

A blocked tear duct is usually present at birth and is thought to be due to a plug of mucous or cells being left behind during the development of fetus *in utero*. It can be up to a month before it becomes obvious that your baby has a blocked tear duct.

A blocked tear duct gets better without treatment, in most instances, as the lower end of the tear duct expands. Regularly cleaning your baby's eyes is usually the only treatment needed.

CONJUNCTIVITIS

Conjunctivitis is inflammation of the *conjunctiva* (the clear membrane that covers the white part of the eye and lines the inner surface of the eyelids). There can be many causes, including:

- Irritant conjunctivitis – caused by chemicals such as soaps, washing detergents or air pollutants such as smoke and fumes. This is not an infectious condition.
- Allergic conjunctivitis – is more common with people who have allergic conditions. Both eyes are usually affected, and may be itchy, red and discharging fluid. If it is an allergic reaction, they may also have an itchy nose and sneeze regularly. This is not an infectious condition.
- Infectious conjunctivitis – due to bacteria or viruses. The infection usually starts in one eye, then is transferred to the other eye. The eyes will look red, itchy and watery. Conjunctivitis is spread by direct contact with eye secretions, or through contact with items that have been contaminated with eye secretions, e.g. washcloths, tissues and towels. It is an infectious condition while there is any discharge from the eyes.

Treatment
Keeping your baby's eyes clean is a good starting point. Gently wipe your baby's eyes several times a day using a cotton wool ball soaked in tepid water. Wipe from the inside of the eye outwards.

Conjunctivitis can be very contagious, so wash your hands after cleaning your child's eye. Wash your hands and your child's hands regularly. Makes sure no one uses your baby's towel.

If your baby is experiencing infectious conjunctivitis they will be excluded from childcare until the discharge from their eye has stopped. Your doctor may prescribe antibiotic eye drops or ointments.

STRABISMUS

Strabismus is often called a turned eye, lazy eye, crossed eye or squint. The eyes are looking in different directions – when one eye is looking forward the other is pointed out, in or up. A strabismus may be present at birth or appear later. It may not be noticeable all the time.

Treatment
As children do not grow out of having strabismus, treatment may include a combination of glasses, exercises, patching or surgery. Early intervention is necessary to ensure the best possible outcome.

TORTICOLLIS (wry neck)

Some babies constantly hold their head to one side, with their chin pointing to the opposite side. There is limited neck movement. This is either something a baby is born with, or it is an acquired condition. If you think your baby has limited movement of their head and neck, have your baby checked by the doctor.

Treatment
Stretching exercises and regularly changing your baby's position are the usual treatment.

UMBILICAL HERNIA

An umbilical hernia is common in babies due to the delayed closure of a small opening in the abdominal wall at the umbilicus (belly button). They rarely cause serious problems, but can take several years to close naturally. If the hernia has not gone by the time the child is five years of age, an operation to repair the hernia may be necessary. Strapping the skin over the hernia does not help it close more quickly and can be dangerous. If an infection occurs it can become systemic, spreading into the bloodstream and resulting in septicemia.

Treatment
See your doctor if you are concerned.

INGUINAL HERNIA

An inguinal hernia is the result of the bowel sliding through an open canal into a pouch in the groin. This hernia appears as a lump in the groin. In some babies it can appear in the scrotum (boys) or the labium (girls). Inguinal hernias are common in childhood. They are not as a result of letting a baby cry, though they are usually more noticeable when a baby cries.

Treatment
An inguinal hernia does not go away on its own – an operation will be required. This operation is done as soon as the hernia appears in babies as there is a risk the bowel will get caught in the hernia and be damaged.

UNDESCENDED TESTES

The testes are formed inside the abdomen of the male fetus. Both testes then move down into the scrotum by the time of birth, so they can develop normally. If one or both testes do not descend into the scrotum, it is called *undescended teste(s)*. Some testes can temporarily retract out of the scrotum – these are referred to as *retractile testes*.

Treatment

If the testes are not in the scrotum by the time a baby is six months old, an operation will be necessary to ensure they are in the correct position.

URINARY TRACT INFECTION

Urinary tract infection is common in babies. Your baby may be only mildly ill or very unwell. It is due to the growth of bacteria in the bladder and sometimes in the kidneys. A urinary tract infection can result in painful, frequent passing of urine. There may be blood in the urine. Your baby may not be able to adequately communicate their discomfort or pain. They may become very unwell, with a high fever and they may be very irritable and unsettled.

Treatment

Medical treatment is essential without delay. Your doctor will organise a urine test. Antibiotics are usually prescribed. Offer your baby regular feeds to ensure an adequate fluid intake.

MOSQUITO-BORNE INFECTIONS

Mosquitoes are responsible for spreading diseases from infected humans and animals. Common mosquito-borne infections include Ross River virus and dengue fever. Other mosquito-borne infections that are rare in Australia include malaria, Japanese encephalitis and Murray Valley encephalitis.

These infections are not spread from person to person so your baby does not need to be excluded from contact with other children or adults. The infection is transmitted by the mosquito. Importantly not all mosquito bites will result in an infection.

Infection symptoms may include:
- Fever
- Muscle and joint pain and swelling
- Intense headache
- Vomiting and diarrhoea

- Skin rash as the fever subsides
- Extreme tiredness.

Treatment
If you are concerned your baby might have been infected it is important you seek medical advice.

Prevention
To prevent or reduce the risk of your baby being bitten:
- If possible keep your baby indoors during peak times of mosquito activity; most mosquitos are active for two to three hours around sunrise and sunset.
- Make sure insect screens are in good condition.
- Dress your baby in long sleeves and pants, loose and light coloured clothing that covers as much of the body as possible.

It is far better to stop the mosquito population growth by:
- Emptying any garden pots or dishes containing water.
- Removing equipment or objects from the garden that will hold rainwater.
- Emptying paddling pools daily and turning over.
- Emptying pet water containers and birdbaths at least weekly.
- Placing a screen over water inlets to rainwater tanks. The holes in the screen need to be less than one millimetre in diameter.
- Keeping small native fish that will eat mosquito larva in ponds.

INFECTIOUS DISEASE

Your baby will be exposed to an infectious disease or a disease that is caused by a germ (virus or bacteria) that can be spread from one human to another. Our first line of defence is to regularly wash our hands (see Chapter 14) and practise cough and sneeze etiquette. The difficulty is that when babies venture into the outside world and have contact with others the risk of infection is impossible to avoid whether it is the common cold or a more serious infectious disease such as measles or whooping cough.

The second line of defence is immunisation. Fortunately, as discussed in Chapter 14, immunisations are available to protect babies, children and adults from several infectious diseases that once devastated communities, often resulting in death or disability. Unfortunately, it is still possible for babies to contract life-threatening illnesses if they have not received adequate immunisation coverage because of their age, pre-existing illnesses or in some instances because their parents make a choice not to immunise their baby or child. These illnesses include: hepatitis B, measles, pertussis (whooping cough), rotavirus, diphtheria, tetanus, and polio. Some of these infectious diseases will be discussed along with other diseases that commonly occur once your baby commences childcare or has increased contact with other children and adults.

PERTUSSIS (whooping cough)

Pertussis is a disease that causes parents a great deal of distress and concern as they watch their baby or young child struggle to breathe. Pertussis is a highly infectious disease that is caused by the *Bordetella pertussis* bacterium. Pertussis is very serious in infants under 12 months of age.

It is spread by airborne droplets as well as indirectly through contact with surfaces that have been contaminated by the airborne droplets such as used tissues, toys, hands and eating utensils.

Pertussis usually starts with cold-like symptoms – a runny nose, tiredness and in some cases a mild fever. The baby then develops a cough that can have a deep whooping sound that can last up to three months. Not everyone makes this sound and it is more common in non-immunised children. The incubation period ranges from nine to 10 days, but may range from six to 20 days. The period where they are infectious is from the beginning of the flu-like symptoms up to three weeks if not treated, or five days once they start taking the appropriate antibiotics.

Babies can stop breathing and sometimes turn blue. A high proportion of children (one in four) will develop pneumonia, some babies and children develop encephalitis (inflammation of the brain) and have convulsions. Most babies require hospitalisation.

Prevention

- Ensure your baby's, yours and other family members' and carers' immunisations remain up-to-date.
- You will need to notify family, friends and other people who may have had contact with your baby.
- Keep your baby at home (if not admitted to hospital) until they are no longer infectious. Avoid contact with other children during this time.
- Encourage cough and sneeze etiquette and hand washing at home.

HEPATITIS B

A virus that is mainly found in the blood of an infected person causes hepatitis B. It can also be found in body secretions: breastmilk, saliva, vaginal fluids and semen; 90% of children don't develop symptoms when they are first infected. If symptoms do occur they include loss of appetite, nausea, fever, tiredness, joint pain, abdominal discomfort, dark urine and yellow skin and eyes (jaundice).

Hepatitis B is not spread through water, food or ordinary social contact (shaking hands). Infection occurs through infected body fluids or blood or body fluids that come in contact with mucous membranes (e.g. mouth, nose, eyes and genitals). It can also be spread by injection or needle stick injuries or through broken skin.

There is no specific treatment for acute hepatitis B.

Prevention

- Ensure infants and children are immunised.
- Always take precautions when handling blood or body fluid contaminated products.
- Cover any open sores, cuts or abrasions that are weeping or moist.

RUBELLA

Rubella (German measles) is in most instances a mild viral illness. Cold-like symptoms are present – slight fever, sore throat and enlarged neck glands. A characteristic rash appears two to three days later. It starts on the face and spreads to the trunk. The pale pink spots merge to form patches. The rash only lasts a couple of days.

Rubella is extremely dangerous for unborn babies especially within the first 20 weeks of pregnancy. They are likely to have severe birth defects. Thankfully rubella is very rare in Australia because of the immunisation program.

Rubella is spread via airborne droplets, or through direct contact with throat or nose secretions of infected people. The incubation period is between 14 to 21 days. The infectious period begins seven days before the rash appears and lasts at least four days after the rash appears. There is no specific treatment for rubella.

Prevention
- Ensure your baby is immunised at the appropriate times.
- Practise cough and sneeze etiquette and handwashing.

ROTAVIRUS

Internationally, rotavirus is the most common childhood infectious disease. Before the introduction of the rotavirus immunisation in 2007, there were a significant number of Australian children hospitalised – it is estimated around 10,000 per year. It usually affects babies and young children up to three years and the onset is sudden. The rotavirus is passed on through food that has been contaminated when being prepared or served or after changing a nappy – effective handwashing hasn't occurred. It can also occur through touching contaminated surfaces such as toys, benches and feeding equipment.

The symptoms include vomiting, watery diarrhoea and fever. The virus is excreted in faeces from 1–2 days before the symptoms appear and up to eight days after the symptoms appear. There is no specific treatment for rotavirus infections. Importantly, care needs to be taken not to infect other family members or friends.

Prevention
- Ensure your baby's immunisations are up-to-date.
- Ensure adequate and appropriate handwashing. Take special care after changing your baby's nappy, or after going to the toilet or when preparing and serving food.
- Your baby's contact with other people should be restricted until they have been free from symptoms for 24 hours.

MEASLES

Measles is a serious and highly infectious disease that can result in serious complications such as brain inflammation and pneumonia. It is encouraging to see that the number of Australian cases of measles has fallen over the past decade as a result of the National Immunisation Program.

Measles is easily spread by mouth-to-mouth contact and airborne droplets landing on such things as toys, hands, food equipment and tissues. The measles virus is very infectious and can stay in the air for up to two hours after an infected person has left the room.

The symptoms of measles include a rash that has reddish blotches that are large and flat. These blotches often join up and completely cover the skin and spread over the entire body. It usually lasts for six days. The infectious period is from approximately four to five days before the rash begins until four days after the rash appears. There is no specific treatment.

Prevention
- Make sure your baby's immunisations are up-to-date.
- Ensure cough and sneeze etiquette.
- Practise regular handwashing.
- Contact family, friends and other people who have contact with your baby to inform them your baby has measles. This is essential if anyone has a compromised immune system.

HAND, FOOT-AND-MOUTH DISEASE

A common viral infection, hand, foot-and-mouth disease causes tiny blisters on varying parts of the body, including: the mouth, palms of hands, fingers, buttocks, nappy area, soles of feet, upper arms or upper legs. The incubation period is three days. This disease has no relationship to the cattle foot-and-mouth disease.

The blisters last for just over a week. There may be a fever, sore throat, runny nose and cough. The mouth blisters are usually the most painful and troublesome, making it difficult for a baby to drink and eat. The virus can be found in faeces.

The virus is spread in fluid from the blisters. Do not deliberately burst the blisters; allow to dry naturally. It can become airborne through coughing, singing and talking. It is often a problem in childcare centres. If your baby becomes infected, they will be excluded until all the blisters have dried.

Treatment

There is no specific treatment, other than keeping your baby comfortable.

To prevent the spread of the virus, careful handwashing and teaching other young children about cough and sneeze etiquette:

- Cough or sneeze into their inner elbow rather than their hand.
- Using a tissue to cover their nose or mouth when sneezing or coughing. Put the tissue straight into the bin. Don't reuse.
- Wash hands straight away.

ROSEOLA (*exanthum subitum*, sixth disease)

Roseola is a common and mild disease in children aged six months to three years of age. It is caused by the herpes virus and is spread by airborne droplets from the nose and throat and by direct contact with infected saliva on surfaces such as hands, eating equipment and toys. The first sign will be a sudden onset of a high fever that will last from three to five days. A rash will then appear and their temperature starts to go back to normal. The rash can last for several hours to days and will appear first on their trunk. The rash is usually fine, raised and red. The most infectious period is just before the rash appears until several days after the rash appears. There is no specific treatment.

Prevention

- Practise cough and sneeze etiquette and handwashing.
- Regular cleaning of toys and items your baby will place in their mouths.

HOSPITAL ADMISSION

Babies sometimes need to be admitted to hospital. Parents are now encouraged and very welcome to stay with their babies while in hospital. The amount of care you provide for your baby will be up to you. Continuing to breastfeed is an important way of supporting your baby's recovery.

Ask the nurses or your doctor what you can do to help soothe your baby and make them feel as safe as possible. Write down your questions as this will help you remember what you need to know when you are discussing your baby's condition with hospital staff.

Some parents are unable to stay with their babies as they have other young children at home and do not have anyone who can provide childcare. Visiting regularly is essential even if you and your partner take it in turns. Continuing to breastfeed and bringing in expressed breastmilk will make a positive contribution to your baby's recovery.

CHAPTER SUMMARY

- Babies have immature immune systems, making them prone to numerous periods of illness during their first 12 months of life.
- Ensure your baby is immunised to protect against many of the very serious infectious diseases.
- Handwashing is a vital technique to reduce your baby's risk of illness.
- Practise cough and sneeze etiquette.
- Learning first-aid skills will assist you to manage minor illnesses and accidents.
- Develop a list of key contact numbers for use in an emergency or when you are caring for a sick baby.
- If you are concerned about the health of your baby, contact your doctor or take baby to your local hospital emergency unit.

Chapter Seventeen
LEAVING YOUR BABY

DURING THE FIRST YEAR of your baby's life there will be times when you need to leave your baby. Be prepared that the very first time you do this, you might feel quite emotional. Whether you're leaving baby for a few hours or to start full-time work, it can be very difficult. Not only mothers, but fathers also can become distressed the first few times they have to leave their baby. The ability of your baby to manage separations will depend on their age, temperament and their familiarity with the person who will be caring for them, and whether the setting is familiar or not.

Babies at around seven months can become reluctant to engage with new and, sometimes, well-known people like grandparents, and often even their fathers. This can be very upsetting as going back to paid work or having medical treatment at this time cannot always be avoided.

Regardless of whether you are a stay-at-home mum or dad or you intend going back to paid work, parenting is a balancing act, requiring lots of support, patience and energy. Feeling confident with the childcare you are using for your baby is very important.

An important health safeguard is being up-to-date with their immunisations. This will help protect your baby if there is an outbreak of a highly contagious disease such as measles or whooping cough. If you make the decision not to immunise your baby, be prepared to organise alternative childcare to limit their contact with children who may have been infected and to limit the spread of the disease.

For many decades a constant issue and concern for many parents has been whether childcare is bad or good for children. Many health professionals and researchers would argue that the important concern is the type and quality of care, and that it suits the child and their family. Some parents have no option but to return to work, while other parents find they are able to be more emotionally available to their children if they go back to work. Other parents use childcare to have time out or to undertake further studies.

There are strategies that can make your life easier:

- Set realistic and achievable goals for you, your baby and other family members.
- Clearly communicate your needs for physical and emotional help and support during the early days of learning to separate from your infant.
- Ask for help and learn to accept offers of help.
- Change your expectations and priorities around the house.
- Involve other supportive adults in the planning and sharing of parenting and household responsibilities.
- Be realistic about what can be achieved each day.

In this chapter we will explore ways to make this separation easier for both you and your baby. Planning is one of the keys to making the separation less distressing for everyone concerned.

PLANNING AHEAD

Allowing your baby the experience of regular short periods of separation can be helpful so that it makes it easier to prepare your baby and you for longer periods away from each other. Start with family and friends that you feel are competent to care for your baby. If you have friends with similar aged children, you might even consider making an agreement to support one another by providing each other with regular babysitting time.

HAVING TIME-OUT

Have some time-out to do things you enjoy. Other time-out periods might be when you need to do tasks where it is not reasonable, convenient or safe to take your baby with you, such as going to the dentist, hairdresser or shopping. Having time-out allows you to recharge your batteries so you are refreshed and ready to provide the best possible care for your baby.

RETURNING TO PAID WORK

All parents are working parents, regardless of whether you are a stay-at-home mum, do volunteer work, do paid work from home, or are returning to the workforce outside the home. You will find having a routine is essential. Having an unpredictable lifestyle is time consuming and unsettling for everyone. Young children become frustrated, overwhelmed, and can feel insecure when routines are frequently changing. The upside is that they are reasonably resilient. So whenever possible try to be organised, but don't be too hard on yourself if some days do not go to plan, because there's sure to be moments that don't conform to attempts at organisation. If you have a less than perfect day, try not to get upset but start afresh the next day.

Talk to your partner about household responsibilities and expectations as a parent and adult household member. Make sure communication with your partner and other support people remains open and honest. Having support with household responsibilities will assist you in making the transition into the paid workforce as a parent with a baby.

Try to start and finish the day on a happy note with these tips:

- Give yourself extra time in the morning even if it means getting up half an hour earlier than your baby to enjoy a quiet morning tea or coffee.
- Rethink what has to be done before leaving the house each morning.
- Pack your work and childcare bags the night before.
- Organise the next day's clothing the night before, for you and your baby.
- Use the time in the car as a valuable opportunity to connect with your child, both on the way to childcare and on the way home. Sing songs and listen to your child when they talk to you, but be careful this doesn't become a distraction when you're driving.
- Most importantly, leave work stresses at work. It is not always possible to put boundaries between work and home. It is worth speaking to your employer if you find work responsibilities are encroaching on your time with your baby.
- Avoid conflicts and fights in the morning – it is always a no win situation for everyone.
- Getting your baby to bed early ensures they have adequate sleep for their development and growth.

Feeding the family does not need to be stressful:

- Prepare double amounts of food and freeze for later.
- Invest in a slow cooker and put dinner on before you leave for work.
- Remember your evening meal does not have to be a hot meal.
- Depending on the age of your child, try to enjoy dinner around the table, with the television off and all family members present. This is a good habit to get into as it provides a great opportunity to interact as a family.
- Consider a no TV rule in the morning as this can distract everyone from getting ready.

Washing:

- Wash and hang out the clothes the night before.
- Fold washing carefully to avoid having to iron.

Shopping:
- Add an extra hour to childcare for shopping later in the day.
- Avoid taking a tired and hungry baby shopping.
- Consider shopping on-line or in the evening, or ask your partner to do the shopping.
- Make a list so you avoid wasting time thinking about what you need to buy.
- Do a big weekly shop to avoid the need to shop everyday.

Babies get sick when you least expect it:
- Let your employer know that you are a new parent, so if your baby does become sick you can take leave.
- Either arrange for your partner to care of your baby, or have a backup plan such as a grandparent or a good friend on standby.

Maintaining family harmony and thinking of yourself:
- Take time-out for yourself and your partner to connect and maintain a healthy relationship.
- Go for a walk, taking time to talk and listen to each other, even if it is only for a short time.
- Plan regular enjoyable family activities that are simple (i.e. go to the park with a picnic lunch). It is these activities that provide your baby with family memories later in life!
- Continue or start a regular exercise program. This will give you more energy to care for your baby and you'll feel better too.
- Babysitting clubs are a great idea if you want to go out at night with no extra childcare costs. However, you do need to 'repay' the hours and babysit other people's children. Try and join a club where you're likely to know a few families or set one up within your own network.

CHOOSING CHILDCARE

If you are expected to return to paid work or study at a pre-agreed time, it is important that you sign your baby up early for a place at the centre you want or with the family daycare scheme. In some areas there can be a limited choice of centres or family day care workers who will care for babies. Not surprisingly, the most popular centres are quickly filled. Importantly, all official forms of childcare require the carers to have a 'working with children' check.

Childcare services (e.g. childcare centres, kindergartens, family day care) must meet the standards set by the Australian Children's Education and Care Quality Authority. Australian childcare services are rated and assessed against the seven National Quality Standards. These standards are in the following area of educational program and practice:

- Children's health and safety
- Physical environment
- Staffing arrangements
- Relationships with children
- Collaborative partnerships with families and communities
- Leadership and service management.

The aim of these standards is to promote:

- Safety, health and wellbeing of children
- Focus on achieving outcomes for children through high-quality education programs
- Families understanding what distinguishes a quality service.

Things to consider when choosing childcare:

- Do you feel your baby will be safe in the care of this person or the staff who work in the childcare centre?
- What are the number of staff to babies or children? It must be at least one educator/carer to every four children (0–2 years old).
- What qualifications do the staff have? Is there always someone working with an Early Childhood Education qualification? Are there other staff with a childcare or nursing qualification?
- Is there always a staff member on duty who has a first-aid certificate?
- Is the centre accredited to ensure it meets all safety and quality standards for childcare? The accreditation certificate is usually displayed.
- Are you made to feel welcome? Are the staff happy for you to stay with you baby so that they get used to this new experience? Is there an orientation program for your baby and you?
- Are staff actively involved with the babies and children? Are the staff playing with the children?
- Do the children look happy?
- Do the staff look happy?
- Is there a general routine or flow to the day?
- Are staff happy to discuss your baby's needs and issues about your baby's care?
- Does the centre look clean?
- Does the centre look safe? Are general and play equipment in good condition?
- What type of snacks or food is provided (if any)? Do you need to provide your baby's food?
- What are the staff's expectations of you as the parent?
- Is the location of the centre or carer workable to enable easy drop off and pickup of your baby?

CHILDCARE OPTIONS

There are several childcare options:

A *family member or friend* is a great option for young babies. It provides your child with someone they already know to look after them. If older people, such as grandparents, have agreed to look after your baby, make sure you show them how grateful you are – sometimes grandparents feel a little taken for granted. A small treat occasionally and a thank you, often makes a difference. Remember that they may find it very tiring looking after a little one for an extended period of time.

Babysitting is a common beginning step for many parents. It is usually an irregular and casual arrangement. Most parents find their child's babysitter through recommendation from family or friends. Teenagers are often employed in this role as they earn pocket money. Always agree on a fee before any childcare takes place. You might want to check the cost through an agency, so you have some idea of the current rate for casual childcare. A carer with a qualification will expect a higher hourly rate than someone without any qualifications. Always ask for references and check them prior to committing to employing the babysitter. Be very clear about your expectations.

Occasional care can be a great way to get used to being separated from your baby, and for your baby to get used to unfamiliar people and lots of noise and movement. It is available in many communities on a casual basis and is usually very affordable. Some community-based occasional care requires payment in the form of time to help at the centre. This is how the service keeps costs affordable. The time available each week is usually very limited.

Family Day Care is provided by an approved carer in their home. There is a limit to the number of children one carer can be responsible for in their home. For 0–2 year olds this is one carer to four children. The positive aspect for your baby is that there is usually only one carer. Family Day Care, depending on the carer, can be more flexible than centre-based care. Many local councils and non-profit organisations are responsible for providing supervision of this type of care. Carers' homes require safety inspections and some training is provided. Some of the carers have a childcare qualification. They are required to complete regular education sessions. Remember to ask if there is access to alternative care if the family day carer becomes unwell and is unable to care for your baby.

Centre-based care provides full-day care and a few rare centres even provide night-time care for shift workers. The real value of these centres is the provision of a developmentally appropriate education program, managed by a qualified early childhood educator. Centres should clearly identify if they have met the National Quality Standards set by the Australian Children's Education and Care Quality Authority.

In-home-care using a *nanny* is an easier option for some families especially if there is more than one child. Some families with babies and young children join forces and hire a nanny together. This can make it much more affordable.

Using a nanny service to contract a nanny is usually a safer option than going through the local newspaper. The nanny service will be responsible for vetting the carers before sending them to you to interview. This will include completing a 'working with children' check. Using a service will also help you deal with any concerns you may have with the nanny.

LEAVING YOUR BABY FOR THE FIRST FEW TIMES

Helping your baby to get used to being left with other family members, friends or in more formal childcare is best done gradually for short periods of time.

For best results:

- Make sure your baby is having a happy day and they are not unwell.
- If possible stay with your baby for the first time in childcare, or limit the time you leave them to a short period.
- Leave a familiar object with your baby, such as a special rug or blanket.
- Leave their food or bottle/cup for them to be fed if they are staying during a meal time.
- Dress them in comfortable clothes and leave spare clothes in case of accidents.
- If you have to leave, introduce them to their carer.
- Regardless of their age, always say goodbye and reinforce you will be back to take them home. Never 'just disappear'.

ESTABLISHING RULES

It is a good idea to communicate clear messages to your baby's carers about what is expected of them while caring for your baby. The following will provide some areas to consider:

- No use of alcohol or smoking while caring for your baby.
- No swearing in front of your baby.
- Not allowing your baby to be left to cry if distressed.
- Never to shake your baby.
- Any form of physical discipline.
- No sleeping with the baby, including napping on the lounge while holding your baby (there is a significant risk of SIDS with this behaviour).
- Not taking the baby in a car without permission.

- Not travelling in a car without an appropriate safety seat.
- Not having personal visits while they are caring for your baby.
- Type of foods and drinks you want or do not want your baby to be given.

If at any stage you feel uncomfortable, unsure or mistrustful of your baby's carer, it is time either to raise the issue with your baby's carer or change carers. Ensuring your baby's safety is paramount. Unfortunately, not every person is a suitable carer for babies and young infants.

EMERGENCY PLAN

An emergency plan is essential. A carer can get sick, children get sick, you can get stuck in traffic or have a flat tyre, just to name a few of the common everyday dramas that cause parents childcare stress. So rather than thinking this may not happen, it is better to expect that your baby will need alternative care at some time through the year and start planning for it.

Problem 1: Your baby is unable to attend childcare because they are unwell

Your baby will not be allowed to attend out-of-home childcare if they are unwell. Unfortunately, babies and young children can have up to 8–10 unwell episodes once they commence childcare due to their exposure to other babies and young children.

Problem 2: The childcare centre gets closed

A childcare service may be temporarily closed because of an outbreak of an infectious disease.

Problem 3: The carer becomes unwell

If you have a private childcare arrangement and the carer becomes unwell, it will be an issue, especially if it becomes a regular event. You definitely do not want your child to be cared for by someone who is unreliable or who may be distracted because of illness.

Problem 4: You get held up at work or something delays you being able to pick up your baby from the childcare centre before closing time

Childcare centres have very clear policies about the collection of children at the end of the day. You can also expect a financial penalty that can be quite expensive if you are late.

EMERGENCY STRATEGIES

Being prepared will make any unexpected childcare problem a lot easier to manage. Some suggestions to discuss with your partner or family could include:

- Parents alternating who stays home each time their baby is unwell. This shares the load and minimises the impact on one parent's employment.
- Discussing with grandparents, other family members or friends about their availability and willingness to help with emergency babysitting.
- Talking to your employer about the possibility of taking your baby (if well) to work or working from home if you encounter childcare issues.
- Investigating the availability and cost of hiring a nanny for the day.
- Organising family or friends who can pick your child up if you are going to be late for any reason. This might be another parent who also uses the childcare centre. You may develop a reciprocal arrangement that you both benefit from. Remember, whoever picks your baby up will have to have an appropriate child car seat restraint if taking your baby in their car.

Most childcare centres will request a list of people who can pick your baby up from the centre. They will also be required to show some identification.

EMERGENCY CONTACT LIST

Write up a list of contact numbers for your baby's minders to use in an emergency. Place this list in a prominent position, e.g. on the fridge.

Items to include:
- Your mobile number
- Partner's mobile number
- Ambulance/fire/police emergency number: 000
- Nearest cross street
- Poisons information service: 13 11 26 (Australia wide)
- Your doctor's number
- Child and family health nurse
- Chemist
- Tresillian Parent Help Line 02 9787 0855
  or 1800 637 357 outside Sydney
- Support person
- Neighbour
- Occasional care
- Other important contact numbers

CHAPTER SUMMARY

- Around the age of seven months babies become reluctant to engage with new and sometimes well-known people like grandparents and often even their dad.
- Regardless of whether you work at home or go out into the paid workforce, at some stage you will need to leave your baby for short or extended periods of time. Preparing your baby for separation can help minimise their level of distress.
- Returning to the paid workforce can at first be very stressful. So it is important to have realistic and achievable goals for your baby, yourself and others.
- To manage the new demands of returning to your work, clearly communicate your need for physical and emotional help and support in the early days of learning to separate from your baby.
- Leave your baby for short periods to get them use to the periods of separation.
- Always tell your baby you are leaving and will be back soon; never sneak away.
- When choosing a childcare centre for your baby make sure that it meets the standards set by the Australian Children's Education and Care Quality Authority.
- Leave a contact list beside your telephone.

YOUR FIRST TRIP with your newborn baby will be from hospital to home. This will require you having the baby capsule correctly fitted and knowing how to position your baby safely in the capsule. The timing and distance you need to travel is important as you may require a break in the trip to feed your baby and do a nappy change. If you are using infant formula to feed your baby you may need to pack feeding equipment and a couple of nappies and baby wipes to clean your baby's bottom. It's also a good idea to decide well in advance of your homecoming whether or not you want grandparents or friends waiting at home. Leaving hospital with your baby can be stressful as you both adjust to being at home and you don't want any added stressors.

When putting your baby in their baby capsule:
- Always lay them on their back. No extra padding is needed.
- Make sure the latches are secure.
- If a cold day, strap baby into the capsule and then place a baby blanket or wrap over them.

Strategies to make your trip as hassle free as possible:
- Carry your baby in a pouch facing towards you, so your hands are free and your baby can easily see your face if they need reassurance.
- Change your baby's nappy just before entering the plane, train or car. Disposable nappies, baby wipes, a plastic change mat and plastic bags to dispose of any dirty nappies are essential.
- Take a small bottle of sanitising lotion to clean your hands, if running water and soap are not available.
- If you are breastfeeding, a wrap or shawl will provide you with some privacy and reduce distractions for your baby.
- If your baby is fed an infant formula make sure you have bottles with the powdered formula in each bottle. The airline will provide you with boiled water (do not accept bottled water). If you are travelling on a train or in a car carry the water in the bottles and the powdered formula in pre-measured packs. Bring extra formula just in case of unexpected delays.
- The amount of clothing you take will depend on the length of the trip. Make sure the clothing is comfortable and appropriate to the season. Layering is always an efficient way to ensure your baby is comfortable.
- Depending on your baby's age, pack a couple of toys that can be used to entertain or distract your baby. If travelling on a plane or public transport ensure the toys do not have a high irritation factor (e.g. squeaky toys or loud rattles) that will cause discomfort to your fellow travellers.

BABY'S DAY OUT

Taking your baby out into the world is an exciting part of being a parent, as well as being extremely important for your baby's physical, cognitive, social and emotional development and wellbeing. Babies are never too young to go on outings. Very young babies often settle down and fall asleep with the movement of their pram or being strapped into a baby pouch that allows them to nestle into their parent's chest. Older babies, however, really enjoy the change of scenery and social interaction with their parents and other people. For parents it is a wonderful opportunity to show off your beautiful baby and have some social contact with other adults.

Nevertheless, travelling with your baby can be a daunting prospect. It might be your first trip home from the hospital, a first trip on public transport, a weekend stay with relatives or an overseas holiday. Whatever the reason for your trip, planning is the key for success.

Babies will usually adapt to their new environments if you take some familiar items on the trip. A favourite toy, blanket or food will often provide comfort and reassurance for your baby. Reassuring words, gentle touch and lots of smiles will help soothe your baby. Asking friends, relatives and even strangers to avoid overwhelming your baby with attention when they first meet your baby is also helpful. In other words, ask them to go at your baby's pace and provide space and time for your baby to feel comfortable in their new environment.

PLANNING

The type of trip you are going to make, and the amount of time away from home, will govern how much planning will need to be done. Things to consider before leaving home include:
- ✓ How long will you be away from home?
- ✓ Who will be travelling with you?
- ✓ Will you be using your car or travelling by public transport or in a family member's or friend's car?

- ✓ If not using your car, how will you access a baby capsule or car seat to transport your baby in someone else's car or taxi? Does the car have the appropriate anchor point for the baby capsule or car seat?
- ✓ How long will you be travelling in the car, on public transport or on a plane?
- ✓ What is the weather like?
- ✓ Do you need to pack a change or multiple changes of baby clothes, nappies and changing equipment?
- ✓ Will there be clothe washing facilities?
- ✓ Where will your baby sleep?
- ✓ Do you need a shawl to provide you with privacy if breastfeeding your baby in public?
- ✓ Do you need to take infant formula? Will you be able to purchase the same brand of infant formula at your destination?
- ✓ Do you need to take food for your baby?
- ✓ Will there be a safe water supply? If not, will you have access to bottled water? Will you be able to boil water? (Bottled water is not sterile and like tap water needs to be boiled before use for your baby.)
- ✓ Will you need toys and books to help distract your baby?

If travelling overseas:
- ✓ Do you and your baby need vaccinations?
- ✓ Have you applied for a passport for your baby?
- ✓ Do you need a visa?

Travelling with your baby may seem very daunting at first, but with practice and planning it does become much easier.

ROUTINES

Sticking to your baby's daily routine when you travel would be the ideal. However, we don't live in an ideal world, so compromise and flexibility become very important when travelling. If you are crossing international time zones, it is a challenge even for the most organised parent with a baby who has an easy-going temperament.

Don't despair if your baby's routine gets totally mucked up. Over the next couple of days, if you restart the routine, your baby will usually become more settled.

TRAVELLING WITH MORE THAN ONE BABY

If you are travelling with more than one baby or have a toddler, preschooler or primary school child/children, and especially if travelling on public transport or on a plane, be prepared to:

- Be vigilant at all times so that the children do not wander away.
- Manage your baby and other children as well as multiple suitcases.

This can be especially difficult when negotiating large public spaces with lots of people, noise and movement. Young children can become overwhelmed or distracted by the noises, colours and hectic movement that is occurring.

Using an inward facing pouch for your baby will leave you with free hands to manage baggage and other children. A harness or wrist strap can be a useful safety measure for an adventurous toddler or preschooler to stop them wandering off.

Check with your airline or transport company to investigate the type of assistance they may provide for boarding and leaving the plane, bus or train. If travelling to a new destination search relevant airport, bus or train websites to locate the exits and where you will need to go to connect with your next flight or with other public transport or taxis to get to your final destination.

CAR TRAVEL

Car travel is a way of life for many Australian families, from short trips to the shopping centre to much longer interstate trips. Car safety is essential (see Chapter 3 car seat safety). Fatigue is a significant cause of road accidents. Having a break every two hours will make for a much safer trip. Giving your baby a change of position, for even just a short period of time, will make the trip less stressful for your baby. Long trips that were no problem prior to being a parent may not be as realistic with a baby in the car. Breaking the trip into smaller segments can be a useful strategy.

Buy a shade screen for your car to reduce the sunlight coming through the windows and directly onto your baby. A shade screen will reduce the glare and some of the heat while travelling. Babies can easily become sunburnt through a window.

If your baby needs to be removed from the car safety capsule or seat to be fed, changed or for any other reason, you must stop the car. Having to listen to a distressed crying baby while driving can be very distracting.

Shopping or travelling with a child in a car can be difficult, and there will be times that it would be easier and very tempting to leave your baby in the car, even for a very short period of time. Leaving a child in a car unattended or inappropriately supervised (by another child) is illegal and you can be charged with an offence. Of more importance is that it is life threatening for your baby.

In Australia, on a typical summer day the temperature inside a car can be 30 to 40 degrees higher. Babies very quickly become hyperthermic (heat stressed) and dehydrate rapidly, causing death. The temperature within a car can very quickly exceed the outside temperature. It is estimated that 75% of the temperature rise in a car occurs within five minutes. The temperature rises as quickly in large cars as it does in small cars. The greater the amount of glass in a car, the quicker the rise in temperature. Having the windows down only reduces the temperature slightly.

WARNING: Never leave your baby in the car unattended or inappropriately supervised!

PUBLIC TRANSPORT

Travelling on public transport can be difficult and time consuming at the best of times, but when you are travelling with a baby it increases the difficulty, especially as you learn to maneuvre a pram and a baby. Thankfully most people are helpful and will assist you to lift the pram onto the bus or train. If at all possible, travel outside of peak hours. Most state transport websites now have trip planning tools that enable you to identify the quickest route to get to your destination.

Long distance train or bus trips will require lots of planning. Many of the planning issues are identified in the following air travel section. Even though there are not as many checking-in requirements, it is important that you provide adequate time to settle yourself and your baby on the train. Depending on the age of your baby, take several toys and books to help pass the time. A plastic change mat can be useful to provide a clean surface to change your baby on and plastic bags to dispose of the nappies. Prepare enough food to eat during the trip. This is especially important if you are travelling on your own with your baby as it may not always be easy or convenient to purchase a meal or snack.

If you are travelling by taxi make sure it has the appropriate child safety equipment to protect your baby. This equipment will need to be ordered at the time of booking the taxi.

AIR TRAVEL

A baby can travel once they are seven days old without medical clearance. If you can wait a little longer it will be much safer for your baby as their immunity has increased or they have commenced their immunisations.

If you need to travel before your baby is a week old, you will need to gain permission from your doctor. Check with your airline to see if they have a special form that needs to be completed. Most airlines have useful information about travelling with children on their website. If you are travelling with more than one child or travelling on your own with your baby or babies, it is worthwhile investigating with your travel agent or with the airline the type of support they will provide you at the airport and getting onto the plane.

Check with your doctor when travelling overseas if immunisations are needed or advised for the countries you are visiting. Allowing several weeks prior to travelling will ensure your baby has recovered from any side effects. Try to avoid plane travel if your baby has a cold as the fall in air pressure may cause ear pain. If unavoidable see your doctor for advice prior to travelling. Offering a feed or a dummy during take off and landing will assist in equalising the pressure in your baby's ear and it may reduce the pain.

Most airlines are supportive of parents travelling with babies and young children, often allowing them to board the plane prior to other passengers. Pre-book bulkhead seats if possible; sometimes these have a foldout bassinet that will accommodate your baby once the plane has taken off. On domestic flights the bassinets usually take a baby up to six months of age, while on international flights the bassinets are suitable for babies up to 18 months. Bassinets are limited, so it is important to book as early as possible so you can request one.

Even though most airlines provide a limited range of baby foods, it is probably safer to take your baby's food. If travelling across time zones, it may take time for your baby to adjust to changed feeding and sleeping patterns.

To make your trip as stress free as possible:
- Make a list of the articles you will need to take. Ensure you keep within the baggage allowance.

- Check in to your flight prior to leaving home, this can usually be accomplished 24 hours before.
- If you have not booked in online, arrive at the airport early enough to be near the head of the queue, so you are not standing in line for a long time.
- Put all your travel documents in one bag – always carry these on you for safety.
- Most babies will suffer discomfort and even pain in their ears during take off and landing. If possible breastfeed your baby or offer your baby a bottle or a dummy. Sucking assists equalising the pressure in their ears.

WATER TRAVEL

Travelling by water on a public transport ferry with a baby is usually very enjoyable, especially for older babies. However, we recommend that babies 12 months and younger do not go on other types of boats. This restriction appears to be due to the lack of available life jackets suitable for babies under 12 months.

ARRIVING AT YOUR DESTINATION

When arriving at your destination there are several activities to make your stay enjoyable and safe:
- If travelling by public transport or airplane, having pre-arranged transport to get to your accommodation will considerably reduce your stress level.
- If your baby is mobile, make sure the room or house is safe. Remove any small objects and any water sources that may be a safety concern.
- Is the water supply safe? If not, do you have access to bottled water (you will need to boil and cool before giving to your baby)? Is there a jug to boil water?
- Where will you sleep your baby? Is the bassinet or cot safe?

- Do you need to use a mosquito net to protect your baby?
- Make sure you wash your hands before handling your baby, after changing their nappy, preparing food or feeding your baby.
- Wash and peel all fruit and vegetables if you are not going to cook them.

CHAPTER SUMMARY

- If travelling in a car make sure the baby capsule or seat is correctly attached to the car and your baby is strapped in.
- Always stop the car if you need to remove your baby from the baby capsule or seat to feed or attend to them.
- Never leave your baby in a car where there is no adult supervision.
- If travelling by plane check with the airline to investigate the type of assistance they can provide.
- Travelling often disrupts routines, so compromise and flexibility are important.
- Don't despair if your baby's routine gets totally mucked up. Over the next couple of days, if you restart the routine, your baby will usually become more settled.
- Babies should not go onto boats other than ferries unless there is an appropriate size and type of life jacket available.
- If using public transport investigate via the internet the route you will take, where taxis are located, and other helpful information that will lessen the confusion or effort of getting to your final destination.

Chapter Nineteen
FREQUENTLY ASKED QUESTIONS

WORK AND WEANING

'I have to return to work four days each week in two months' time. My baby is now four months old and we both really enjoy breastfeeding. I hate the thought of having to wean Zoe.'

It's a shame to have to interrupt such an enjoyable routine, yet it's quite possible to continue to breastfeed. Some mothers are able to continue to fully or partially breastfeed their baby for many months after returning to work. It does take some pre-planning, but it's worth the effort. Don't be put off easily. Discussing your desire to breastfeed with your employer may help to gain some support.

Express. Start by expressing extra breastmilk and freezing it (see Chapter 10). If you haven't been expressing, it might take a little while to build up your milk supply to be able to express more than a few millilitres of milk each time you express. Hiring an electric breast pump may make the process easier. And quicker, too.

You may need to express at work to keep your breasts comfortable. Keep the milk refrigerated and bring it home in an insulated cool bag. Some mothers find regular expressing difficult to maintain. However, your baby can be offered an infant formula when you are at work, and still be breastfed at home. Many mothers and babies are able to continue to partially breastfeed for many months with this more flexible arrangement.

Bottle. If your baby hasn't had a bottle before, start by giving your baby expressed breastmilk from the bottle. If you don't want to use a bottle, a feeding cup may be an option from around six months of age (see Chapter 12).

Feeding routine. When you return to paid work, feed before you leave home, when you come home, and then just before your baby's bedtime. On days when you are not working, revert back to your normal feeding routine. At six months you will be able to start feeding your baby solid foods and this will reduce your baby's need for breastmilk.

The important thing is to relax and enjoy the time with your baby.

DISTRESSED BABY

'My baby seems to get really upset and distressed. It takes a very long time to get him to calm down.'

Crying is the main way infants have of communicating their needs. Babies provide us with lots of cues, such as crying, to show how they are feeling and what they want us to do to help them regulate their emotions.

They can't tell you in words or actions how lonely, uncomfortable, frustrated or hungry they may be. It's normal for babies to cry daily at some point. Learning to de-code and watching for cues as to what your baby wants from you, will make your job as a parent easier (see Chapter 5).

Crying can be due to:

- Hunger, thirst, being hot or cold, a wet or soiled nappy
- Being overtired, excited or frightened
- A need for comfort (to soothe your baby back into a calm state).

Keep in mind that your baby may also have unsettled periods where they are fussing and crying for no apparent reason. If your baby is otherwise well you can consider other options. For example, offer a 'top up' breastfeed within 30 minutes of the last feed (babies up to three months); cuddle; rhythmical movement, walk using pram, sling; play some music; offer a dummy; offer cooled boiled water (babies over six months); baby massage or deep relaxation bath.

If your baby still finds it hard to settle, a wrap may help. It is thought a wrap lessens baby's involuntary movements giving a sense of security and promoting a state of calm. Use a light material (usually cotton) ensuring arms are above waist level and hip movement is not restricted.

Respond. Learn to respond to your baby's cues before they become totally distressed and overwhelmed. If you watch your baby closely you will notice some subtle disengagement cues (looking away, fast breathing, frowning, increased sucking noises) and potent disengagements cues (arching their back, pulling away, crying, turning head away). This is your baby's way of telling you that they need either a couple of moments to calm down or that they are tired and need help to get to a quiet alert or drowsy state so they can go to sleep.

If the strategies listed above are not working and baby continues to cry for long periods of time, you need to rule out that your baby is not ill, has colic, or other potential medical conditions. Visit your child and family health nurse who may give you a referral to a day stay unit or a residential early parenting centre (such as Tresillian Family Care Centres). These services offer families the chance to have a more thorough assessment from a child and family health health nurse over a longer period of time. They will also support you while you try new strategies with your baby.

Meanwhile, hang in there.

FEAR OF HURTING MY BABY

'Sometimes I get so upset and angry when I can't calm my baby. It really scares me that I might hurt him.'

No matter how upset and angry you are, never shake your baby! Shaking can result in permanent brain damage and life-threatening injuries (see Chapter 5).

If you feel you are losing self-control this is one of the times that it is okay to leave your baby to cry. Place them in to a safe place until you calm down and regain self-control.

Get help. While baby is in a safe place, such as the cot or pram, ring your partner, a family member or friend to come and give you some support or ring a professional helpline such as the Tresillian Parent's Help Line. Have a cup of tea or coffee or have a shower to relax (see Chapter 2).

If you are unable to get someone to come over, put your baby in the pram and go for a walk (if it's daytime). This can have a calming effect on both of you. Do not drive if you are distressed.

Talk to your child and family health nurse or doctor about professional parenting and community support services that may be available to you and enable you to gain practical assistance or emotional support.

IMMUNISATIONS ARE DANGEROUS!

'One of the mothers in our mothers' group said that she was not going to have her baby immunised as it was really dangerous.'

By immunising your baby you are protecting them against highly infectious diseases that are far more dangerous than the vaccines used to prevent them. For the vast majority of babies, reactions to immunisations are extremely mild. Try to encourage the other mums in your mothers' group to immunise their children so that, if there is an outbreak of a disease (for example, whooping cough), your baby (and theirs) will be protected from it.

It is also important that your baby's immunisation courses are completed and kept up-to-date (see Chapter 15).

If you live in New South Wales, immunising your baby is necessary if you intend enrolling them in childcare. Laws were introduced in 2012 that childcare operators have the right to exclude unvaccinated children from state-run childcare facilities. This ruling is expected to extend Australia-wide.

Of course there are always exemptions. If your baby has a medical condition or you have an objection to your child being immunised on religious grounds, you can apply for an exemption to your GP, but only after receiving counselling.

TUMMY TIME BLUES

'The child and family health nurse has strongly suggested that I let my six week old baby have time on his tummy each day. But he gets so upset.'

Make it fun. At first most babies don't seem to enjoy being on their tummy. Having Mummy or Daddy there with them will reassure them. Gently talking to them using soothing words and sounds can help calm them. A brightly coloured toy to look up at can also help.

Importantly, never leave your baby unattended during tummy time as all babies are at risk of SIDS if they fall asleep while on their tummy.

When a baby lies on their tummy, they are able to use a whole range of important muscles that will help with their physical and intellectual development. During 'tummy time', your baby is actually learning to lift their head and use their arms, shoulder and legs in a very different way than when they are lying on their back. They will also see a very different view of their world. Tummy time becomes even more important as your baby grows and develops and starts crawling and exploring the world (see Chapters 7 and 8).

Regular 'tummy time' each day helps to prevent flat or misshapen skull development. This comes about as a result of babies sleeping on their backs in order to help prevent SIDS (see Chapter 5).

I FEEL SAD

'I often feel really sad and anxious during the day. Some days I just sit and feel sad. I know I should feel happy that I have a healthy beautiful baby, but I just can't. I always thought I would really enjoy being a mother.'

There are things that can be done to help you feel much better so you can really start enjoying motherhood.

Firstly, ask yourself some of these questions:

Are you getting enough sleep? Remember, the housework can wait, sleep when baby sleeps.

Are you eating a well balanced diet? There are many online companies that deliver fresh fruit and vegetables and groceries to your door. Take advantage of the convenience.

Do you have regular time to yourself away from your baby? (An hour a week will do and if you don't have family, contact the Occasional Care Centre in your neighbourhood.)

Have you connected with other mums in a similar position to you? If not, your child and family health nurse can suggest some options, such as mothers' groups, etc.

Are you exercising each day? Taking your baby in the pram for a walk each day, even for half and hour, will make the world of difference.

Try and make time to play with your baby and enjoy those toothy grins. You are your baby's best friend.

If you continue to feel sad, don't bottle up your feelings, **talk about it** with your partner, a close friend or family member as you may have the early stages of postnatal depression and the sooner you get help, the sooner you can receive treatment. But do **talk about it** and tell those close to you how you're feeling. You'd be surprised at how many other women also go through the same feelings. Then make an appointment to see either your child and family health nurse or doctor to discuss the options for treatment.

Some mothers require medication in addition to counselling to speed up the emotional recovery process. Medication on its own is usually not as effective so don't be tempted to put off the counselling. Keep in mind that it can take up to a month for the medication to positively impact on how you are feeling.

MY PARTNER HAS PND

'My partner has just been diagnosed as having postnatal depression. What can I do to help her feel better?'

This can be a really difficult and confusing time for partners and families. Your partner may have mood swings and be extremely critical and complaining that you are not helping enough. Yet when you ask what you can do to help she becomes upset. Make sure that you don't stop trying. Keep the communication channels wide open.

Useful strategies. Rather than asking what you can do to help, sit together and make a list of the things that need to be done around the house. This way when you are both feeling tired, you have the list to remind you the important tasks that need to be done. Put it on the fridge and refer to it, crossing out or ticking jobs done.

Arrange for time-out for your partner, as well as time-out together. If this is not possible, be creative. Perhaps go for a walk together taking the baby. Arrange a picnic lunch or dinner, especially in summer. Encourage your partner to join a mothers' group, so she will feel less disconnected and isolated. Help more with the care of the baby and other children – without being asked to do so.

For more information see Chapter 2.

SIBLING TANTRUMS

'Since our new baby arrived our 2½ year old has started to become very demanding and has regular tantrums. His naughty behaviour usually occurs when I am trying to feed my baby.'

Going from being the centre of attention to having to share attention with another can be very difficult when you are 2½ years old (see Chapter 1).

Ideas to distract and soothe. Organise a snack for your 2½ year old child to have while your baby is feeding. Make the snack fun by putting the food into a lunch box and adding interesting healthy foods. Place a rug on the floor so he can have a picnic.

Having a special DVD or television show to put on while you feed can help keep your toddler occupied and happy. Have a special book to read or toy to play with during feeding time. This can act as a distraction and make feeding a special time. Tell your son that you will spend some time playing with him when you have put the baby down to sleep. Make sure you carry through with any promises you make to spend time with your son.

Providing some structured attention with Mummy or Daddy can really make a difference as does encouraging extended family and friends to share some of their attention with both your son and baby.

If these strategies are not working it is important that you visit your child and family health nurse to have the situation assessed and gain additional support to manage the behaviours.

BOTTLE IS THE SOLUTION

'My mother keeps telling me I need to put my two month old baby on to a bottle because she cries for several hours every afternoon and is often difficult to get to sleep.'

Most babies have an unsettled period each day that can vary from one to three hours.

Giving your baby a bottle is usually not the answer. In fact, it may even make your baby more unsettled. Firstly, start by visiting your child and family health nurse and asking her to assess one of your feeds. The nurse will observe a breastfeed and possibly also weigh your baby. She may suggest strategies to increase your milk supply if your baby is not gaining adequate weight.

These might include increasing the number of times you breastfeed, expressing a small amount of milk before the feed, resting more and drinking more water. However, the issue may be the way you are currently settling your baby to sleep. So it would also be worthwhile explaining to the nurse how you put baby to sleep (for example, do you wrap baby, and are you consistent in the way you put baby to sleep every time?) Again, your child and family health nurse can advise you on some new strategies to try at home (see Chapters 5 and 10).

The nurse may ask you to visit your doctor to check there is not a medical reason behind your baby's crying. However, once any medical cause is ruled out, parents can be reassured that normal crying peaks at this age and will decrease naturally from about five months of age.

SURGERY AND BREASTFEEDING DILEMMA

'I have to go into hospital for an operation in about two weeks' time. I will be in hospital for two days. My baby is only eight weeks old and I am still breastfeeding. My doctor said I will be able to continue to breastfeed once the anaesthetic has worn off.'

As you have a couple of weeks until you are admitted to hospital, building up a supply of breastmilk in your freezer will provide milk for your baby when you are unable to feed (see Chapter 10 expressing and storage of breastmilk).

In hospital. Arrange ahead for your baby to room in with you (as per hospital policies to promote, protect and support breastfeeding), with the support of your partner or alternatively to be brought into you at regular intervals to breastfeed.

When you are being admitted, talk to the nurses about your needs as a breastfeeding mother. You may need to ask for assistance to sit up to breastfeed or to express when you have returned from the operation.

At home – Your baby may be a little fussy or even refuse the breast when they are reintroduced to the breast. This may be a reaction to the emotional and physical separation of mother and baby and if the baby needed to be temporarily offered milk feeds from a bottle. Gently persist in offering the breast, as it may take a little while before baby settles back into a good feeding pattern (see Chapter 12).

MY BABY WON'T SLEEP

'Some of the mothers in my mothers' group keep saying that their three month old babies are sleeping through the night. I feel a bit of a failure because my baby wakes at least once or twice during the night.'

There are lots of variations in the sleep patterns of infants. No two babies are alike. For many babies waking once or twice during the night is normal. If you are breastfeeding, it's a positive outcome as it provides regular stimulation and emptying of your breasts (see Chapter 10).

Perhaps you could ask the mothers what they mean by 'sleeping through the night'. You might find that they feed before midnight and again at around 4 or 5 a.m.

THE SOLID FOODS RULE

'My mother said that I should introduce solid foods to my baby very slowly and meat should be one of the last things I offer my daughter.'

The process of introducing solid foods is much more relaxed these days, with the advice now to offer iron-rich food (iron-fortified rice cereal, red meat) from around six months of age. As long as meat and other foods are pureed, your baby will be able to accept them. See Chapter 13 for more details.

TRESILLIAN FAMILY CARE CENTRES

tresillian.net

Tresillian Family Care Centres have a range of support services for families who may be experiencing difficulties with their baby or toddler. Whether the issue is settling baby, breastfeeding, toddler behaviour, managing multiple births or postnatal depression and anxiety, Tresillian's child and family health professionals can provide specialist advice, support and education.

Essentially, Tresillian's aim is to give parents the tools they need to feel confident in their own parenting abilities and to connect them with child and family health services in their local community.

There are similar services to Tresillian in most states of Australia. For full details visit:

http://www.tresillian.net/family-resources/useful-websites/other-family-care-centres-around-australia.html

HOW DO I CONTACT TRESILLIAN?

Parents with concerns for their baby are encouraged to call the Tresillian's Parent's Help Line on 02 9787 0855 (Sydney) or 1800 637 357 (Freecall within NSW) to speak to a Tresillian child and family health nurse or go online to Tresillian Live Advice, available using Facebook, by visiting tresillian.net

The benefit of using Tresillian Live Advice is that you can print out your conversation afterwards and refer back to it later.

Both services are **free of charge**.

CAN I BOOK MYSELF INTO A TRESILLIAN FAMILY CARE CENTRE?

No, however, if you feel you would benefit from our Residential, Outreach or Day Stay services, a referral is required from a health professional such as your child and family health nurse, general practitioner, paediatrician, Family Care Cottage, hospital staff or counselling professionals (social worker, psychologist or psychiatrist).

HOW DO I ORGANISE A RESIDENTIAL STAY AT TRESILLIAN?

If you live in the Sydney metropolitan area you need to have attended a Family Care Centre or specialist service or had a visit from Tresillian's Outreach or Day Stay team, prior to admission to our Residential unit.

Rural families can contact their specialist (e.g. paediatrician) or health professional such as a child and family health nurse or local doctor to obtain a referral to our Residential program. However, if your case is classified as urgent, admission may be as soon as 48 hours.

WHAT IF MY BABY OR FAMILY IS SICK?

Tresillian is a 'well-baby facility'. This means that you and your baby must be well at the time of admission. Usually, a baby who has an ongoing medical problem and is being managed by a general practitioner or paediatrician and who is unlikely to require acute medical intervention during admission will be admitted.

If you or anyone in your family is suffering an infectious disease, your admission will need to be re-scheduled. If you or your child develop an illness during your stay, it is Tresillian's policy to discharge you as soon as possible to decrease the risk of cross-infection.

HOW IS TRESILLIAN FUNDED?

While the majority of our funding comes from the NSW Ministry for Health we do rely on the generosity of the corporate sector and individual donors to assist us with special projects.

HOW MUCH DOES IT COST?

Clinical services in the Residential Units are covered by Medicare or the family's private health fund. Parents pay a small accommodation and meals charge per day. Prior to admission you will be advised of the current rate. Tresillian's Outreach and Day Stay services are free.

WHICH AGE GROUP DOES TRESILLIAN SPECIALISE IN?

Our services specialise in caring for families with young children in different age-groups – for more information contact your nearest Tresillian Centre.

Tresillian Canterbury
Residential Unit – children aged up to 2 years
Day Stay Unit – children aged up to 2 years
Outreach Unit – children aged up to 3 years

Tresillian Nepean
Residential Unit – children aged up to 3 years
Day Stay Unit – children aged up to 3 years

Tresillian Willoughby
Residential Unit – children aged up to 2 years

Tresillian Wollstonecraft
Day Stay Unit – children aged up to 12 months
Outreach Unit – children aged up to 2 years

DOES TRESILLIAN SUPPORT BREASTFEEDING?

Tresillian staff acknowledge that breastfeeding provides the best possible nutritional start for babies under the age of six months and thereafter up to two years of age or beyond, to complement a child's solid diet. Our nurses and paediatricians are committed to supporting breastfeeding if this is the mother's chosen method of feeding her baby.

Breastfeeding encouragement, education and support are provided to mothers striving to overcome difficulties breastfeeding. However, if a mother makes the decision to wean this will be respected and supported.

If a mother chooses to give her baby an infant formula or has to wean for whatever reason, the nurses will support and help the mother to ensure that infant feeding is an important and pleasurable experience for both her and the baby.

DOES TRESILLIAN BELIEVE IN CONTROLLED CRYING?

Tresillian does not recommend or use control crying. Parents are encouraged to learn to identify their baby's cues and state of wakefulness and recognise the intensity of the baby's cry. The parent is encouraged to respond to the baby in an appropriate manner. This may include picking the baby up and cuddling, softly crooning or singing to their baby, repositioning and patting their baby and offering a feed or trying to settle at a later time. For more information about settling your baby see Chapter 5.

Chapter Twenty
YOUR BABY'S FIRST FOODS
– RECIPE IDEAS

START BY OFFERING your baby a smooth puree consistency, introducing one food at a time, until they are eating a variety of foods from all the food groups. It is important to watch for any reactions to the foods.

As your baby masters pureed foods, gradually increase the texture and consistency from fine to lumpy (coarse), mashed, then minced, and then chopped by 12 months. This increase in texture and consistency may take many months.

By eight to 12 months babies should be starting to eat a 'baby adapted version' of the main family meal. At the end of this section there are several recipes that the whole family may enjoy.

Remember to always supervise your baby while they are eating to keep them safe. For further information see Chapter 14.

The following recipes will provide you with some ideas as to the types and consistency of foods you can offer your baby. Many of the recipes will provide more food than your baby will eat, so freeze for another day.

BABY BANANA SMOOTHIE

This healthy fruit snack provides your baby with the nutrients of potassium and iron.

Ingredients
½ banana
1–2 tablespoons of breastmilk or infant formula
1 teaspoon of iron enriched baby rice cereal (or for older infants cooked rice)

Method
1. Peel the banana.
2. Place it into a blender with the breastmilk or infant formula until the food resembles a puree consistency.
3. Add a teaspoon of rice cereal and mix thoroughly.

BROCCOLI AND CARROT MASH

Ingredients
1 head of broccoli (with stalk removed)
1 carrot
½ potato peeled (use either Desiree or 'old' potatoes)
Sprinkling of grated cheese (optional)
¼ cup boiled water or breastmilk

Method
1. Wash all vegetables thoroughly.
2. Peel the potato and carrot and chop off the ends.
3. Steam the vegetables until fully cooked and place in the blender with about ¼ cup of boiled water or breastmilk.
4. Blend to a puree.
5. You can add a sprinkling of grated tasty cheese to vary this dish.

MINI BEEF STEW

Ingredients
200g diced lean beef (either mince or rump, fish, veal, pork or chicken can replace the beef, or the meat can be replaced by additional vegetables)
1 small portion of cooked pumpkin
½ zucchini cooked
½ potato peeled (use either Desiree or 'old' potatoes)

Method
1. Wash all vegetables thoroughly.
2. Cook the beef in a frypan in ½ teaspoon of olive oil.
3. Peel pumpkin and chop the ends off the zucchini.
4. Steam the vegetables until fully cooked and place in the blender with about ¼ cup of boiled water.
5. Place cooked meat with vegetables and boiled water into the blender.
6. Blend to a puree.

MINI LAMB CURRY

Ingredients
200g diced lean lamb (i.e. either mince or backstrap: fish, beef, veal, pork or chicken can replace the lamb)
¼ peeled onion
¼ cup diced beans (ends removed)
½ peeled and diced potato (use either Desiree or 'old' potatoes)
¼ tin tomatoes
dash of garlic
pinch of ground cumin
pinch of fresh coriander

Method
1. Wash all vegetables thoroughly.
2. Cook the garlic, cumin and coriander with the onion in a frypan in ½ teaspoon of olive oil.
3. Add the finely chopped lamb to the frypan and cook till just done.
4. Add beans, diced potato and tomato to the frypan
5. Cook till just soft.
6. Mash rather than puree.

AVOCADO SMASH

Ingredients
Squeeze garlic
½ avocado
1 small banana
1 tablespoon natural yoghurt
2 teaspoons rice bran

Method
1. Peel the banana and scoop out flesh from avocado.
2. Mix all ingredients together to form a mash.

VEGIE SURPRISE

Ingredients

½ cup chopped yellow squash

1 tablespoon cooked peas (or beans)

2 tablespoons tinned tomatoes

sprinkle of dried parsley

½ peeled and cooked sweet potato

Method

1. Wash all vegetables thoroughly.
2. Steam the vegetables until fully cooked.
3. Add peas, tomatoes and finely chopped sweet potato.
4. Let simmer till soft.
5. Add a sprinkle of dried parsley.
6. Mash with a fork.

CHICKEN WITH QUINOA

Ingredients

½ cup diced chicken (beef, veal, pork or lamb can replace the chicken, or you can replace the meat with tofu, legumes or more vegetables)

¼ onion, peeled, diced and cooked

squeeze of garlic

½ cup zucchini

2 tablespoons tinned tomatoes

fresh basil or mint finely chopped

½ cup quinoa

Method

1. Cook onion and chicken in the frypan in ½ teaspoon olive oil
2. Add zucchini and tomatoes to chicken mixture.
3. Run heat to low and simmer for 10 minutes.
4. Using a sieve, rinse quinoa in water. Simmer in 1½ cups of water until the quinoa is the same consistency as rice.
5. Mix all ingredients with finely chopped basil or mint.

BABY MACARONI

Ingredients

500g lean beef mince (lamb, pork or chicken can replace the beef,
or you can replace the meat with more vegetables or legumes)

½ red onion

squeeze garlic

½ cup grated zucchini

½ cup grated carrot

2 tablespoons tomato paste

fresh parsley

1 cup beef stock (if using stock cubes make sure they are salt free
or reduced salt)

1 cup macaroni

dash Worcestershire sauce

grated cheese

Method

1. Cook onion in ½ teaspoon olive oil in frypan.
2. Add lean mince and cook.
3. Add vegetables and parsley to pan.
4. Add tomato paste.
4. Let simmer till soft.
5. Add beef stock.
6. In a separate saucepan, cook macaroni in 2 cups water.
7. Once macaroni is soft, strain through.
8. Serve with grated cheese.

FISH DISH

Ingredients
250g white boneless, skinless fish or salmon
½ onion
½ cup finely chopped celery
½ cup grated carrot
10g butter
1 teaspoon flour
½ cup milk
1 teaspoon fresh parsley
1 potato (cooked in boiling water and mashed)
(In a separate saucepan, make a white sauce by melting the butter and then adding flour. Whisk in milk and add grated cheese.)

Method
1. Cook onion in ½ teaspoon olive oil in frypan.
2. Add fish and cook.
3. Add vegetables and parsley to pan.
4. Let simmer till soft.
5. Cook white sauce in separate saucepan.
6. Cook potato in boiling water then mash.
7. Serve fish and vegetables on mash with white sauce over.

The following recipes can be used for the rest of the family.

BEEF & SWEET POTATO COTTAGE PIE

Serves 4
Preparation time: 20 minutes
Cooking Time: 2 hours

Ingredients
600g beef chuck steak, trimmed of fat, diced (chicken or veal can
replace the chuck steak; or the meat can be replaced by additional
vegetables or legumes)
1 tablespoon olive oil
1 onion, roughly chopped
2 stalks celery, chopped into 2cm pieces
1 carrot, peeled and cut into 2cm pieces
1 clove garlic, minced
400g can diced tomatoes (no added salt)
750mL beef stock (salt reduced)

Sweet potato topping
700g sweet potatoes, peeled and thinly sliced
(potato can replace the sweet potato)
¼ bunch parsley, chopped
2 tablespoons margarine spread, melted
steamed broccoli and green peas to serve

Method
1. Heat oil in a large heavy-based oven ready casserole pot over a medium
   heat. Brown the meat in two batches and set aside. Add onion, celery
   and garlic and cook for 3 minutes. Add canned tomatoes and simmer
   for 8 minutes until reduced slightly and thick.
2. Return beef to the pot, add 750mL stock and bring to the boil.
   Reduce heat and gently simmer for 1½ hours. Then add carrot and
   cover with the lid and continue cooking for a further ½ hour.
3. Meanwhile, preheat oven to 220°C and place sweet potato slices in
   a saucepan with 2 cups stock and parsley. Bring to the boil and cook
   for 10–15 minutes.

4. Drain stock and layer the potatoes evenly over the top of the meat casserole, brush lightly with melted margarine. Place in an oven at 220°C and bake for 20 minutes until top is golden.
5. Serve with steamed broccoli and green peas.

Use the cooked ingredients to adapt the family meal for different developmental stages.

Fine puree
Blend ⅓ cup casserole with juices and ¼ cup of the sweet potato topping until smooth. Serve with a spoonful of pureed broccoli and peas.

Finely mashed
Pulse ½ cup casserole with juices and ⅓ cup of the sweet potato topping in a blender until partially smooth or mash with a fork. Serve with a spoonful of fork mashed broccoli and peas.

Finger Food
Put ½ cup of casserole in a small bowl and top with the sweet potato topping. Surround with a couple of broccoli stems and green peas.

Toddlers
Spoon ¾ cup of casserole into a small bowl and top with sweet potato topping. Surround with broccoli stems and green peas and encourage your toddler to eat with a fork.

LAMB AND VEGIE ROAST WITH POTATO WEDGES

Serves: 4
Preparation time: 20 minutes
Cooking time: 40 minutes–1 hour

Ingredients
500g lamb mini roast, trimmed of fat (beef, chicken or veal can replace
the lamb)
2 tablespoons olive oil
800g potatoes, peeled, cut into wedges (you can substitute sweet potato
for the potato)
500g pumpkin, peeled, cut into 2cm pieces (other vegetables could be
parsnip or carrots)
250g cherry tomatoes
2 bunches asparagus, cut into bite size lengths

Method
1. Preheat oven to 200°C. Rub lamb with 2 teaspoons of oil and brown
   in a non-stick frying pan over high heat. Place on baking tray lined
   with baking paper.
2. Toss potatoes and pumpkin in remaining oil and place on another
   baking tray lined with baking paper. Place wedges on one side
   and pumpkin on the other. Bake for 1 hour adding tomatoes and
   asparagus for the last 15 minutes of cooking.
3. Meanwhile bake browned lamb for 20–25 minutes. Remove from
   oven when cooked while potatoes and vegetables finish cooking.
   Loosely cover lamb with foil and rest for 10 minutes before carving.
4. Carve lamb into thin slices. Serve with wedges and roasted
   vegetables.

Fine puree

Blend small slice of lamb (25g), 1 potato wedge (25g) and 1 tablespoon of roasted pumpkin (35g) for a smooth puree. Add 1 tbsp of boiled water if needed.

Finely mashed

Pulse a slice of lamb in blender with 1 tablespoon of boiled water until partially smooth. With a fork mash 1 potato wedge and 2 tablespoons of roasted pumpkin. Combine with blended lamb.

Finger Food

Cut a slice of lamb into thin strips. Cut 3 wedges and some vegetables into pieces for small fingers.

Toddlers

Cut potato into mini wedges before baking. Cut lamb into strips and roll around asparagus tips and sliced pumpkin into wheels. Serve with halves of the roasted cherry tomatoes. (Remove skin if preferred.)

SPINACH AND BEEF CANNELLONI

Serves 4
Preparation time: 15 minutes
Cooking Time: 25 minutes

Ingredients
400g lean beef mince (you could also use chicken, pork or veal mince)
1 tablespoons olive oil
1 × 250g packet frozen spinach, thawed and liquid drained
250g fresh ricotta
¼ tsp nutmeg
½ cup grated parmesan cheese
3 × fresh lasagne sheets (10cm × 17cm)
750mL bottled tomato passata
2 tablespoons tomato paste
Roasted pumpkin and steamed cauliflower to serve

Method
1. Preheat oven to 180°C. Lightly grease a large ovenproof baking dish. Heat oil in a large frying pan and cook mince for approximately 3 minutes over high heat until browned.
2. Stir in spinach, ricotta, nutmeg and ¼ cup of the parmesan cheese.
3. Cut 3 lasagne sheets in half. Spoon filling onto one end of each lasagne sheet, roll up and place seam side down in the baking dish.
4. Combine tomato paste and passata in a bowl and spoon over cannelloni. Top with extra parmesan cheese and bake for 25–30 minutes. Serve with roasted or steamed pumpkin pieces.

Use the cooked ingredients to adapt the family meal for different developmental stages.

Fine puree
Blend ⅓ of a cannelloni with a little of the tomato sauce and 1 piece pumpkin and 1 cauliflower floret until smooth.

Finely mashed
Take ½ cannelloni and finely cut up or pulse with a stick blender until lumpy. Mash 1 piece pumpkin and 1 cauliflower floret into the mixture.

Finger Food
Cut up 1 cannelloni into small pieces. Serve with pumpkin cubes and small cauliflower florets.

Toddlers
Cut up 1 cannelloni into biggish chunks and serve with pumpkin pieces and cauliflower florets on a plate with a fork.

WEBSITES

There is a great deal of information about parenting and child health available on the internet. The following are reputable national and international websites that may be of interest and assistance.

TRESILLIAN FAMILY CARE CENTRES

http://www.tresillian.net
The Tresillian site describes the services available for parents and how to access them. Additional, regularly updated parenting information is available on this site.

PARENTING

Australian Government Infant Nutrition
Infant Feeding Guidelines: information for health workers (2012)
http://www.nhmrc.gov.au/guidelines/publications/n56
You can find the latest Australian Government infant nutrition guidelines on this site. These guidelines have formed the basis for Section 3 in this book.

Australian Breastfeeding Association (ABA)
https://www.breastfeeding.asn.au
This site provides a valuable source of breastfeeding advice and information about how to access the ABA services.

Healthy Start – parenting resources for parents with an intellectual disability
http://www.healthystart.net.au/for-parents
Healthy Start originates from Sydney University and is dedicated to providing evidence-based information and resources for parents with an intellectual disability and their families.

Immunise Australia Program
http://www.immunise.health.gov.au
Immunise Australia is an Australian Government site. Best practice information and other useful resources including the current immunisation schedule are available.

Farm Safe Australia
http://www.farmsafe.org.au/index.php?article=content/home
Safety information and resources are available on this site for families living in rural Australia.

Kidsafe NSW
http://www.kidsafensw.org
Child safety information and resources are provided. This site is regularly updated.

NSW Poisons Information Centre
http://www.chw.edu.au/poisons/

ACT Poisons Information Centre
http://www.health.act.gov.au/c/health?a=sp&pid=1316133581&site=67611&servicecategory=42

Victorian Poisons Information Centre
http://www.vic.gov.au/contactsandservices/directory/?ea0_lfz99_120.&service&54baf353-3d9a-4dc2-acba-69ca2564328b

Queensland Poisons Information Centre
http://www.health.qld.gov.au/poisonsinformationcentre/
There are four Australian Poisons Information Centres. These centres provide phone information as well as factsheets.

Raising Children Network: The Australian Parenting Website
http://raisingchildren.net.au
This Australian Government funded site provides a wide range of parenting information and resources. This information includes the primary school and adolescent years.

Staying Healthy: Preventing infectious diseases in early childhood education and care services (5th Edition)

http://www.nhmrc.gov.au/guidelines/publications/ch55

This site provides access to the latest health publications used by childcare centres to manage the child health practices within centres. It is especially useful for the information provided about the management of a range of infectious diseases.

Stepfamilies Australia

http://www.stepfamily.org.au

This site is devoted to providing information and resources for stepfamilies.

CHILD GROWTH AND DEVELOPMENT

Begin before birth

www.beginbeforebirth.org

A range of resources and information for parents that focus on the latest research about the development of the fetus. The website was developed by the Institute of Reproductive and Developmental Biology, Imperial College, London.

Centre of Excellence for Early Childhood Development:

www.excellence-earlychildhood.ca/home.asp

Up-to-date child development and health information. This centre is located at the University of Montreal, Canada. The aim of this website is to disseminate scientific information about early childhood development.

Center on the Developing Child: Harvard University

www.developingchild.net

On this site you will find video clips, fact sheets, and academic papers on early brain development. Some of the world's leading neuroscientists contribute to the resources available on this site. Importantly the science information has been translated into easy to access and understand video clips, fact sheets, and academic papers on early brain development. The Centre is located at Harvard University, USA.

Zero to Three
http://www.zerotothree.org

This internationally-renowned organisation provides a wide range of information about child development and behaviour.

Early Childhood Learning Resource Project
http://deewr.gov.au/early-childhood-learning-resources-project

The Early Childhood Learning Resources Project has been developed to assist parents to introduce and develop early literacy and numeracy learning for their young children. The Australian Government has provided funding for this project.

Hearing Australia
http://www.hearing.com.au/children

Hearing Australia is an Australian Government funded organisation that aims to look after the hearing needs of Australian children who have a permanent or long-term hearing loss. The organisation works with children with all degrees of hearing loss from birth up to the age of 26 years.

NCAST
http://www.ncast.org

This organisation is located at the University of Washington in Seattle, USA. The site provides links to other reputable child development sites as well as resources for health professionals working with young children. The work of Professor Kathryn Barnard has been influential in informing the practice of Tresillian nurses, in particular the understanding of infant cues and parent-child interaction assessment.

CHILD CARE

Australian Government My Child: childcare services
http://www.mychild.gov.au

My Child is an Australian Government site that aims to assist parents to find childcare for their young children.

Family Day Care Australia
http://www.familydaycare.com.au/index.php/main/Home#M55
Family Day Care Australia is a national peak body which supports, enhances and resources family day care services.

The Australian Child Care Index: listings of childcare options available in each state
http://www.echildcare.com.au
This site provides a national search engine for all forms of childcare.

BABY EQUIPMENT SAFETY

Product Safety Australia website for safety information
www.productsafety.gov.au
Product recall: provides information about equipment that has been recalled due to safety problems at http://www.recalls.gov.au.
These two sites provide valuable baby equipment safety information for parents. Well worth checking prior to going shopping for any type of baby equipment.

Choice: The People's Watchdog
http://www.choice.com.au
Choice is a renowned Australian consumer organisation, providing information about product testing and comparison. Access is often available to their magazine or website at your local library.

HEALTH

Australian Cancer Council
(for sun protection and quit smoking information)
http://www.cancer.org.au
Important information and products to assist in minimising the risk of cancer. It is especially useful to check the latest information on baby sun protection products.

Australian Government Quit Now – quit smoking program
http://www.quitnow.gov.au
This site provides lots of information and resources if you want to quit smoking.

Australian Red Cross – first aid courses
http://www.redcross.org.au/ourservices_acrossaustralia_firstaid_courses.htm

St John first aid courses
http://www.stjohn.org.au/index.php?option=com_content&view=article&id=14&Itemid=25
The Australian Red Cross and St John Ambulance are reputable organisations that provide first aid courses for parents.

Domestic Violence – Australian Government site
http://www.humanservices.gov.au/customer/subjects/domestic-and-family-violence
If you or someone you know is experiencing domestic violence, this Australian Government site provides important information to assist you to change your situation.

Healthy and Active Australia
http://www.healthyactive.gov.au
With the increasing concern about obesity and its health implications, this Australian Government site provides a wide range of support to develop healthier lifestyle behaviours.

Health Direct Australia – free health advice
http://www.healthdirect.org.au
Health Direct makes available health-related resources and contact numbers to gain personalised health information.

HealthInsite – Australian Government health information site
http://www.healthinsite.gov.au
This Australian Government provides a wide range of health and lifestyle information.

Managing your Money – Australian Government site

http://www.humanservices.gov.au/customer/subjects/managing-your-money

Managing your money information is available from this Australian Government site. Importantly, it provides information about available payments families may be eligible to receive.

Measure Up – Australian Government weightloss site

http://www.measureup.gov.au/internet/abhi/publishing.nsf/content/home

If you are wanting to lose weight and need some support and information, this Australian Government site may help motivate you to develop healthier lifestyle behaviours.

Men's Health Australia

http://www.menshealthaustralia.net

This organisation provides information and resources relevant for boys and men.

Mothersafe

http://www.mothersafe.org.au

This is a free telephone service for NSW mothers. It provides information about the use of drugs, both prescription and non-prescription, and other toxins. The site has a list of services for mothers in other states.

NPS Medicinewise

http://www.nps.org.au

NPS site is dedicated to helping Australians make wise choices about their medicine use by providing evidence-based information.

Sexual Health and Family Planning Australia

http://www.shfpa.org.au

Sexual Health and Family Planning Australia provides sexual health and family planning services, education and resources for Australian women and men.

MENTAL HEALTH RESOURCES

BeyondBlue: www.beyondblue.org.au
The Black Dog Institute: www.blackdoginstitute.org.au

Both BeyondBlue and the Black Dog Institute are funded by the Australian Government and provide a wide range of Mental Health resources for the Australian community. Each organisation provides information about perinatal mental health.

Gidget Foundation
http://www.gidgetfoundation.com.au

A NSW-based not-for-profit organisation whose mission is to promote awareness of perinatal anxiety and depression amongst women and their families. There are numerous resources available for women and families on the Gidget site.

Lifeline
http://www.lifeline.org.au

Lifeline provides 24-hour crisis and suicide prevention services. The telephone number is: 13 11 14

PANDA – Postnatal and Antenatal Depression Association
http://www.panda.org.au

PANDA provides Australia-wide services to support women and their families experiencing perinatal depression and anxiety.

MensLine Australia
http://www.mensline.org.au/Home.html

MensLine Australia is a professional telephone and online support, information and referral service, helping men to deal with relationship problems in a practical and effective way. It is funded by the Australian Government.

Relationship Australia
http://www.relationships.org.au

Relationship Australia provides a range of relationship focused services and education. Relationship Australia is a non-profit, government supported organisation.

Country Women's Association of Australia
http://www.cwaa.org.au
The Country Women's Association of Australia is an important part of the support network provided to women living and working in rural Australia.

AUSTRALIAN RESEARCH

Australian Institute of Family Studies
http://www.aifs.gov.au
The Australian Institute of Family Studies (AIFS) is the Australian Government's key research body in the area of family wellbeing. Its role is to increase understanding of factors affecting how Australian families function by: conducting research; and disseminating findings. The Institute's work provides an evidence base for developing policy and practice related to the wellbeing of families in Australia.

Growing up in Australia: The longitudinal study of Australian Children
http://www.growingupinaustralia.gov.au
Growing Up in Australia is a major longitudinal study following the development of 10,000 Australian children and families from all parts of Australia.

Australian Institute of Health and Welfare
http://www.aihw.gov.au
The Australian Institute of Health and Welfare is an Australian Government organisation that provides authoritative information and statistics to promote better health and wellbeing.

REFERENCES

Barnard K, (1999), *Beginning rhythms: the emerging process of sleep wake behaviour and self-regulation*, NCAST University of Washington, Seattle.

Baston H & Durward H, (2010), *Examination of the newborn: a practical guide*, Routledge, London.

Bowlby J, 1988, *A secure base: clinical application of attachment theory*, Tavisock/Routledge, London.

Center on the Developing Child at Harvard University, (2010), *The Foundations of Lifelong Health Are Built in Early Childhood*, National Scientific Council on the Developing Child, Cambridge MA. Retrieved from http://www.developingchild.harvard.edu

Center on the Developing Child at Harvard University, (2011), *Building the Brain's "Air Traffic Control" System: How Early Experiences Shape the Development of Executive Function: Working Paper No. 11*. Retrieved from www.developingchild.harvard.edu

Cozolino L, (2006), *The neuroscience of human relationship: attachment and the developing social brain*, W.W. Norton & Company Inc, New York.

Crockenberg, S & Leerkes, E, (2009), Infant social and emotional development in family context, In C. Zeanah, *Handbook of Infant Mental Health* (3rd ed), pp. 60–90, New York, Guilford Press.

Department of Health and Ageing, (2013), National immunisation program schedule, Australian Government, Canberra.

Fraiberg S, (1959), *The magic years: understanding and handling the problems of early childhood*, Charles Scribner's Sons, New York.

Hockenberry M & Wilson D, (2011), *Wong's nursing care of infants and children* (8th ed), Mosby, St Louis.

Lawrence R & Lawrence R, (2011), *Breastfeeding: a guide for the medical profession* (7th ed), Elsevier Mosby, Philadelphia.

Mares S, Newman L & Warren B, (2011), *Clinical skills in infant mental health: The first three years* (2nd ed), ACER Press, Melbourne.

Murray L & Andrews L, (2005), *Your social baby: Understanding babies' communication from birth* (2nd ed), ACER Press, Melbourne.

National Scientific Council on the Developing Child, (2004), *Young Children Develop in an Environment of Relationships: Working Paper No. 1*. Retrieved from http://www.developingchild.harvard.edu

National Scientific Council on the Developing Child, (2004), *Children's Emotional Development Is Built into the Architecture of Their Brains: Working Paper No. 2*. Retrieved from www.developingchild.harvard.edu

National Scientific Council on the Developing Child, (2007), *The Timing and Quality of Early Experiences Combine to Shape Brain Architecture: Working Paper No. 5*. Retrieved from www.developingchild.harvard.edu

National Health & Medical Research Council, (2013), *Australian Dietary Guidelines: Providing the scientific evidence for healthier Australian diets*, Commonwealth Government, Canberra.

National Health & Medical Research Council, (2012), *Infant feeding guidelines: information for health workers*, Commonwealth Government, Canberra.

National Health & Medical Research Council, (2012), *Staying healthy: preventing infectious diseases in early childhood education and care services* (5th ed), Commonwealth Government, Canberra.

Oxford M & Findlay D, (2013), NCAST caregiver/parent-child teaching interaction manual (2nd ed), NCAST Publications, University of Washington, School of Nursing, Seattle.

Rosenblum K, Dayton C & Muzik M, (2009), Infant Social and

Emotional Development – Emerging Competence in a relational context, In Zeanah, C. (Ed) *Handbook of Infant Mental Health* (3rd ed), pp. 80–103, Guilford Press, New York.

Sheridan M, (2008), *From birth to five years: Children's developmental progress,* ACER Press, Melbourne.

Sheridan M (2011), *Play in early childhood: from birth to six years,* ACER Press, Melbourne.

Siegal D, (2012), *The developing mind: how relationships and the brain interact to shape who we are* (2nd ed), Guilford Press, New York.

Slade A, (2005), Parental reflective functioning: An introduction, *Attachment & Human Development, 7*(3), 269–281.

Spietz A, Johnson-Crowley N, Sumner G, & Barnard K, (2008), *Keys to caregiving,* NCAST-AVENUW, Seattle.

Summer G & Spietz A, (1994), NCAST caregiver/parent-child interaction feeding manual, NCAST Publications, University of Washington, School of Nursing, Seattle.

Szalavitz M & Perry B, (2010) *Born for love: Why empathy is essential and endangered,* William Morrow, New York.

The Science of Early Childhood Development, (2007), *The Science of Early Childhood Development: Closing the Gap Between What We Know and What We Do,* National Scientific Council on the Developing Child, Cambridge MA. Retrieved from: http://www.developingchild. harvard.edu

ACKNOWLEDGEMENTS

There are many people who have supported, encouraged and contributed to this book. I would like to thank Tresillian Family Care Centre staff who read many drafts of this book, provided comment, suggested changes and improvements.

Fran Chavasse – Acting Manager, Centre for Education
Leanne Daggar – Acting Director of Nursing and Clinical Services
Dr Penny Field – Director of Medical Services
Caroline Flynn – Nurse Educator and Lactation Consultant
Dr Nick Kowalenko – Child and Adolescent Psychiatrist and President of the Tresillian Council
Lisiane LaTouche – Director of Social Work and Psychology Services
Julie Maddox – Clinical Nurse Consultant
Robert Mills – Chief Executive Officer
Debra Moen – Acting General Manager 2013
Jacqueline Walker – Child and Family Health Nurse
Beulah Warren – Clinical Psychologist and past President Tresillian Council

There were several mothers who read the book and provided insightful comments.

Significant support has been provided by Ann Paton, Tresillian's Public Relations Manager, who managed the production of the book for Tresillian Family Care Centres and contributed to the menu section of the book.

Meat and Livestock Australia, for their contribution to the recipe section.

Paul Higgs of Palmer Higgs who has guided Tresillian management through the overall production of this book.

Of greatest importance was Rose Inserra who has provided writing guidance, critical comment and developed the design and organisation of this book.

Finally I wish to acknowledge my colleagues at the University of Washington, Seattle NCAST programs. Especially Professor Kathryn Barnard and Denise Findlay who have so willing shared their knowledge about infant and parent interactions. This book has been informed by the knowledge I have gained from completing the NCAST courses and becoming a parent-child interaction assessment instructor.